RENEWAL DATE DUE

DATE DUE

Minority

MULTILINGUAL MATTERS SERIES
Series Editor: Professor John Edwards,
St Francis Xavier University, Antigonish, Nova Scotia, Canada

For more details of these or any other of our publications, please contact:
Multilingual Matters, Frankfurt Lodge, Clevedon Hall,
Victoria Road, Clevedon, BS21 7HH, England
http://www.multilingual-matters.com

MULTILINGUAL MATTERS 138
Series Editor: John Edwards

Minority Language Media
Concepts, Critiques and Case Studies

Edited by

Mike Cormack and Niamh Hourigan

MULTILINGUAL MATTERS LTD
Clevedon • Buffalo • Toronto

WITHDRAWN
UTSA Libraries

Library of Congress Cataloging in Publication Data
Minority Language Media: Concepts, Critiques and Case Studies/Edited by Mike
Cormack and Niamh Hourigan.
Multilingual Matters: 138
Includes bibliographical references and index.
1. Ethnic mass media. 2. Linguistic minorities. I. Cormack, Michael J. II. Hourigan,
Niamh
P94.5.M55M56 2007
302.23089–dc22   2006031791

British Library Cataloguing in Publication Data
A catalogue entry for this book is available from the British Library.

ISBN-13: 978-1-85359-964-4 (hbk)
ISBN-13: 978-1-85359-963-7 (pbk)

Multilingual Matters Ltd
UK: Frankfurt Lodge, Clevedon Hall, Victoria Road, Clevedon BS21 7HH.
USA: UTP, 2250 Military Road, Tonawanda, NY 14150, USA.
Canada: UTP, 5201 Dufferin Street, North York, Ontario M3H 5T8, Canada.

The policy of Multilingual Matters/Channel View Publications is to use papers that
are natural, renewable and recyclable products, made from wood grown in
sustainable forests. In the manufacturing process of our books, and to further support
our policy, preference is given to printers that have FSC and PEFC Chain of Custody
certification. The FSC and/or PEFC logos will appear on those books where full
certification has been granted to the printer concerned.

Typeset by Saxon Graphics Ltd.
Printed and bound in Great Britain by the Cromwell Press Ltd.

Contents

     Problems: An Irish Perspective
     Eithne O'Connell 212

13   Signs of Change: Sign Language and Televisual Media
     in the UK
     Paddy Ladd 229

14   Minority Language Media Studies: Key Themes for Future
     Scholarship
     Niamh Hourigan 248

     Contributors 266
     Index 267

Chapter 1
Introduction: Studying Minority Language Media

MIKE CORMACK

What is a minority language? The question is a more complex one than might at first be thought. Various related terms have been used to describe such languages – regional, lesser-used, non-state, subordinated, non-hegemonic. 'Indigenous' has also been used to cover a related but slightly different area. In this book 'minority language' is the preferred term. All the other terms have particular disadvantages. (For other discussions of this issue, see Grin, 2003: 20; Hourigan, 2003: 2). Despite its institutionalisation in the European Charter for Regional or Minority Languages, 'regional' is less than satisfactory since it makes no reference to what the problem for minority languages is – that they are dominated by a surrounding majority language. As François Grin notes, 'referring to a "region" stresses a geographical association, yet defuses a cultural, possibly more essentialist one' (Grin, 2003: 20) and is thus, in effect, a way of deflecting the argument away from linguistic rights. It is also unsatisfactory in that in many minority language communities, there are speakers – and indeed communities of speakers – of the language who live outside the traditional territories. Using 'regional' in relation to media, for example, might lead to media provision in specific areas, but not necessarily in cities containing speakers of the language who have moved away from the traditional areas. It clearly also does not apply to non-territorial languages such as Yiddish and Romany (as Grin notes) and the various varieties of sign language (as will be clear from Ladd's Chapter 13 in this book). Sometimes it has been a preferred term to avoid what are seen by some as the negative connotations of 'minority'.

'Lesser-used' makes no reference to the context of the language. Danish, an officially recognised language of the EU, has fewer speakers (6 million) than Catalan (10 million), but the former is the official language of a fully-fledged state, whereas the latter is not. The term has been institutionalised in the European Bureau for Lesser Used Languages (EBLUL), but François Grin has argued that 'lesser-used' was adopted as a political compromise, 'chiefly in order to avoid the term "minority", which would have not been to the liking of member states that recognise no minorities, autochthonous

1

or otherwise, among their citizens' (Grin, 2003: 20). Even EBLUL's own website uses other terms when it refers to the remit of its Member State Committees as representing 'the interests of the various regional or minority communities within their state'.

Sometimes 'non-state languages' has been preferred. This is closer to the mark, but still fails to be explicit about what the problem actually is – that the language in question is dominated by a much larger language community. It can also lead to confusion. Languages that are official in one state might be a minority language in another (such as Russian in Estonia, Latvia and Lithuania, or Arabic in France). As with 'regional' and 'lesser-used', it is a term largely used to avoid reference to minority communities. 'Subordinated' (as used by Grillo in opposition to 'dominant' languages, see Grillo, 1989) and 'non-hegemonic' are closer to indicating the problem, but here again the precise nature of the relationship between the minority community and the majority one is not made clear. Only the term 'minority' makes explicit what these languages have in common – that they are dominated politically and economically by numerically larger communities within a particular state. It is this that puts Catalan in the same category as Scottish Gaelic (with 58,000 speakers). The political element is made explicit by Monica Heller when she writes: 'The concept of a linguistic minority only makes sense today within an ideological framework of nationalism in which language is central to the construction of the nation' (Heller, 1999: 7). She goes on to note that 'linguistic minorities are created by nationalisms which exclude them' (Heller, 1999: 7). In other words, the concept of a linguistic minority is essentially a political one. If a language group with a small number of speakers was given the same linguistic rights as a large language group, then its status as a minority would be unimportant, and it is the nationalism (whether explicit or not) of the larger group that denies these rights. It is the majority group that makes a 'problem' of the minority. This relates to the notion of 'minoritisation' as the process – political and ideological – by which one community is constructed by another as a minority.

Sometimes, of course, many of these languages are grouped under the heading of 'endangered' languages. Here, however, the element of subjective assessment is very apparent. While few would argue that languages with fewer than 100,000 speakers are endangered, it is a much more controversial term when applied to larger communities, and, of course, some – taking a long-term view of the dominance of English – would see many majority, official, state languages as ultimately endangered.

Another term that has been used in this context is 'indigenous'. As noted below, Donald Browne used this as the central category in his book

Electronic Media and Indigenous Peoples. He defended his use of the term pragmatically while noting its difficulties, and suggested a working definition: 'For my purposes, those who can establish that they have been in the area for the longest time, and continue to live there, would be the indigenous peoples of that area' (Browne, 1996: 4). This may make sense when looking at former colonial territories, such as Australia, Africa and the American continent, but in the European context, such a term is highly problematic. English, Spanish, French and Norwegian are just as indigenous as Irish, Basque, Breton and Sami. It makes little sense to get into arguments about which language was around before others in any particular area.

The Emergence of Minority Language Media Studies

The history of the media developments that have led to the emergence of this area of study are well covered by Browne's Chapter 7 in this book. Alongside these changes in the media has been a gradual increase in the official recognition and institutionalisation of minority languages. In the European context, 1982 saw the establishment by the European parliament of the EBLUL. Its website describes it as 'an independent democratically governed Non-Governmental Organisation working for languages and linguistic diversity'. In 1987 Mercator was established by the European Commission as a forum for the exchange of information and co-operation in relation to minority languages. Of its three parts, one is specifically devoted to media, and since 1995 has been publishing the *Mercator Media Forum* with the aim 'to promote discussion and the flow of information between those who work in the territorially-based non-state languages of the European Union in the field of media' (Thomas, 1995: 3). In 1996 the European Centre for Minority Issues was established. Such bodies have given invaluable support to minority language initiatives in Europe and have made sure that the question of minority languages remains firmly on the political agenda.

Alongside these, there is the recognition given by the European Charter for Regional or Minority Languages of 1992. This has tried to build minority languages into the structure of the 'New Europe'. The development of this Charter (and its full text) is given in Grin, 2003. Most relevant for the media is Article 11 (Grin, 2003: 214–215). There a comprehensive list of media provision is recommended. A minimum standard is established of at least one radio station, one television channel and one newspaper in the relevant language, with governments asked to either 'ensure' or 'facilitate' their setting up. However an escape clause is added, allowing a lower standard of just 'adequate provision' of programmes and the publication of newspaper articles, rather than a whole newspaper in the language. Not surprisingly for such a document, there is no attempt to define just exactly what all this means. If a newspaper is issued weekly is this adequate? Is there a minimum number of hours a day required to constitute a television channel? (For further discussion of these standards of provision, see Cormack, 2005: 112–113, and for discussion of the more general issue of media provision, see Moring's Chapter 2 in this book.) The Charter then goes on to protect cross-border broadcasting, important since many linguistic minorities have been split by state boundaries (this is most obvious in the cases of Basque and Catalan, both crossing the border between Spain and France). (For further discussion of the Charter, see Guyot's Chapter 3 in this book.) In 1996 the Universal Declaration of Linguistic Rights (sometimes known as the Barcelona Declaration) reinforced this argument, deriving norms for media provision from the assertion of linguistic rights. More recently, the 2003 Conference on the Use of Minority Languages in the Broadcast Media resulted in a set of *Guidelines on the Use of Minority Languages in the Broadcast Media*, which gives much more detailed consideration to this issue (the Guidelines, along with other papers from the conference, were published in 2005 in *Mercator Media Forum 8*, in an issue devoted to the *Conference*).

Another impetus to the study of minority languages has been the steadily growing body of academic writing in this area, marked most clearly by the publication of Joshua Fishman's *Reversing Language Shift* in 1991 and his follow-up of a decade later, *Can Threatened Languages Be Saved?* (the latter being a collection of essays by various writers but including important opening and closing essays by Fishman himself). His influential account of the 'Graded Intergenerational Disruption Scale' (GIDS) as a means of measuring the degree of language shift, put the emphasis for language maintenance firmly on the lived experience in the local community (Fishman, 1991: 87–109; Fishman, 2001: 451–483). Fishman's work has stimulated much other writing in what has become a significant academic growth area, and this leads towards the more specific territory of this book – minority language media studies (despite Fishman's own scepticism about the media's role in language maintenance). Several publications during the 1990s established the groundwork for this, alongside a steadily increasing number of studies of media in specific minority language communities.

Although there had been earlier writings dealing with specific languages, the first major step towards developing the study of minority language media was taken with the publication in 1992 of the collection

Ethnic Minority Media: An International Perspective (Riggins, 1992). Despite the fact that the title did not mention them, minority languages featured throughout this book, with essays ranging from media in Greenlandic to Aboriginal broadcasting in Australia, from Basque radio in France to Spanish language media in New York. Again and again in these essays, language emerges as a crucial factor in minority community media. However, perhaps the most significant contributions were the two generalising essays by the editor, Stephen H. Riggins, at the start ('The Media Imperative: Ethnic Minority Survival in the Age of Mass Communication') and at the end ('The Promise and Limits of Ethnic Minority Media'). In these he laid out some principles that began to identify the ground on which the study of minority language media could be built, even though this was not the declared aim of the book.

In the introduction he describes what he terms 'the media imperative': 'What better strategy could there be for ensuring minority survival than the development by minorities of their own media conveying their own point of view in their own language?' (Riggins, 1992: 3). But against this he notes that 'ethnic minority media may also unintentionally encourage the assimilation of their audiences to mainstream values', thus revealing the 'dual role' of ethnic media (Riggins, 1992: 4). He also describes five models of state support for ethnic minority media, which make clear the variety of reasons that a state may have for supporting a minority (and are useful to bear in mind when reading the historical account given in Browne's Chapter 7 in this book): the integrationist model (media designed to integrate the minority into the majority culture), the economic model (assimilating the minority by economic pressure), the divisive model (setting different minorities against each other), the pre-emptive model (pre-empting more radical media from within the minority community itself), and the proselytism model (assimilating the minority into the majority's values). These are important as a first attempt at a descriptive categorisation of minority media and work as well for minority languages as they do for other types of minority. They also show an awareness of the dangers of state support that European writers would do well to take to heart.

From Riggins' comments generally, five points can be extracted that indicate key elements in any study of minority language media, but that, at the same time, indicate key problems.

(1) *The media imperative* – This is the need that minorities have to express their own values and culture in the media.

(2) *The limits of media power* – 'It appears that the long-term effect of ethnic minority media is neither total assimilation nor total cultural

preservation but some moderate degree of preservation that represents a compromise between these two extremes' (Riggins, 1992: 276).
Importantly, he goes on to note that 'the actual impact of the media on
ethnic minority survival remains problematic' (Riggins, 1992: 277).

(3)   *The political context* – 'The crucial importance of the political context
       of ethnic minority media is evident in all the case studies presented
       here' (Riggins, 1992: 276). This point has been argued elsewhere for
       minority languages in general (May, 2001) and minority language
       media in particular (Cormack, 1998), and is noted in several of the
       chapters in this book, notably Chapter 3 by Guyot.

(4)   *Minority empowerment* – This stresses differences, and, of course,
       while acknowledgement of difference may be what the minority
       community seeks, it may also be profoundly unsettling for the
       majority community, upsetting the myth of the homogeneous nature
       of the nation-state (this is most apparent in France, although it is also
       evident in reactions to developments in the 20th century in Spain
       and in the UK).

(5)   *Minority control of the media for the benefit of the community* – Riggins
       notes that 'it is essential for minorities to have full control over the
       financing and administration of their own media' (Riggins, 1992:
       285) and that 'minority media should be designed in response to the
       informational needs and preferences of the community' (Riggins,
       1992: 286). These might seem very obvious points but they indicate
       an essential problem – if finance is coming from the majority
       community (inevitable given the cost of television in particular),
       how is overall power and control to be disentangled from this, while
       appropriate accountability is retained?

From all of this it will be clear that Riggins takes an unashamedly pragmatic view of minority media. He is not so much concerned with theoretical issues as with the practicalities of media production. In taking this
approach, he is not alone. Minority language media studies are energised
by two sources – on the one hand the practicalities of how the media can
be used to support languages under threat, and on the other hand, the
rather more academic view of minority language media as an intriguing
example of the media's role in society. It is probably fair to say that the
former is the underlying concern of most of those involved in minority
language media studies, but the latter provides the link with more mainstream media studies.

    After Riggins, the next significant step came in 1996 in another book
whose title did not focus explicitly on language issues: Donald Browne's

Electronic Media and Indigenous Peoples: A Voice of Our Own? Once again language issues permeated the book, although here, unlike *Ethnic Minority Media*, there was a chapter specifically on minority language broadcasting. Again, some important points were developed that were to feed into later writings. Like Riggins, Browne emphasises the limitations of the media: 'The preservation or restoration of a language, and a culture in a larger sense, is not the task of the media alone' (Browne, 1996: 7). Browne based his book on cultural dependency theory, and in particular on two issues: (1) the point that 'receivers of imported material may not be aware of their dependency' (Browne, 1996: 11) and may regard the importation of broadcast programming to be quite natural; (2) the question of how 'majority culture (colonial or otherwise) models of professional conduct by broadcast staff [have] influenced indigenous staff members' (Browne, 1996: 11). Both remain highly relevant issues for minority language media, and have not been given the saliency that they deserve. Browne goes on to note (1996: 59) seven purposes for indigenous media: (1) to rescue the language; (2) to increase self-esteem; (3) to combat negative images; (4) to work for greater cohesiveness and, through this, for political influence; (5) to provide a visible and audible symbol of indigenous society; (6) to provide an outlet for creative production; (7) to provide a source of employment. These still stand as appropriate aims for minority language media, as much as for indigenous media generally.

The section in Browne's book specifically on language issues starts with an important point: 'There is virtually no "hard" (scientific) evidence to indicate that the initiation of an indigenous language media service helps to restore or revive its usage, but all stations broadcasting substantial amounts of such languages certainly have that hope and expectation' (1996: 169). (Some of the implications of this are discussed in Cormack's Chapter 4 in this book.) Browne then separates out the three aims of reviving languages, preserving languages, and extending languages, and notes five potential problems for minority language media: (1) the use of dialects (such languages seldom have an accepted standardised form); (2) the reshaping of language use by media practitioners; (3) the use of visual languages; (4) the use of languages to establish a separate identity; (5) the use of languages to maintain subordination. He concludes this chapter by writing that 'the chief lesson so far appears to be that whatever is done along those lines will be almost certain to upset or antagonize someone, and sometimes a very influential someone' (Browne, 1996: 189), and it is not just those in the majority language community who may be unsettled by minority language media.

In the final chapter of his book Browne notes seven important elements if indigenous media are to emerge and flourish (Browne, 1996: 233): (1) 'the ability to gather enough committed individuals together'; (2) 'the support of at least one group or organization in majority society'; (3) 'the backing of at least a few influential individuals and organizations from within indigenous society'; (4) 'reasonably favourable publicity through majority culture media on an indigenous group's attempts to develop electronic media outlets'; (5) 'support in the form of advice, training and use of equipment by majority culture electronic media organizations'; (6) 'events that call the attention of society as a whole to the magnitude of injustice, inequality, and other evidences of the discriminatory treatment of indigenous groups within society'; (7) 'a reasonably sound national economy at the time the campaign for indigenous media is in progress'. These emphasise the difficulties of such campaigns and make clear the obstacles in their way (for further discussion on minority language media campaigns, see Hourigan, 2003).

Overall, then, Browne's work is based on the concept of cultural dependency and much of his concern is how to combat this. However his book has been very important in emphasising the limits of minority media, the importance of programming issues (in his third chapter), and the importance of internal problems, such as differences of language use and cultural tradition. The main problem is that the term 'indigenous' does not work in many situations as a contrast between minority and majority linguistic minorities, such as those in Europe, and can confuse by hiding important distinctions.

In these books by Riggins and Browne two strands can be seen. On the one hand, there is an attempt to provide guidance to minority media practitioners. On the other hand, the authors are attempting to make sense of what is happening in this area by applying analytical categories to it. This relates to the two sources of interest in minority language media noted earlier – language activism and academic understanding.

Although the books of Riggins and Browne were the most relevant for the development of minority language media studies, another book, published in 1995, is worth noting: Frachon and Vargaftig's *European Television: Immigrants and Ethnic Minorities*. Frachon and Vargaftig were concerned with issues of immigration and racial policy. The emphasis was on minority ethnic groups getting access to and fair treatment from dominant media, but (implicitly) in the language of the dominant culture. In one essay, on the guidelines of the Council of Europe, 1972–1992, language is referred to when discussing official guidelines, particularly five points in a report of 1979 (by B. Ducoli and A. Martinow-Remiche) that the writer of the essay has 'encountered time and time again' (Frachon & Vargaftig, 1995: 77). These five points are: (1) 'to help immigrants understand and adapt to the host society'; (2) 'to provide immigrants with information resources in their own language about their country of origin and to enable them to find out more about their own culture'; (3) 'to give immigrants and minorities access to the media'; (4) 'to give society as a whole a better understanding of immigrant communities by familiarizing people with immigration as part of their own history'; (5) 'to encourage understanding in what is now a multicultural and multi-ethnic society'. In the rest of the book, language issues are never emphasised, but yet the book's survey of European television does allow some sense of the region's linguistic diversity to appear. As such it uncovers and gathers useful information in relation to the linguistic variety on European television, including references not just to Arabic, Hindi and Turkish, but also to Romany (Frachon & Vargaftig, 1995: 223), a language even more hidden than other European minorities. Most importantly, this book implicitly raises an issue that has so far been neglected in minority language media studies – the comparison between indigenous minority languages and immigrant minority languages.

With these books as forebears, Cormack (1998) attempted to lay the grounds for minority language media study as such, although in this case, explicitly limited to the Western European examples. His concern was with setting up a basis for comparative study: 'The overall aim is to set up a framework of debate within which specific examples can be investigated and assessed' (Cormack, 1998: 34). He suggested a number of features necessary for minority language media to emerge, and then discussed how the notion of the public sphere applied to such media, and the role of intellectuals. Thus the twin themes of applying analytical categories to the field, along with a more pragmatic involvement with how minority language media might function most successfully were continued. Cormack concluded by putting forward four points: (1) 'that in any discussion of minority language media careful attention needs to be given to the specific context'; (2) 'that central to any discussion of these media must be consideration of the political environment'; (3) 'that not just the cultural and entertainment needs but also the political needs of minority communities...must be considered if minority language media are to be assessed and compared'; (4) 'that an essential part of the study of any minority language media is the role of intellectuals and cultural producers' (Cormack, 1998: 48–49). However, perhaps the most significant aspect of this essay was not the specific suggestions made, but the general attempt to treat minority language media as a category of its own, with distinctive problems and issues, while keeping it within the more general field of comparative media studies.

From these various writings in the 1990s, it is possible to see the beginnings of, if not a theory of minority language media, at least the development of a framework within which such media might be considered. The field is delineated by the politics of language and the media's relation to that. It is driven by the attempt to understand the role of minority languages in contemporary society, thereby intending to contribute to their survival. Along with language survival, a key aim for such media (and therefore a key topic for research) is cultural and political self-representation, thus linking these issues into identity politics. Such work can feed into policy development, at both the organisational and production levels, giving this field of study a very direct practical application.

Minority Language Media as a Field of Study

If so much is clear, the conceptual constituents of the field are less so. It differs from both language study and media studies in important ways, but also makes use of contributions from other disciplines, such as sociology, politics and economics. It differs from language study (such as sociolinguistics) in its engagement with the problematics of media studies – debates concerning media impact, media economics, media organisation, and media analysis. However it also differs from conventional media studies in its reliance on the concepts and, indeed, the insights, of language study, particularly in the area of language planning.

Looking through writing on this subject, the key concepts become clear: community, the public sphere, linguistic normalisation, cultural identity, globalisation, new social movements. Each of these suggests a different context, a different way of looking at media in minority language communities, and a different way of assessing such media. 'Community' is a much debated term within sociology. One current dictionary of sociological terms makes clear both the attraction of the term and its problems. On the one hand 'the concept of community concerns a particularly constituted set of social relationships based on something which the participants have in common – usually a common sense of identity'; on the other hand, 'there is no clear and widely accepted definition of just what characteristic features of social interaction constitute the solidaristic relations typical of so-called communities' (Marshall, 1998: 97). Using the term in relation to linguistic groups at least makes clear the basis for the group's identity – the language itself. However that in itself can cause problems. Many minority languages are based not just in the traditional areas where the language has a long history, but are also represented in large, industrialised urban areas, and may also have a diaspora. The emergence of the term 'virtual community' in relation to the Internet adds to an already confusing concept.

The use of Habermas's notion of the public sphere, as a domain for public discussion on public issues, has now a long history in media studies (see, for example, Dahlgren, 1995). In the current volume it is fundamental to Guyot's analysis in Chapter 3. There are however limitations associated with this term (see Hourigan's criticisms in Hourigan, 2003). The problems associated with using this term in relation to minority languages are simply the problems of the term in general, but writ large, given the centrality of language to the idea of the public sphere. The concept sets up an ideal of public communication, and public participation in communication, which is impossibly high, particularly in these days of commercially driven media. However alongside this is its usefulness as a critical term, a basis from which to assess actual media provision.

Although not yet, perhaps, a familiar term in many countries, the notion of 'linguistic normalisation' has proved to be a useful term, particularly in the Catalan and Basque contexts (see the chapters by Arana, Azpillaga and Narbaiza (Chapter 9) and Corominas Piulats (Chapter 10) in this book). As a way of generalising about language planning, it puts the emphasis on the processes by which minority languages are not merely rescued and maintained, but are incorporated into everyday life. The media's ability to construct our sense of everyday life is thereby put into the foreground and the debate then centres on how both media outlets and media content contribute best to this. Clearly, this is closely linked to the public sphere.

Notions of culture and cultural identity have been central in many discussions of minority languages and their media. This does however show up a specific problem – what is the nature of the relationship between culture and language? (See May, 2001: 132–137 for a useful discussion of this.) With media being language-dependent and both contributors to, and bearers of, culture (by most definitions of that notoriously complex term), this issue is of central importance for minority language media. It is difficult to get far in discussions of either minority language media content or arguments in favour of such media without notions of culture being invoked.

Globalisation sets the international context for minority language media and constructs this as both threat and opportunity (see Hourigan's conclusion to this book (Chapter 14)). The threat is that of cultural imperialism and dependency. Despite the criticisms that have been made of the notion of cultural imperialism (Tomlinson, 2000), the phenomena which that term attempts to conceptualise are very familiar to minority language groups. The opportunity is the ease by which contemporary electronic media – both the Internet and digital broadcasting – can be used. There are media spaces there for minorities of all kinds, although the technology which allows the use of new media by minority languages also allows the availability of majority languages to increase.

With the analytical approach of new social movements (Hourigan, 2003), the postmodern context of contemporary minority languages is made explicit. This gives a context in which minority languages are seen not as some dubious throwback to a pre-modern age, but rather as part of the new identity politics. It also helps to explain why claims for minority language media began to be more widely recognised and even partially satisfied at a particular historical moment.

In addition to these approaches, the economic approach associated with the work of François Grin deserves mention (Grin, 2003; Grin & Moring, 2003; Grin & Vaillancourt, 1999). Although not reflected directly in any of the chapters in this book, Grin's work provides an important counterpoint to other approaches, and one that is rooted firmly in empirical detail.

As this field of study develops, however, other analytical concepts will be introduced and play their part. This will be clear from the remainder of this book. It will also be clear that, despite the common interests of many working in this field, there is no single dominant approach. The one factor that might be said to unite this work is a concern for, and belief in, the importance of minority languages, allied with a conviction of the importance of the media for such languages. Arguments in favour of these languages, whether based in human rights or in theories of cultural diversity, inevitably imply an important role for the media (Cormack, 2005).

The Rest of the Book

The essays in this book are designed to demonstrate current work in this field in various ways, as indicated by the subtitle: concepts, critiques and case studies. The essays sum up current writing on minority language media and set the stage for future research. The core of the book developed out of the First Mercator International Symposium on Minority Languages and Research, held at the University of Wales Aberystwyth in April 2003. The book's European origins will be clear – most of the chapters are based on the experiences of the European minority languages. Future research will determine how generally applicable this experience is.

The first part of the book consists of essays on general topics in the field of minority language media. It begins with Tom Moring who uses the concepts of 'institutional completeness' (a full range of media) and 'functional completeness' (the audience being fully satisfied by the media on offer) to examine the media needs of minority language communities. He demonstrates how a full range of media provision is necessary in a minority language if the (usually bilingual) audience is not to move to the richer (in all senses) media of the majority. This has major implications for the rather tokenistic practices of many European media providers in relation to minorities. Jacques Guyot then focuses on political factors, looking first at the legal situation of minority languages and their media, and then at the idea of the public sphere and how this relates to multiculturalism and linguistic diversity, ending with the outline of a multimedia strategy for minority languages. Put together these points emphasise the importance of minority language access to the public sphere of debate and comment. Following this Mike Cormack focuses of the specific issue of the media's role in language maintenance, raising questions about how this can be understood, and emphasising our current lack of knowledge in this field. He goes on to suggest a way of researching this based on the notion of an ecology of language. Campaigns for minority language media have frequently been considered as if they were isolated phenomena. However Niamh Hourigan in her chapter looks at how some of these campaigns have learnt from each other. She examines the three Celtic campaigns for minority language television – in Wales, Ireland and Scotland – and shows how networking operated across the three campaigns. This chapter points to the way that minority language groups – at least in Europe – have become increasingly aware of each other in recent years. Glyn Williams then looks at the 'knowledge economy' of digital multimedia. He discusses the transformations required in media work organisation, with the introduction of Digital Asset Management Systems, and emphasises the implications this has for minority languages. The threats and opportunities that the digital revolution pose for minority languages appear in every aspect of the media from production through distribution to consumption. Williams makes us aware that this will involve fundamental changes in the media workplace. Following this Donald R. Browne gives the first published history of minority language broadcasting, drawing on a wide range of examples from around the world, and showing the range of factors involved in this development. His work gives a worldwide context for the other chapters, as well as, in various ways, emphasising the importance of politics in the development of such media.

The second part of the book looks at more specific issues. Daniel Cunliffe considers new media and tackles head on a topic that is becoming increasingly important in relation to minority languages (see, for example, some of the contributions to issues 5, 6 and 7 of the *Mercator Media Forum*): the role of the Internet. He notes how the Internet offers minority cultures the opportunity to be producers of media content, and indeed to form communities of media producers, rather than being merely consumers of majority mass media, but he also argues that it is not clear how a minority culture can make best use of the technologies available, and which of these technologies are the most effective in maintaining and revitalising minority cultures.

After this three geographically based chapters assess aspects of the media in the three areas in Western Europe that are often seen as the most successful as far as minority language broadcasting is concerned, all having established television channels in the local language in the early 1980s – the Basque Country, Catalonia and Wales. First Edorta Arana, Patxi Azpillaga and Beatriz Narbaiza look at the role played by the media in the Basque Country, with particular emphasis on the role of local television. They show that although television can be of great importance in supporting a minority language at the level of the local community, there are dangers when such local media become commercialised and succumb to economic pressures to abandon the minority language in favour of the more lucrative majority audience. Next Maria Corominas Piulats looks at media policy and linguistic policy in Catalonia, with particular concern for the balance between Catalan and Spanish in the media. Not only has Catalonia the most highly developed media system in any minority language in Europe, but it also represents the most sustained attempt by a government to develop a linguistic policy of normalisation, that is, making the language a part of normal everyday life in all social contexts. The media's role in this has been crucial. Corominas Piulats' chapter shows how this process has worked, but also contains some words of warning, particularly in relation to the Internet. Then Elin Haf Gruffydd Jones examines the representativeness of television programming in Welsh. With a limited amount of programming, the question of how minority language broadcasters represent the community as a whole becomes important. Indeed one of the arguments in favour of minority language television is that it can be used to give the minority community some power over the way in which it is represented. Jones uses the locations shown within programmes as a guide to representativeness and looks at Welsh language broadcast fiction over a four-year period, and then at programming in general over much shorter periods. Her results are encouraging in that she finds that, by this measure at least, Welsh television can truly claim to be representing the whole community of Welsh speakers.

The next two chapters shift the emphasis from area studies to more general topics. Eithne O'Connell discusses issues of translation, so often important in minority language media, noting that the act of translation is never neutral, with the result that translation practice needs to be critically investigated. Choices concerned with dubbing, subtitling and indeed even whether material imported from other languages and cultures should be used at all in a minority language all deserve more attention than they have so far had in the study of minority language media. More generally she argues cogently for the seeming paradox that the study of minority language media has so far not paid enough attention to specifically linguistic issues. Paddy Ladd then puts sign language firmly on the minority language media agenda. His account of the battle for sign language on British television will strike many familiar notes to those with experience of other minority languages – the struggle for media visibility, the paternalism of the national broadcasters, the desire for self-representation in television drama, arguments within the minority community as to the quality of the language used on television, the centrality of children's programming, particularly in earlier years, the importance of television as a career option, the prestige and self-confidence that television can bring, and the current aim of a digital channel devoted to sign language.

Finally, Niamh Hourigan's conclusion draws together a number of threads and looks towards future research. She discusses four areas on which minority language media research can fruitfully be focused: (1) the comparison between 'indigenous' minority language media and those for 'new' or 'immigrant' languages; (2) the relationship with global languages; (3) the digital divide and how it impacts upon minority language communities; (4) the broad issue of globalisation. Her comments build upon the rest of the book, all of which makes clear that minority language media studies can now be seen as an established field of study, one with its own research agenda, and one that is energised by the awareness of the fragility of the situations of many minority languages.

References

Browne, D. (1996) *Electronic Media and Indigenous Peoples: A Voice of Our Own?* Ames, IA: Iowa State University Press.

Cormack, M. (1998) Minority language media in Western Europe: Preliminary considerations. *European Journal of Communication* 13 (1), 33–52.

Cormack, M. (2005) The cultural politics of minority language media. *International Journal of Media and Cultural Politics* 1 (1), 107–122.

Dahlgren, P. (1995) *Television and the Public Sphere: Citizenship, Democracy and the Media*. London: Sage.

Fishman, J. (1991) *Reversing Language Shift: Theoretical and Empirical Foundations of Assistance to Threatened Languages.* Clevedon: Multilingual Matters.

Fishman, J. (ed.) (2001) *Can Threatened Languages Be Saved? Reversing Language Shift, Revisited: A 21st Century Perspective.* Clevedon: Multilingual Matters.

Frachon, C. and Vargaftig, M. (eds) (1995) *European Television: Immigrants and Ethnic Minorities.* London: John Libbey.

Grillo, R. (1989) *Dominant Languages: Language and Hierarchy in Britain and France.* Cambridge: Cambridge University Press.

Grin, F. (2003) *Language Policy Evaluation and the European Charter for Regional or Minority Languages.* Basingstoke: Palgrave Macmillan.

Grin, F. and Moring, T. (with Gorter, D., Häggman, J., Ó Riagáin, D. and Strubell, M.) (2003) *Support for Minority Languages in Europe.* Final report on a project financed by the European Commission, Directorate Education and Culture. On www at: http://europa.eu.int/comm/education/policies/lang/langmin/support.pdf.

Grin, F. and Vaillancourt, F. (1999) *The Cost-Effectiveness Evaluation of Minority Language Policies: Case Studies on Wales, Ireland, and the Basque Country.* ECMI Monograph No. 2. Flensburg: ECMI.

Heller, M. (1999) *Linguistic Minorities and Modernity: A Sociolinguistic Ethnography.* London: Longman.

Hourigan, N. (2003) *Escaping the Global Village: Media, Language and Protest.* Lanham, MD: Lexington Books.

Marshall, G. (ed.) (1998) *A Dictionary of Sociology* (2nd edn). Oxford: Oxford University Press.

May, S. (2001) *Language and Minority Rights: Ethnicity, Nationalism and the Politics of Language.* Harlow: Pearson Education.

Riggins, S.H. (ed.) (1992) *Ethnic Minority Media: An International Perspective.* London: Sage.

Thomas, N. (1995) The Mercator Media Forum. *Mercator Media Forum* 1, 2–11.

Tomlinson, J. (2000) *Cultural Imperialism.* London: Continuum.

Websites

European Bureau for Lesser Used Languages: ww2.eblul.org
European Charter for Regional or Minority Languages:
http://conventions.coe.int/treaty/en/Treaties/Html/148.htm
Universal Declaration of Linguistic Rights:
www.linguistic-declaration.org/index-gb.htm

Chapter 2
Functional Completeness in Minority Language Media

TOM MORING

It is often said that the media are important, but precisely how they are important is not so clear. The cultural effects of the media *in general* are notoriously difficult to distinguish from effects originating from other aspects of social life. The quest into the cultural pertinence of daily mass media becomes even more challenging when we talk about media in minority languages. However, from the view of a researcher – or a policy-maker – this question is of the greatest importance. Why and how should society distribute scarce resources to this field? What do we know about the specific effects of specific media in specific situations? The fact is that we do not know very much. We lack the important tools that are required to make the reliable predictions that are needed to support with credibility claims for improvements in the media landscape that may mean development or depravation – if not life or death – to language communities.

This chapter presents an effort to provide a structure that can be of help when addressing such matters. The chapter first addresses shortcomings of media research so far in this field. It then considers what media provision is necessary if the minority audience is not to move to majority language media (the need for institutional completeness, which can allow the audience to have functional completeness). It does this by discussing the individual significance of different media, and the need for different kinds of content (genre completeness). Finally it looks at what influences the viewing preferences of bilingual viewers.

A basic point underpinning the entire reasoning in the chapter is that media carry language. They also operate through language. And further-more, they develop language. Specific types of media display different features in this aspect. To language minorities this makes an under-standing of the more complex nature of this field all the more important. Although these points are evident in those milieus where a minority language is spoken, media research and language sociology have not taken this issue on board with the weight it deserves.

Edward Sapir noted that 'anthropologists have been in the habit of studying man under the three rubrics of race, language and culture'

(Sapir, 1963: 207). In international media research the focus was for many decades on ethnicity, race and class. In more recent times, popular culture has risen into a major position in international research. However, the question of language has had a less prominent position and it has often been set aside altogether, particularly in the very influential research that has been carried out in the English-speaking part of the world. Also the speakers of other major languages have been rather uninterested in the language dimension. It seems as if the predominance of the monolingualism of Anglo-American, French or German culture too often has led mainstream research to leave out language as a variable (Moring, 2000a: 206–207; Patten & Kymlicka, 2003: 1, 6–7).

This essay is not the first one to point to the lack of analysis regarding minority language media and its impact. For example Mike Cormack (1998: 34) and Brigitta Busch (1999: 3; 2004: 13) have specifically pointed to the problem of a lack in theorising research on media, minority language and collective identity. They have also made commendable efforts to take the analysis to a new level. And there are indeed studies that help us to understand how the media landscape contributes – negatively and positively – to the development of the particular type of cultural identity that relates to minority languages.

Sociologists and historians who take language seriously tend to claim that language is at the core of identity formation in Europe (Allardt & Starck, 1981: 22; Schöpflin, 2000: 116–127). But the central question remains: how does speaking a language (in this case a minority language) in the media interact with the survival and development of the language itself? This chapter accepts the general assumption that the availability of media to support a language matters greatly. The particular aim of the chapter is to develop the discussion about the conditions under which minority language media will exist and be used.

A Functional Perspective on Media Use

The point of departure of this chapter is that any language community – and minority languages are no exception – would strive to develop a state of *functional completeness* (or *normalisation*, see Chapter 1 of this volume, also Grin, 2003: 201–203) regarding the use of the language. This means that speakers of the language, if they so choose, can live their life in and through the language without having to resort to other languages, at least within the confines of everyday matters in their community. A necessary but not sufficient condition for such a functional completeness is the *institutional completeness* (Breton, 1964; Kymlicka, 1995, 2004) of different providers of services and functions in a language, that is, that there are media platforms available in the minority language for each type of media.

As we shall see, regarding media use there is a complex relationship between the institutional aspects and the functional aspects of completeness. Depending on the status of the language, the level of bilingualism among the speakers, and also on the territorial distribution of the speakers of a language, even high levels of institutional completeness may not lead to functional completeness. It is, however, evident that low levels of institutional completeness will always tend to foster patterns of incomplete media use in the language, and a movement among the speakers of this language towards media offered in the majority language and languages in global use.

Even some state languages today are afraid of not fulfilling all aspects of functional completeness (see, for example, the declaration on a Nordic language policy, *Deklaration om nordisk språkpolitik*, 2005). Only a few minority languages can credibly claim a high functional level in the media sector. Such examples of relatively good media landscapes are Catalan and Basque in parts of Spain, German in South Tyrol and Swedish in Finland. In all these communities there are at least one television channel, one radio station and one newspaper functioning in the regional or minority language. Other communities, such as Welsh in UK and Frisian in the Netherlands, are well served by broadcasting (mainly as part of a public service remit) but less well served by printed media such as newspapers. Furthermore, it appears as if in all situations where there exists a good supply in the broadcast media, the media services on the web will also be rather well developed.

Such media systems can be called more or less institutionally complete. A further prerequisite for institutional completeness is, however, that each of these platforms can provide at least one distinguishable full service alternative in the minority language of a quality that is at the level of the services available in the majority language. As a consequence of the fast development of commercial television and radio since the late 1980s, attention has increasingly been raised also towards the availability of a variety of genres of content in the minority language as a prerequisite of institutional completeness.

The dynamics of the media field in this sense have been well known in media research for a long time. Harold Innis has pointed to the divisions between community-building media of an old and traditional form that were oral or hand-written and modern mass media. According to Innis (1973), modern mass media would favour commercialism and imperialism.

This is a finding well in line with what has been observed by researchers who have studied the use of minority language media (cf. Busch, 2001, Jackson & Rosenberg, 2004). The overall effect of media tends rather to undermine than support minority identity in the sense that mainstream media accelerate language shift and assimilation of minority communities. In most cases, minority language media serve as a defensive tool, balancing the impact of the language(s) that dominate the media landscape.

Policy-makers have expressed an understanding of the restitutionary character of media policies when they have created the legal instruments in this field. Most clearly this is expressed in the European Charter for Regional or Minority Languages (1992) (Council of Europe, European Treaty Series (ETS) 148 – hence referred to as the Charter). Its explanatory report (paragraph 10) makes explicit the point that where regional or minority languages have suffered from unfavourable conditions in the past, they should be compensated. State support to media in minority languages can thus be seen as an effort to counterbalance the damage made to language-based cultures by modern mass media.

In addition to such quantifying and qualifying conditions regarding the media field as a whole, there is also a need to look at specific types of media more closely. In the footsteps of Innis, Marshall McLuhan developed an argument about how different media differ in character. The specific discourse presented by McLuhan (1967, and elsewhere) on the characteristics of different media is not the most relevant aspect here, but the more wide-ranging insight implied by this reasoning is essential: media have fundamentally different characteristics that affect us in distinct ways and serve different senses and different cultural functions. For institutional completeness, minority language audiences would have to have access to them all in their own language.

The Dangers of Substitutive Strategies

Minority languages are frequently forced to accept a situation where the media offerings are all but complete. As resources are limited, those who work with enhancing the languages face difficult choices. Representatives of minority language speakers are frequently faced with questions about whether to offer their own services on separate radio stations or television channels with very meagre resources, or rather to resign the broadcasting of programmes in their languages to slots (often called 'windows') on a service offered in the majority language. The latter situation prevails, for example, for radio and television in minority languages in Germany, Hungary, Slovenia (except for Italian language) and Croatia, and for television broadcasting in Scottish Gaelic in UK or in the Sami languages in the Nordic countries. Minority language speakers are also often confronted with a demand to be modest in their desire for a presence in competitive and more expensive platforms (such as nation-wide television) and instead use their scarce resources on local radio or on the Internet. The Internet is also often suggested as an alternative to print media, because of lower production and distribution costs. Such substitutive practices are not, however, at all ideal, as the different media fulfil different and distinct functions.

Starting with radio, a quite common state of affairs in smaller minority language communities is the existence of a radio station and some television programmes on a regional station, in addition to a weekly or monthly community newspaper. Under such circumstances radio has proven to be an indispensable tool for developing, for example, a common oral language standard. Such effects have been reported by studies made in Ireland (Grin & Moring, 2003), and witness of the same effect is born in communications to the Committee of Experts of the Charter (for example regarding Scottish Gaelic). Whereas this is not always welcomed by speakers of local varieties of languages, it has indisputably positive effects with regard to the status of the language itself. Radio is also a good conveyor of news in the minority language, and it is an excellent contact medium connecting members in the community itself. The shortcomings of radio have to do with its transient character and its inaccessibility for speakers of other languages. Radio broadcasts evaporate fast, leaving less trace than print media, and the broadcasts are not easy to follow for speakers of other languages who may live in the same household.

Television also has a particular role when it comes to organising the minority around a common experience. It also is unbeatable as a medium that gives prestige and visibility to the minority language and its culture in the eyes of the majority. Purely due to its technical quality (where subti-tling is used), it allows for shared experiences in bilingual families where part of the family is capable of understanding the minority language. This is due to the simultaneous use of the elements of visuality and language, which Busch (2004: 51–55, 281–282) calls multimodality. Television also supports image construction and popularisation, which is required if a community is to develop its own representations, for example in the field of popular culture.

The printed press is essential for daily stimulation in a reading culture. Where a local or regional press exists, the newspaper is also in a key role with respect to organising the community. Maintaining a presence that is physical in a different sense from the radio or the television programme (and also normally in comparison with a news page on the web), it is essential for the community's short-term memory. In this sense, the newspaper today appears to fill some of the time-binding functions that Harold Innis linked to oral tradition and hand-written media.

Considering the Internet, the opportunities and flexibility in geographical terms may be without limits, while other constraints (generational, educational, time-use etc.) come into play (see also Cunliffe's Chapter 8 in this book). There are indications, for example in audience research carried out among Finnish speakers in Sweden, that some minorities are more active Internet users than the rest of the population. This feature has been discussed also with respect to immigrant communities with a kin-state that carries extensive services in their language.

If we compare the media supply to traditional linguistic minorities with the supply to speakers of immigrant languages, an interesting difference becomes apparent. In many cases immigrant language communities are served by satellite television from the original homeland of the language, complemented by material on the Internet, which also is predominantly produced abroad. Media that connect to the local community in the new homeland are scarce and produced at low cost: often community radio and some local websites, only seldom community TV (Christiansen, 2003; Moring & Malmgren, 2004: 21; Sreberny, 2000). This type of media supply is likely to affect the processes of identity formation within the immigrant community, keeping it culturally distinct. In situations where the immigrants are not fluent in the language of the state that they have moved to, the Internet in combination with satellite television may lessen the contacts between cultures and even isolate the immigrants within cultural *sphericules* instead of fostering a common public sphere (Downing & Husband, 2005: 211). This would be expected to occur particularly if the minority was subjected to social segregation. In the case of national minorities with (predominantly) good understanding of the majority language and a habit of using media in the minority language and the majority language side by side, this type of problem does not, however, occur. In addition the policy of public service media usually runs counter to such developments.

The Internet was at the start considered by some to be the death stroke to other media, particularly the press. Media research has, however, demonstrated that technological development usually does not mean that old media die; they seek ways to adjust (Pool, 1983: 5–7). This finding has proven to be true (at least so far) also for the Internet. Irrespective of media convergence and the appearance of the new web platform, press, radio and television are still very much alive as different entities with different functions. Efforts to plant old media functions into the Internet have not so far been entirely successful, while it has developed distinct features of its own. Somewhat counter-intuitively, a positive correlation between use of the printed press and use of Internet has been detected in Nordic media studies (Carlsson & Harrie, 2001).

These findings have immediate consequences with respect to media policies for language minorities. If, in society at large, substitutive media use has not commonly developed, can people who speak a minority language be expected to act differently? It would seem not. It is therefore of the utmost importance that minority language media are allowed to follow suit. As minority language communities are predominantly bilingual, people that have access to an incomplete set of media outlets in their own (minority) language would not only be tempted (by market mechanisms) but actually forced to turn to media in the majority language to compensate missing parts.

Time-use studies tend to show that different media become predominant at different times of the day. In Scandinavia, for example, newspapers, radio and television dominate the media habits of the morning, radio and internet dominate the day, whereas television, the Internet, and to some extent newspapers are the main media in the evening. The time distribution patterns vary, depending on, for example, distribution routines of the newspapers, but in most societies similar patterns can be observed.

It is not reasonable to assume that the needs of minority language speakers can be satisfied by media policies by which one type of media is expected to substitute for another type. And it should not have to be, from the point of view of language enhancement. In other words, it is a rash assumption to think that a bilingual speaker of, for example, Scottish Gaelic, or Sami, would seek compensation for his/her television viewing with listening to radio, or substitute newspaper reading with reading Internet sites instead. The same argument holds also for situations in which services in minority languages have been established on platforms that are not normally used in that society, such as East Europe FM frequencies (minority language radio programmes in Hungary) or DAB radio (Finnish radio in Sweden). Instead of going out of their way to find a substitute media in their own language, bilingual speakers are drawn into the mainstream media in the majority language. This is counter-productive with regard to the objective of enhancing the minority language (Moring, 2000b).

The Relevance of Genre Completeness

A similar problem can be found with respect to media formats or media genres. Developments in media research have contributed to our understanding of identity effects of the media. The critique of mass culture by Theodor W. Adorno, Max Horkheimer and other founding fathers of critical theory has been followed by more elaborate understandings of the dynamism between media production and consumption (e.g., Ang, 1986; Dahlgren & Sparks, 1991; Neuman, 1991). Media research has become much more sensitive to the use of different types of media content. Where earlier studies mainly evolved around news and information programming, newer research has demonstrated that people use all types of media material in their daily life, and that they are capable of sense-making when they reflect on popular culture. The interest in the mechanisms connecting media and culture has broadened, and researchers have also learned to apply anthropological methods and take a more constructivist approach to the understanding of how media affects culture (Busch, 2004: 17–18; Grin, 2003: 19).

In his book *Imagined Communities*, Benedict Anderson vividly describes how vernacular languages that were not national languages were suppressed from the imaginary of the people. Taking Ernest Renan's *Qu'est-ce qu'une nation?* as his example, he writes

> ... 'thirteenth-century massacres of the Midi' blurs unnamed victims and assassins behind the pure Frenchness of 'Midi'. No need to remind the readers that most of the murdered Albigensians spoke Provençal or Catalan, and that their murderers came from many parts of Western Europe. The effect of this tropology is to figure episodes in the colossal religious conflicts of medieval and early modern Europe as reassuringly fratricidal wars between – who else? – fellow Frenchmen... [W]e become aware of a systematic historiographical campaign deployed by the state mainly through the state's school system to 'remind' every young Frenchwoman and Frenchman of a series of antique slaughters which are now inscribed as 'family history'. (Anderson, 1991: 200–201)

Anderson sees the nation as an *imagined* political community. While the members will never know most of their fellow members, 'yet in the minds of each lives the image of their communion' (Anderson, 1991: 6). On the same note, the Finnish poet and writer Paavo Haavikko describes Finnishness as constructed through an incorporation of some Karelian – that is, Byzantine – cultures into regional cultures within a Finnish identity (Haavikko, 1988). A crucial vehicle in this process was an illustrated book that was read in schools by many generations, depicting Finland's history, people, countryside and geography (Topelius, 1875).

Specific studies have been made regarding the impact of different contents and forms (Altheide, 1985; Altheide & Snow, 1979; Isin & Wood, 1999). As noted by David L. Altheide:

> I am proposing a much broader view of media than the popular generic distinction such as 'print' or 'electronic,' or even specific types such as newspapers, radio, or television. Rather, I suggest that a medium is any social or technological procedure or device that is used for the selection, transmission, and reception of information... The definition considerably broadens the range of interest beyond the mere information media. This perspective opens things up to include architecture, calendars, dance, conversation, automobiles, and a host of other objects and processes... [T]his conception of media offers a perspective for understanding the use and significance of social time and space. (Altheide, 1985: 15)

Altheide's argument points to the importance of *format*. This is seen as a kind of meta-communication, or communication about communication. The rules and logic have to be understood before the substantive meaning and significance become understandable (Altheide, 1985: 136). A consequence of this would be that it is not only important to ask whether a community maintains a medium in a certain language, but also that the different formats carried by that medium would be of similar relevance. In this sense, the concept of format comes close to the concept of *genre*.

Much of the research relating to particular media genres, such as the genres associated with popular culture (Ang, 1986; Schrøder, 2000) or the news genre (Ridell, 1998), is about the social functions that a variety of genres can fulfil. Whereas media in majority languages offer a broad range of programme and newspaper genres, it is customary in states where only limited offerings are available in the minority language to focus on news, some programmes reflecting events within the minority community, and in the best case some programmes for children (cf. television programmes available in Sami language in Sweden and Finland).

In the light of the development of popular programming on commercial radio and television, however, the availability of programme formats that are attractive to young audiences are increasingly important as well. An example from Finland has shown that such media investment can actually prove to be both successful from the point of view of diversity related objectives and, at the same time, cost effective in terms of unit costs for achieving such goals (Grin & Moring, 2003).

From the examples above, it becomes evident that a low level of institutional completeness *in each type of media*, and *in each genre of content*, leads to negative results to the development of the minority language. It increases the tendency towards a complementary use of media in the minority language, lowering the level of *functional completeness* of these media.

In all but the biggest minority language communities there is a problem concerning the lack of commercially driven offerings in the minority language (the privileged exceptions being Catalan, to some extent Basque and Welsh, the Breton TV channel being a particular case, see Guyot's Chapter 3 in this volume). This means that even in relatively strong minority language communities, much of the content that supports popular culture and youth culture is available almost only in the majority language or in English – if it is not available as cross-border supply from a nearby 'kin-state' (that is, a state in which a language that is a minority language in another country is the majority state language).

From the point of view of functional completeness, this situation is of course not satisfactory. A responsible policy-maker would be expected to act in favour of an institutionally more complete range of media offerings, including different formats that support varying functional needs of a minority language community. Sadly, this is often not the case. Authorities and regulatory bodies tend to leave it to the minorities themselves to demand resources and regulated space within which to operate on a public service platform, and to the market to decide how to serve minorities with popular culture. It is evident that particularly the latter part of this equation usually does not work at all.

The minority groups will then have to do the best they can on the basis of scarce resources. This may foster entrepreneurship and efficacy, but as Charles Husband (2005) reminds us, it also fosters amateurism and frustration from having to meet professional requirements with insufficient means.

The Relevance of Spatiality and of Territorial Divisions

The spatial aspects of the linguistic community are of immediate relevance to media use as well. Alan Patten (Patten & Kymlicka, 2003: 299–305) distinguishes between three types of language divide. In territories with perfect concentration, the area where the language is spoken is unilingual and has a clear border (for example, the divide between Flemish and French in Belgium, except for Brussels). In territories with imperfect concentration, the territories are divided into areas where the language is strong, sometimes even dominating, and outlying areas where the language is dispersed into a population speaking another language (for example, Basque in the Basque Country on the one hand, and in Navarra in Spain and the border areas in France on the other). In territories with bilingual districts, the areas where the language is spoken form clusters in local communities where it is more or less concentrated, but has no unifying territorial stronghold (for example, Irish in the Republic of Ireland).

Media are affected by territorial aspects from many points of view, not least their physical distribution. This, again, reflects the spatial focus of their content. In territories with perfect concentration, the language community can be expected to form a relatively uniform cultural community as well. If there is imperfect concentration, media would have to respond to asymmetric tasks as some of the speakers would be within a (more or less) unified linguistic culture whereas other parts would be culturally mixed with the majority population. Bilingual districts, finally, would form a culturally mixed context for the minority media to operate within, the strongholds of which might or might not form separate local communities.

There are also technological and economic aspects of distribution, relating to the economic rationale of the distribution system as well the economic interests of the advertisers. It may be economically viable for even quite small newspapers that locally have a relatively strong concentration of readers to find an economic rationale that satisfies both aspects, and vice versa, if the speakers are widely dispersed, the logistics of both aspects suffer.

Distribution logistics of radio and television have similar, though not identical, problems. From a commercial point of view, the economic viability of regional broadcasts in areas with a high concentration of minority language speakers would not form a problem. But in situations where a large part of the minority language speakers are bilingual, and in addition form a minority of the local market, the economic viability of broadcasting in minority language is low or even non-existent (Moring & Salmi, 1998).

This particular feature is of special relevance in situations where commercial broadcasters are supposed to serve minority audiences. A not unusual case (such as for Scottish Gaelic on private television in the UK, Sami on private television in Norway, or Breton on private television in France) is that the broadcaster, due to cultural reasons, licensing agreements, or on the basis of extra funding, is expected to carry services in the minority language. Whereas the presence of minority language programmes on private channels has many advantages (one being the popular culture aspect mentioned above), this also often creates problems.

In a competitive environment, the broadcaster does not want to lose audiences that are turned off by programmes in minority languages. The broadcaster is tempted to place minority language programmes at off-peak hours during the day or late at night. The problem is, of course, that those who speak the minority language work and sleep with the same rhythm as the rest of the population, and are not served well by broadcasts in their own language at awkward hours. In the worst case, audience ratings are then used as a tool to show that the audience for these broadcasts is negligible. While such reasoning is totally circular, the programme supply may still be negatively affected.

The Strict Preference Condition

The content requirements that minority language media are expected to live up to are notoriously high. As has been indicated at several instances earlier in this chapter, in most contexts minority media exist side by side with an extensive supply of media in the majority language. Normally, speakers of minority languages with a traditional presence in the state where the language is spoken are bilingual. A not unusual situation is that families are formed between speakers of a minority language and speakers of a majority language. For example, in Southern Finland, more than half of the partnership relations formed where at least one of the parents speaks the minority language (Swedish) are bilingual. In Ostrobothnia where Swedish has a stronger position this share approaches one-third (Finnäs, 1998).

Research in Finland has shown that the challenge for minority language media to achieve a position in the household grows dramatically if one of the spouses speaks the majority language as a mother tongue. In such situations, the *strict preference condition* becomes particularly relevant, and difficult to meet: to what extent will the minority language speaker use media in the minority language, and to what extent will he/she prefer to lean on the majority language outlets in conformity with the majority? And will the minority language media also be present as an alternative for the children in the family? That is, is there a strict preference for the minority language and can that preference be met?

The strict preference condition implies that the target public, all other things being equal, will display a net preference for carrying out at least some of their activities in the minority language rather than in the majority language. If this condition is not met, or only weakly, protection and promotional measures will be ineffectual (Grin & Moring, 2003: 190; Grin & Vallaincourt, 1999: 98 ff.). If the minority language media become a hobby only for the minority language speaking parent, the media will be useless as an instrument to support the language in the long run, and ineffective in reversing language shift.

The answer to whether the strict preference condition is met or not will have to be sought in empirical research in particular contexts and the results will evidently vary. For example, in research conducted in Finland (Moring & Nordqvist, 2002), three factors were used to position individuals with respect to their language: a personal dimension (self-reported familiarity with using the minority language and the majority language respectively); a relational component (the composition of the household as monolingual or bilingual); and a spatial component (the composition of the surrounding community as bilingual or dominated by the majority or minority languages respectively). The findings show that there indeed is a dramatic difference between how persons in these different positions (and different combinations of these positions) use minority language media. As noted earlier in this chapter (see also Moring, 2002), the Swedish language media landscape in Finland is institutionally complete to an unusual level in spite of the fact that the number of Swedish speakers in Finland is not very high (fewer than 300,000 speakers). This situation allows persons who live in monolingual families to lean mainly on Swedish language media, if they so choose. In monolingual families more than 70% read a Swedish language newspaper, 80% of radio listening time is to stations broadcasting in Swedish and (in Ostrobothnia where television supply is complete also with respect to commercial supply, thanks to relay broadcasts from Sweden) almost the same share of television viewing is to Swedish channels. In bilingual households, the share of media use in Swedish of the Swedish-speaking family members is in all these fields reduced to half of what it is in the monolingual family.

The two other variables, personal command of the majority language, and the social strength of the language in the outside community, proved to influence media habits less. These factors mainly strengthened the tendencies that were basically established through the linguistic composition of the household.

This research shows that media use is to a great extent relational and socially embedded. Under favourable conditions, persons in a minority position demonstrate a preference to lean predominantly on the minority language media outlets if they are (at least to some extent) institutionally complete and qualitatively competitive. Also in situations where the context (composition of family, neighbourhood etc.) is less favourable, the

strict preference condition was met to a relevant extent, though functionally complementary patterns of use were gaining ground.

In another study, including different policy fields (Grin & Moring,
2003), a general preference to use minority language was detected. The
media examples studied were related to an increase in the amount of
supply (increased services on Irish language radio in the Irish Republic)
and increase in genre complexity (the establishing of a youth-oriented
radio channel in Swedish in Finland, referred to earlier in this chapter).
Particularly in the latter case the increased supply of youth-oriented
programmes was matched by an even bigger relative increase of the use of
radio in Swedish. This result would point to a possibility of 'domain
conquest' for minority language media, as opposed to the often discussed
'domain losses'.

In situations where the media supply in the minority language is scarce,
the complementary functions of media use gain ground. Brigitta Busch
has studied listening to Slovenian language radio in Carinthia, finding
listening habits among Slovenian speakers to be of a complementary
nature, while the overall media habits of the speakers of the language
resemble those of the majority (Busch, 2001: 37). The missing parts would
thus be filled with media in German language. It is likely that the same
would be the case in most settings where minority language media supply
is scarce and the population to a large extent is bilingual. Busch, however,
notes that there is a lack of research regarding the behaviour of minority
language audiences (Busch, 2004: 281).

Conclusion

The point of departure for this chapter was the lack of the appropriate
knowledge that could guide systematic efforts to develop media in
minority languages. The chapter has pointed towards several paths
leading to a more levelled and systematic approach in this field. Two
fundamental concepts have been introduced to structure the discourse:
institutional completeness – meaning a fully developed set of media of all
types, and *functional completeness* – referring to the actual use, among
minority language speakers, of media in their own language.

A conclusion is that there should be a respect for the need to develop
institutionally complete – or as institutionally complete as possible –
media landscapes in minority languages. An institutionally complete
media supply is a necessary, but not sufficient, condition for functional
completeness. There is little room for substitutive practices, where one
type of media is expected to take on functions from another type of media

in the service of minority language speakers. This type of policy has not emerged in services in the majority languages. If they were applied solely to minority languages they would immediately lead to less functionally complete use of media in the minority language.

Attention should be given to the availability of different genres of content in minority language media, including content that takes on the functions of popular culture. Also the development of quality of supply in minority languages is a matter of concern. Such features are part of institutional completeness and have a particular importance with respect to the willingness of speakers of minority media to actually use the services they are offered in their language – what here has been called the *strict preference condition*.

Acknowledgement

The author recognises that the research for this chapter has been supported by the project *European Public Sphere(s): Uniting and Dividing* and written as part of its sub-project *Public Sphere and Sphericules: Ethnic and Linguistic Minorities in an Integrating Europe.* This project is financed by the Academy of Finland (2005–2007).

References

Allardt, E. and Starck, C. (1981) *Språkgränser och samhällsstruktur: Finlandssvenskarna i ett jämførande perspektiv.* Stockholm: Almqvist&Wiksell förlag.
Altheide, David L. (1985) *Media Power.* Beverly Hills, CA: Sage.
Altheide, David L. and Snow, Robert P. (1979) *Media Logic.* Beverly Hills, CA: Sage.
Anderson, Benedict (1991) *Imagined Communities: Reflections on the Origin and Spread of Nationalism.* London: Verso.
Ang, Ien (1986) *Watching Dallas: Soap Opera and the Melodramatic Imagination.* London: Methuen.
Breton, Raymond (1964) Insituational completeness of ethnic communities and the personal relations of immigrants. *The American Journal of Sociology* 70, 193–205.
Busch, Brigitta (1999) Von Minderheitenmedien zu Medien in multilingualen & multikulturellen Situationen: Versuch eines Überblicks über das Forschungsfeld. *Medien Journal* 2, 3–12.
Busch, Brigitta (2001) The virtual village square: Media in minority languages in the process of media diversification and globalization: An example from Southern Carinthia (Austria). In C. Moseley, N. Ostler and H. Ouzzate (eds) *Endangered Languages and the Media. Proceedings of the Fifth Conference of the Foundation for Endangered Languages (FEL), Agadir, Morocco 20–23 September 2001* (pp. 35–39).
Busch, B. (2004) *Sprachen im Disput: Medien und Öffentlichkeit in multilingualen Gesellschaften.* Klagenfurt: Drava Diskurs.
Carlsson, U. and Harrie, E. (eds) (2001) Media trends 200 in Denmark, Finland, Iceland, Norway and Sweden. *Nordic Media Trends 6.* Göteborg: Nordicom.

Christiansen, C.C. (2003) TV-nyheder fra hjemlandet – integration eller ghettois-ering? In T. Tufte (ed.) Medierne, *minoriteterne og det multikulturelle samfund.* *Skandinaviske perspektiver* (pp. 157–179). Göteborg: Nordicom.
Cormack, M. (1998) Minority language media in Western Europe: Preliminary considerations. *European Journal of Communication* 13 (1), 33–52.
Dahlgren, P. and Sparks, C. (eds) (1991) *Communication and Citizenship. Journalism and the Public Sphere.* London: Routledge.
Deklaration om nordisk språkpolitik (2005) Förslag antaget av Nordens språkråd – NSR, 3.2.2005. (Declaration on Nordic Language Policy, approved by the Language Council of the Nordic countries – NSR on February 3, 2005). On www at: http://www.spraknamnden.se/aktuellt/Utkastdeklarationpublik.pdf
Downing, John and Husband, Charles (2005) *Representing 'Race'.* London: Sage.
European Charter for Regional or Minority Languages (1992) ETS 148. On www at: http://www.coe.int/T/E/Legal Affairs/Local and regional Democracy/ Regional or Minority languages/1 The Charter/List Charter versions.asp
Finnäs, F. (1998). *Finlandssvenskarna 1996 – en statistisk "versikt.* Finlandssvensk rapport nr. 37. Helsingfors: Svenska Finlands Folkting.
Grin, F. (with Jensdóttir, R. and Ó Riagáin, D. (2003) *Language Policy Evaluation and the European Charter for Regional or Minority Languages.* Houndmills, Basingstoke and New York: Palgrave Macmillan.
Grin, F. and Moring, T. (with Gorter, D., Häggman, J., Ó Riagáin, D. and Strubell, M.) (2003) *Support for Minority Languages in Europe.* Final report on a project financed by the European Commission, Directorate Education and Culture. On www at: http://europa.eu.int/comm/education/policies/lang/langmin/support.pdf
Grin, F. and Vaillancourt, F. (1999) *The Cost-effectiveness Evaluation of Minority Language Policies: Case studies on Wales, Ireland and the Basque Country.* ECMI Monograph No. 2. Flensburg: European Centre for Minority Issues.
Haavikko, P. (1988) *Erään opportunistin iltapäivä.* Juva: Art House, WSOY.
Husband, C. (2005) Minority ethnic media as communities of practice: Professionalism and identity politics in interaction. *Journal of Ethnic and Migration Studies* 31 (3), 461–479.
Innis, H. (1973) *The Bias of Communication.* Toronto: University of Toronto Press.
Isin, E.F. and Wood, P.K. (1999) *Citizenship and Identity.* London: Sage.
Jackson, J.D. and Rosenberg, M. (2004) *Recognition and Mis-recognition: Radio as Interlocutor – A Study of 2nd Generation Immigrant Use of Radio.* Research report sponsored by Multiculturalism, Department of Canadian Heritage, Government of Canada. Montreal: Centre for Broadcasting Studies, Concordia University (mimeo).
Kymlicka, W. (1995) *Multicultural Citizenship: A Liberal Theory of Minority Rights.* Oxford: Oxford University Press.
Kymlicka, W. (2004) Culturally responsive policies. Background paper for UNHDR 2004, Human Development Report Office, UN Development Programme. Occasional paper 2004/5.
McLuhan, M. (1967) *The Medium is the Massage.* New York: Random House.
Moring, T. (2000a) Euroopan vähemmistökielet ja uusi viestintä: uhka ja mahdol-lisuudet. In H. Tapper (ed.) *Me median maisemissa. Reflektioita identiteettiin ja mediaan* (pp. 204–227). Helsinki: Palmenia –kustannus.
Moring, T. (2000b) Minority broadcasting in Scandinavia. *Communications: The European Journal of Communication Research* 25 (2), 187–207.

Moring, T. (2002) The Swedish press in Finland: A record in readership? *Mercator Media Forum* 6, 26–36.

Moring, T. and Nordqvist, A. (eds) (2002) *Svenska medier i Finland*. SSKH Skrifter Nr 13. Helsingfors: Forskningsinstitutet, Svenska social- och kommunalhögskolan vid Helsingfors universitet.

Moring, T. and Salmi, J. (1998) Public service radio programming for minority language audience(s) in a competitive market: The case of the Swedish-speaking minority in Finland. *Gazette* 60 (4), 325–342.

Moring, T. and Malmgren, U. (eds) (2004) *Minority Languages, Media and Journalism. Proceedings from the European Journalism Conference, Helsinki 8–11.5.2003*. SSKH Meddelanden 67. Helsinki: Swedish School of Social Sciences at the University of Helsinki.

Neuman, W.R. (1991) *The Future of the Mass Audience*. Cambridge: Cambridge University Press.

Patten A. and Kymlicka, W. (2003) Context, issues and approaches. In W. Kymlicka and A. Patten (eds) *Language Rights and Political Theory* (pp. 1–51). Oxford: Oxford University Press.

Pool, I. de Sola (1983) *Technologies of Freedom: On Free Speech in an Electronic Age*. Cambridge, MA: The Belknap Press, Harvard University Press.

Ridell, S. (1998) Beyond the pendulum: Critical genre analysis of media-audience relations. *Nordicom Review* 19 (1), 125–133

Sapir, E. (1963) *Language: An Introduction to the Study of Speech*. London: Hart-Davis.

Schrøder, K.C. (2000) Making sense of audience discourses: Towards a multidimensional model of mass media reception. *The European Journal of Cultural Studies* 3 (2), 233–258.

Schöpflin, G. (2000) *Nations, Identity, Power: The New Politics of Europe*. London: C. Hurst & Co.

Sreberny, A. (2000) Media and diasporic consciousness: An exploration among Iranians in London. In S. Cottle (ed.) *Ethnic Minorities and the Media*. Milton Keynes: Open University Press.

Topelius, Zacharias (1875) *Läsebok för de lägsta läroverken i Finland. II kursen: Boken om vårt land (Reading Book for the Lowest Secondary Schools in Finland. II course: The Book about Our Country)*.

Chapter 3
Minority Language Media and the Public Sphere

JACQUES GUYOT

Since the mid-1990s, the development of audiovisual and multimedia technologies has been providing a vast variety of worldwide channels of communication, opening up outlets and prospects for alternative and community media. In the meantime, as a reaction against state-centralised policies as well as against the deterritorialisation of traditional cultural and social spaces caused by the internationalisation of communication systems, a new consciousness in favour of cultural diversity has gradually appeared (Mattelart, 1994). This new situation holds for the entire planet, not just in Europe where, until recently, the variety of languages spoken in the different countries was considered a serious drawback to the creation of unity (see Benda, 1933, 1947). In many regions throughout the world, linguistic minorities are making strong claims for the right to be present in the audiovisual media. For many endangered languages, this expresses the concern to legitimise their cause and to reach a wider audience thanks to digital networks.

Sometimes considered only as cultural phenomena, linguistic issues are a very political matter. Indeed, they frequently convert into demands for official recognition by states as well as by supranational authorities (for example, the European Union (EU)). Above all, they question the public sphere[1] and imply a redefinition of the social contract that links citizens. They also require special attention from political authorities, quite apart from specific policies. The unrest in 2004 in Bolivia and Peru, in which Aymara communities were opposed to their local corrupt politicians, shows how the lack of interest from their respective states can drive the Indians – long considered as second-class citizens – to violent actions.

In this chapter, I will tackle two complementary sides of the question: on the one hand, the legal framework set by political institutions in order to organise or restrict the expression of minority languages in the media; on the other hand, a critical survey of some of the theories that discuss issues of linguistic and cultural diversity, multiculturalism and citizenship in relation to the public sphere of the media. Taken together these demonstrate the importance of the concept of the public sphere in relation to minority languages. In fact, the two sides are closely related: political and academic debates are deeply marked by national historical traditions, thus affecting the legal or institutional solutions established in different countries. Following these discussions will be some comments on the use of specific media in the development of a public sphere in a minority language. Most of the examples are taken from the European context which illustrates very clearly the ongoing relationships between national and supranational political authorities and their linguistic minorities.

The Development of Legislative Frameworks for Minority Language Media

Historically speaking, two factors played an important part in the fate of minority languages: the construction of modern states and successive waves of immigrants. In many countries, the choice of one official language is the direct result of the creation of the modern nation-state from the 18th century onwards. Within newly unified geopolitical spaces, many official languages were in fact former vernaculars that could help build (in Benedict Anderson's phrase) 'imagined communities' based on a common idea of nationality (Anderson, 1983; Hobsbawm, 1990). In view of the linguistic variety, many native vernaculars were hit directly as they could not attain national status. As for the immigrants, in their quest to integrate with their host countries, they tended to switch to the official language, at least for their children, keeping their mother tongue within the private, domestic sphere. Democracies were in a paradoxical situation since the state institutions had to promote a common language for communication and education while protecting the cultural heritage of different language groups, at least in theory. History reveals moments of progress balanced against periods of harsh decline in the relationships between states and their linguistic minorities.

As a matter of fact, the continuing existence of minority languages has generally come from the obstinacy of militants or close-knit communities struggling for official recognition. However, whatever conflicts existed – and still do exist – between linguistic minorities and state authorities over the granting of rights, minority language issues have been a continuing part of public debate, at least in Europe. Each state represents a specific historical construction, which means that the laws passed to allow minority language expression are different from one country to another and determine the way minority languages are taken into account in the media, generally (at least in the European context) through public service broadcasting.

Specificities and limitations of public service broadcasting in Europe

When dealing with the organisation of minority language media, one of the clearest features is the clear-cut distinction between the press and the audiovisual media. The existence of newspapers and magazines dedicated to minority languages has almost always been left to the initiative of the linguistic groups themselves. Although some minorities launched their own papers (such as *Avui*, the Catalan daily newspaper), they usually benefit from the regional press in the majority language, which frequently publishes articles using the local language: Asturian in four Spanish regional papers, Corsican in *La Corse* or *Corse Matin*, Frisian in *Het Friesch Dagblad* and *Leeuwarden Courant* or Friulan in *Messagero Veneto* and *Il Gazzettino*. As for immigrant minorities, they generally turn to the daily press from their home country. On the whole, the situation is pitiful and, for minority languages, the press can be considered as neglected media.

As far as audiovisual media are concerned, there is a distinctiveness in the European situation as most countries there opted for a public service broadcasting system. Within that context, a number of public aims were defined in the legal articles that constituted these broadcasters, creating a situation quite different to that of the press. Typically, public service broadcasting guarantees political pluralism, religious expression, access for political parties or union representatives, and quotas of national or European audiovisual works. In many countries, particular obligations referring to 'regional' languages were also integrated into public service missions, sometimes after a period of experimentation (in France, for example, the situation became official when the regional network *France 3* was created in 1973). The change appears at the regional level thanks to local opt-out 'windows' within existing radio and television stations.

Radio started providing programmes in Irish (1945), in Sami in Norway (1946) and Finland (1947), in Welsh on BBC (1950s), in Frisian on *Omrop Fryslân* (1950s) (Moragas Spà *et al.*, 1999), and in Breton (1959). Following radio by a few years, television also opened such windows to minority languages: Irish in Ireland (1960), Welsh in the United Kingdom (1964), Breton (1964) and Basque (1971) in France, Frisian in the Netherlands (1979) (for more detail, see Browne's Chapter 7 in this book).

In spite of these advances, which actually only concerned a small number of European public media, minority linguistic communities were not satisfied with their lot. Indeed, the amount of broadcast programmes was far less than they demanded. Whatever the media – radio or television – minority languages get a very small share of programming:

commonly just a few hours every week with no real hope of development, that is, an amount that is too low to contribute much to revitalising a language. Two reasons account for this situation. First of all, when dealing with minority languages, national public service legislation shows its limitations. In the list of aims commonly assigned to public service media, linguistic issues are just one of many obligations and usually no quotas are fixed. This means that in order to ensure political and social cohesion, priority tends to be given to content with a common national cultural background, thus leaving aside language diversity. Secondly, it is always difficult to promote a 'regional' language within a national media system. Even if most countries have a regional network, few give their regional or local channels any real autonomy. This is why many minority language production units suffer from lack of funding or, at least, from a dependence on subsidies and public institutions (Guyot *et al.*, 2000: 73).

Political and technological changes after the 1970s

As noted already, before the 1980s, very few countries developed linguistic variety in the media, although for quite different reasons. For instance, Spain was still under Franco's dictatorship while Italian public media were facing severe competition from local and private television channels. In an apparently stable context, three phenomena brought significant changes to the audiovisual media: (1) the general deregulation process that put an end to many state broadcasting monopolies (apart from Great Britain and Finland, all other European countries had the audiovisual broadcast media under state control until the 1980s); (2) the devolution policies that were applied in Great Britain and Spain; and (3) the arrival of digital technologies.

The consequences are important for the organisation and workings of the media: more democracy with an opening to the private sector and legalisation for community media, a variety of news channels, and the development of the Internet. The other side of the coin is that media profusion does not necessarily bring plurality. Indeed, the integration of the means of communication in the hands of major industrial groups is a general trend at the international level. Bertelsmann and Berlusconi's Fininvest are obvious European examples. But this recent development is worrying as the main activity of such new companies in the cultural industries may have nothing to do with media and culture. In France, the multimedia group TF1 belongs to the building contractor Bouygues; in 2004, Dassault and Lagardère, two firms involved in the arms industry, took control of 80% of French publishing.

Radio was an early beneficiary of this situation. Radio is a medium that has many advantages: low operating and production costs, cheap transmitters and receivers, a broadcasting range that fits well with the local or regional dimension, a simple technology with light, mobile equipment. Typically, launching a radio station is within a small community's means. This is why, long before national legislative policies, the ground had been occupied by pirate commercial or alternative radio stations, thus preparing for future developments. During the 1980s, local and regional stations flourished, including those dedicated to minority languages. One interesting feature is that the stations are operated by all kinds of broadcasters. Four major categories can be distinguished. The first one includes the 'historical' public service broadcasters through their regional networks: for example, *BBC Wales* and *BBC Scotland* in the United Kingdom; *RAI* in Italy for Ladin and Slovene; *France 3* for Alsatian, Basque, Breton, Catalan, Corsican and Occitan; *Omrop Fryslân* in the Netherlands for Frisian. The space offered to minority languages is usually limited. The second category consists of private commercial broadcasters operating on a local or regional scale, such as *Radio Onde Furlane* for the Friulan community, *Cadena Nova* in Catalonia, *Radio Ceredigion* in Wales and *Radio Ser* in Asturia. The third category includes local radio stations run and financed by municipalities. Most of these appear in regions that have gained autonomy, such as Catalonia and the Basque country in Spain: the figures are impressive according to the Mercator Media database (2004) with respectively 180 and 120 local radio stations (and see also the chapters in this book by Arana, Azpillaga and Narbaiza (Chapter (9) and Corominas Piulats (Chapter 10)). The last category consists of independent radio stations created by voluntary associations. They are often subsidised by cultural organisations or public institutions. They reveal the capacity many minority groups have to mobilise themselves in order to revitalise their languages. Indeed, if independent radio is not always monolingual, many stations broadcast a high volume of programmes using the native language. As far as minority language stakes are concerned, independent radio stations launched by minorities undoubtedly constitute the most equally distributed and developed media in Europe.

Television and the quest for legitimacy

As for television, except for Spain, the situation is far from satisfactory for linguistic minorities. After a short period of competitive spirit with optimistic promises from public and private media, the volume of programmes quickly came to a standstill. Brittany is a good example of this stimulating but short period. On the one hand, the creation of a private channel, *TV Breizh*, by the French multimedia group Bouygues TF1, spurred the regional television network *France 3* to increase the volume of Breton programmes, particularly those aimed at children and teenagers. On the other hand, the original project of launching bilingual private television soon came to a sudden end, revealing that the ambition displayed by TF1 had little to do with the defence of Breton language and culture. This was noted by the newspaper *Libération* when reporting that the percentage of programmes in Breton was seriously declining (*Libération*, 2003). But close attention to the different press conferences held between 1998 and 2000 by TF1"s chairman Patrick Le Lay shows that his intention had always been perfectly clear and had little to do with the defence of Breton language and culture: as a matter of fact, *TV Breizh* was designed as a technological and commercial tool to test the Breton consumers and to provide a presence at the regional level when the invitation to tender for digital terrestrial television channels was launched (Guyot, 2001, 2002: 243). On the whole, nothing much changed in Breton language programmes. In its last report, the French regulating authority even points to the 'insufficient space dedicated to programmes using regional languages, a situation which is against what viewers expect in their regions' – programmes in Breton dropped from 63 hours a year in 2001 to 50 hours in 2002 (Conseil Supérieur de l'Audiovisuel, 2003: 25–26).

Linguistic minorities are of course eager to have access to independent television channels. Television tends to confer legitimacy on any linguistic cause. In this day and age, when so much is assessed according to market value, the interest of the private multimedia group TF1 for a Breton television channel demonstrated how the wealth of a culture can be translated into the economic sphere. Another argument is that, thanks to satellite television, a small community can reach a worldwide audience. After all, *TVG* (*Televisión de Galicia*) has been watched outside Galicia via the Panam satellite by the diaspora living in South America (almost 2 million people) (Guyot *et al.*, 2000: 41). It shows that a virtual social link can be established through satellite networks between members of a community scattered all around the world. More generally, television can revitalise the cultures and languages of minorities.

However, television is a very expensive medium, which explains why the only channels dedicated to minority languages are to be found in countries where political autonomy or devolution were granted to regions: Spain and the United Kingdom. A simple comparison speaks for itself: almost 40 hours a week of Welsh on S4C, 16 hours a day in Galician on *TVG* and less than 300 hours a year on *France 3* for the six regional languages all together (Guyot *et al.*, 2000: 17). Although political devolution in the United Kingdom followed some time after the establishment of S4C in 1982, Wales had retained a distinct political identity that allowed the argument for financial help to be successful.

Multilingualism and the protection of minorities: The role of European authorities

Faced with their own historical contradictions, many countries are still reluctant to accommodate linguistic minorities. They usually maintain a strongly hierarchical organisation of languages in their audiovisual system. However, most nations belong to broader political and economic entities. This is what has happened in Europe since the creation of the Council of Europe in 1949. The Council, which is composed of 44 member states, developed a very active policy in the field of human rights. There is also a concern for the protection of minorities. Compared to other continents, Europe has less minority languages (Grimes, 2000) but, on the whole, they are better protected thanks to the existence of a legal framework.

As the sociolinguist Henri Giordan (2002: 1–2) noted, the awareness of the importance of defending linguistic diversity was not immediate. In fact, this awareness of language issues has evolved in three stages. First, up until the Second World War multilingualism was seen as an obstacle to European development. According to the linguist Antoine Meillet, quoted by Giordan (2002: 1), language diversity was a real evil, and multilingualism – restricted to French, English and German – should be the preserve of elites. The second step came after Hitler's attempt to establish the Third Reich over Europe, when it became obvious that the hegemony of one language was not desirable. The European Cultural Convention, signed in December 1954, illustrates the change in course. Article 2 specifies that each contracting party should 'encourage the study by its own nationals of the languages, history and civilisation of the other contracting parties and grant facilities to those parties to promote such studies in its territory'. Of course, what is taken into account here are the official national languages. The third and most recent stage in the awareness of questions of language began in 1992 when explicit reference to cultural issues appeared in the Maastricht Treaty. As mentioned in Article 128: 'The Community shall contribute to the flowering of the cultures of the Member States, while respecting their national and regional diversity and at the same time bringing the common cultural heritage to the fore.'

The recognition of 'regional diversity' opened up new prospects to minority language activists whose efforts led to two important treaties: the European Charter for Regional or Minority Languages and the Framework Convention for the Protection of National Minorities. The Charter was adopted by the Council on 25 June 1992. It is based on the principle that linguistic rights are part of human rights and that they are fundamental freedoms. It also expresses the awareness that European languages are a precious heritage, contributing to cultural wealth and traditions. It proposes a series of measures aiming at protecting and promoting regional or minority languages in the fields of education, judicial authorities, administrative authorities and public services, media, cultural activities and facilities, economic and social life. It was ratified by five states in 1997. This first ratification led to its official application in 1998. When a state decides to ratify the Charter, it can choose the languages it wishes to protect and 'undertake to apply a minimum of 35 paragraphs or sub-paragraphs chosen from among the provisions of part III of the Charter, including at least three chosen from each of the articles 8 to 12 and one from each of the articles 9, 10, 11 and 12'.

The enforcement of the Charter is each signatory country's responsibility. By the end of 2004, 27 countries had signed the Charter and 14 of them had ratified it. When a particular country does not ratify the Charter, it does not necessarily mean that minority languages will not be taught or appear in the media. Usually, it indicates that some of the Charter's articles are in contradiction to the official constitution of that state. Constitutional changes must then be made by the appropriate national parliaments: this requires internal debate and the negotiation of political tensions. Another point that also needs to be noted is that the languages of migrants are not taken into account. Such an exclusivity may have a serious impact on social integration. On the whole, the advantage of the Charter is that many states use it to set up their linguistic policies. This is particularly important for the 10 countries that joined the EU in 2004. Among other things, the treaty signed by member states includes clauses that can become, for future candidates, criteria of eligibility.

As for the Framework Convention for the Protection of National Minorities, it was signed on 1 February 1995. After its ratification by 12 countries, it came into effect in February 1998. It constitutes another imprecise and vague framework. It is a basic contract offering a minimum acceptable protection of national minorities. It can be considered as a first step towards the recognition of the linguistic factors contained in the Charter. In both cases, European institutions do not have the means to enforce these treaties, but they at least provide a legal basis that gives substance to linguistic issues. The Charter and the Convention establish an institutional link with member states and, above all, they bring linguistic issues into the public sphere.

Linguistic and Cultural Diversity in the Public Sphere

According to Tomazs Goban-Klas (1989: 31), minority media fulfil two main functions. One consists in 'fighting for the rights of minorities', the other helps 'giving minority members a feeling of identity, increasing their social cohesiveness, and providing an escape from homesickness and the isolation of life in a strange or hostile environment'. This second aspect is particularly important because it suggests how media can participate in the social integration of individuals belonging to a minority. Presence in the media also gives public visibility and consequently contributes to full citizenship.

Quite often linguistic diversity is restrained due to economic or socio-political reasons. The vitality of a language is directly related to its use value: some are highly used on the international scene, others are looked down on, along with the people who speak them. Political action is a way to counterbalance this trend.

Linguistic diversity, media and democracy

The existence of a language is linked to its geopolitical and economic situation. This is the 'language market' Louis-Jean Calvet (2002) speaks about when assessing the linguistic effects of globalisation. On a planetary scale, this is particularly true when considering Chinese or Hindi, which, despite their being the first two languages in the world (judged by numbers of native speakers), do not have the international status of English or Spanish. At a national level, the same factors play an important role as far as the mode of existence of minority languages is concerned, and wealthy regions, such as Catalonia, are in a better position to promote the native idiom.

Being rooted in an identifiable territory is also a very favourable point. It bestows visibility on a language and enhances its legitimacy, which considerably helps official recognition. To quote Michel de Certeau, one can say that the territory – with, consequently, all its representative bodies and cultural institutions – is an essential element in developing a strategy: territorialized minorities can speak from 'a *proper*', that is, a place that can stand the test of time and 'serve as the basis for generating relations with an exterior distinct from it (competitors, adversaries, "clientèles", "targets", or "objects" of research)' (de Certeau, 1984: 17–18). The media can fulfil a similar territorialising function. Unfortunately, the languages spoken by nomads and migrants cannot rely on such advantages. Moreover, these social groups are the first to be affected by ostracism and racism. Above all, they are frequently the victims of socio-economic exclusion. This means that there is no point in defending a language without trying to fight against all forms of social, political and economic exclusion. Here again, the linguistic issue is bound up with political considerations.

In Europe, there are also two kinds of non-territorial minorities. The Romany, who arrived from India in the beginning of the 15th century, are a particularly fragile minority. In many countries, they suffer violence, hatred and relegation to the fringes of symbolic and physical space. They demonstrate all the signs of marginalisation: high unemployment, high illiteracy and petty criminality. Romany and its dialectal forms are hardly taught, and have little presence in the media. Any proposal dedicated to the protection of Romany culture must include the social and economic dimensions.

Recent immigrants and their descendants, such as Arabic peoples in France, are likewise often marginalised in the media. In addition, in a context of economic crisis and geopolitical unrest, they are targets for all the resentment of host-country populations (racial discrimination and violence from right-wing political groups). Many Arabic immigrants use their mother tongue at home. They also watch video cassettes and satellite television programmes in Arabic. Video material is often distributed in suburbs by radical Islamic groups. Television programmes are available from satellite networks controlled by countries such as Saudi Arabia. This means that, on the one hand, many host countries are afraid of the spread of Islamic propaganda, but, on the other hand, they do little to offer alternatives through their own media systems. Most European satellite television networks do not offer specific channels to immigrants. On the contrary, they tend to spread a very negative image of immigration. There can be little doubt that European democracies fail to recognise the importance of the languages of immigrants in the public sphere of the media.

The controversies of multiculturalism

If the issues related to the political expression of linguistic diversity are a challenge to democracies, there is no doubt that they also arouse theoretical debates among social scientists. In the 1990s, North American works on multiculturalism became popular, both in the academic community, thanks to the works of Will Kymlicka, Charles Taylor and others (for example, Kymlicka, 1995; Taylor, 1992), and in politics (in the shape of affirmative action programmes and the debate over political correctness). These North American trends, often presented as an apology for differentialism, tend to dominate discussions that try to question the legitimacy of cultural claims in the public sphere.

Indeed, multiculturalism is a very complex and controversial notion, as Pierre Bourdieu and Loïc Wacquant (2000) comment: 'Neither a concept, nor a theory, nor a social or political movement – while pretending being all that at the same time.' The concern for multiculturalism is often considered to be the result of the crisis of modernity. We could also say that the phenomenon of the internationalisation of communications has emphasised this crisis (Semprini, 1997: ch. 7). What is it all about anyway: the return of subjectivity, the revenge of cultures and the saying of things differently, or the existence of binary oppositions such as global/local, universalism/communitarianism, rationality/subjectivity?

Will Kymlicka thinks that minority claims to administrative and/or political rights must be satisfied by political authorities, particularly in the case of 'national minorities' (such as Native Americans, Bretons or Catalans). The liberal theory of minority rights (Kymlicka, 1995) as well as the politics of recognition defended by Taylor (Taylor, 1992) have often been criticised because they postulate that the autonomy of minority groups (considered as sets of responsible and rational individuals) comes first. In other words, their actions are pre-eminent since they determine political choices, thus subjugating the political system to civil society. It also privileges whichever minorities are capable of organising themselves and being heard by authorities: this is the case of the linguistic groups who are the 'historical' inhabitants in a region. But a minority must be a majority locally to enact its linguistic rights (Kymlicka, 1995: ch. 6). On another level, multiculturalism is more concerned with theorising linguistic rights from the perspective of political correctness rather than from the point of view of minority languages. Lastly, what multiculturalism cannot take into account is the socio-political hierarchy of cultural issues: taking the examples mentioned in the preface to the French edition of Kymlicka's book, can the Islamic veil be placed on the same level as territorial autonomy in Corsica? Can French centralized policy be reduced to those two devilish sides with, on the one hand, what is presented as a harmless cultural sign that deserves recognition within what Kymlicka calls 'migration multiculturalism', and on the other hand, the future of a Mediterranean island that will, one way or another, reach some form of devolution?

In short, multiculturalism professes a kind of denial of politics, but it also conveys a very restrictive and essentialist vision of the construction of identity. The Franco-Lebanese novelist, Amin Maalouf (1998), has a more interesting approach based on his own experience: he explains how his identity is the result of a more intercultural pattern, mixing different cultural traditions and thus obtains its real meaning in the adherence to common values. This attitude of being a citizen is what Fred Constant (2000: 89) defines as 'the first rule of a *savoir-faire* in pluralism'.

A European approach to cultural and linguistic plurality

Deeply marked by the North American context, according to Bourdieu and Wacquant (1984: 110), the term multiculturalism 'in Europe has been particularly used to define pluralism within the public sphere while, in the United States, it refers to the persistent aftermath of the exclusion of the black and to the crisis of the national mythology of the "American dream"'. But in this latter case, the notion would not correspond to European realities as the issues dealing with cultural and linguistic plurality are discussed in their relation to the common good. Therefore, the problem is to imagine how linguistic diversity could be better taken into account in public life and the media. In the constitution and legislation adopted by each nation, a variety of choices can be made: some mention linguistic issues (France, in a very exclusive way, Spain and the UK with a more extensive vision), others do not at all (the USA). This is a historical development directly linked to the creation of modern states. All constitutions rest on a number of principles determining what falls within the private domain and what belongs to the public sphere, that is, what needs to be publicised to build public opinion.

Jürgen Habermas analysed how the principle of publicity has been perverted and how the public sphere is being 're-feudalised' (Habermas, 1984, 1989). At the same time, reviving the spirit of the Enlightenment, which associated reason with subjectivity, cultural issues are now part of the public debate. This means that the democratic public sphere must be re-established and Habermas is aware that cultural diversity must be taken into account. But in order to avoid a mere piling up of communities, he thinks that the notion of tolerance should be a model to theorise multicultural societies. This notion, inherited from the aftermath of wars of religion, is interesting because it supposes a social contract between different cultures that are capable of sharing a common vision of the world.

In a more sociological perspective, Michel Wieviorka tackles the problem from the angle of ethnicity. He argues that the debate cannot be reduced to an opposition between tradition and modernity, or 'community' and 'citizenship'. He also points out that in France the assimilation of immigrants was helped considerably by the fact that the community they belonged to was a vital link that allowed them to move from the cultural shock caused by uprooting to full access of French citizenship. Their mother tongues played an important part in the assimilation process. Wieviorka proposes a sociological definition of ethnicity, which he considers as a space organised around three complementary and indissociable poles: (1) individualism and universal values (the legacy of the Enlightenment); (2) subjectivity (cultural identity); (3) communitarianism (community networks) (Wieviorka, 1993: 125–136). This model can be transposed to the many linguistic groups that suffered from modernity and its consequent standardisation of socio-cultural life. It also summarises the tensions and problems social actors are likely to experience when manoeuvring in this 'triangle of ethnicity' (Wieviorka, 1993: 125). In short, some of these theoretical approaches provide models that can be adjusted to different situations and respect both cultural idiosyncrasies and a collective socio-political contract. In that particular context, linguistic issues deserve to be officially recognised and promoted. At the same time, and apart from political action, minorities can use more systematically the existing media in order to promote their culture and language.

A Multimedia Strategy for Developing a Minority Media Public Sphere

Minorities do not always use the full range of media (and see Moring's Chapter 2 in this book for further discussion of this). Examination of what are still called 'mass' media and of some of the most recent developments will make this clear. First, the press, to which the French psycho-sociologist Gabriel Tarde assigned an important role in the construction of public opinion (Tarde, 1989). In many rural areas, where books had little circulation, generations of children, and sometimes adults too, were taught to read and write with the help of the newspaper. At another level, films can strongly echo cultural diversity and help individuals become aware of belonging to a singular community (see, for example, *Atarnajuat: The Fast Runner*, the 1999 feature film about the Inuits produced by Isuma Productions Inc.). As for radio, it is a very flexible means of communication, both from a technical point of view and for economic reasons. It is associated with orality but can be used successfully for literacy campaigns as well. A basic review of the presence of minority languages in 'traditional media' shows that, at best, languages appear marginally in national daily papers, radio and television programmes. When it is a matter of preserving and enhancing their language and culture, minorities have to struggle to set up independent media. They generally face economic problems, mainly because market scale implies meeting a wide audience. For example, the free French daily *Vingt minutes* costs €100,000 to operate everyday for a circulation of 450,000 issues and sells each page of advertising for €12,000.

In the last 20 years, media, telecommunications and data-processing have merged into what we now call multimedia. Regardless of their physical nature, written text, figures, graphics, pictures or sound are processed by computers. Multimedia integrates all these different data, which can be viewed, listened to, transformed, recorded and transmitted through the World Wide Web. With multimedia, traditional means of communication, like the newspaper, radio and even television, take on a new life through the possibility of mixing media content, user-friendliness, disappearance of space and time constraints or low operating costs. (See Williams' Chapter 6 in this book for further implications of this.)

Most minorities do not take full advantage of these new opportunities. There are a number of interesting experiments that have been carried out by cultural groups or linguistic associations, but on the whole, there are no real multimedia strategies. Thus there are very few online daily newspapers in minority languages (Guyot, 2004). Of course, almost half of the languages of the world have no writing. But, if we take the case of Europe, all languages could launch dailies of some kind. In fact, even if few minority languages have a daily printed press (Basque, Catalan, Galician), electronic publishing is now a real possibility. Already some academic institutions and socio-political movements are doing this with a minimum of funding and staff: no heavy structural investments, no need to sub-contract with a printing company and distribution networks, no paper to buy. These expenses account for 40–65% of the retail price.

Another advantage is that Internet technology is useful at targeting small groups, which is particularly important in the case of deterritorialised minorities. In fact, the concept of mass media is no longer appropriate to describe a medium whose networking logic favours more user-friendly, interactive point-to-point links. New media can meet the needs of fragmented audiences.

Last but not least is the archive function. This means that through the Internet, readers can consult old issues. This can prove to be a strong point since minority languages often lack written material for those who wish to learn.

David Crystal (2000) is quite right when, among the six key areas he suggests to help language revitalisation, he mentions access to electronic technology. It may appear utopian, like the dreams of the 1970s of user-friendly, small community media, with the exception that, in this particular case, it involves reasonable resources. The online press represents an interesting alternative, just like radio on the Internet. In that case, the two media can merge into a hybrid solution, which is more faithful to the definition of multimedia: an online paper can integrate sound files. (See Cunliffe's Chapter 8 in this book for further discussion of the issues relating to minority language use of the Internet.)

Conclusion

This chapter has shown the complexities of minority language access to the media and the public sphere. The presence of a linguistic minority in the media is a legitimate claim as the media are integral parts of everyday life in a democracy. The minority's access to media, as a complement to educational policies, is the sign that it is no longer discriminated against, marginalised or invisible. In this sense, the minority's members can be considered as ordinary citizens belonging to groups or associations bound to respect the common rules guiding the media and usually guaranteed by national regulating authorities.

However, the situation is far from satisfactory, particularly in the case of television channels. Whenever the question of setting up new local television stations is raised, the national regulating authorities often tend to favour projects that are brought forth by economically wealthy urban areas rather than those carried by cultural or linguistic communities. Hence the paradox: while the number of channels increases exponentially due to digital technology, the opportunities for cultural and linguistic minorities to express themselves seem to shrink (Cheval, 1996: 210; Morley & Robins, 1996). The economic paradigm leads the development of networks, and digital video broadcasters are mostly interested in solvent customers to whom they can offer international, second-market television productions. Following the example of free radio, there is a danger that local television channels serve, sooner or later, the interests of private groups, particularly in a context of increasing media concentration (Mattelart, 2005). Future solutions should resort to joint action at the regional, national and European levels in order to extend the aims of public service broadcasting and to bring financial support to media projects developed by linguistic minorities.

From an academic point of view, it is obvious that investigation of minority language media still requires a great deal of attention. The issues raised by the media expression of linguistic communities are quite new and are different, for instance, from those relating to alternative media that led to a large variety of studies and research. In a context of internationalisation of media and culture, minority language media deserve special attention from researchers. Indeed, such media reveal some of the paradoxes of internationalisation: within the intersections of market communication flow, they express the 'revenge of cultures', in the words of Mattelart (1994), that is, a particular reaction against the standardisation of cultural content and exchange, against the acceleration of acculturation processes. Minority language media also illustrate one kind of interesting link between the local dimension and global networks: thanks to satellite television and the Internet, regional minorities can reach their diasporas, while immigrants, scattered all over the world, can still have bonds with their home culture and language.

Minority language media issues are a good way to analyse the evolution of cultural and communication practices. They are also relevant to the assessment of the relationships between culture and politics in contemporary democracies. In order to forge specific tools to shed light on these naturally complex and changing phenomena, research focusing on minority language media should be conducted within an interdisciplinary perspective, borrowing concepts from cultural studies, linguistics, information science, communication studies, political science, sociology, law and the political economy of communication.

Note

1. The notion of the *public sphere* is borrowed from Jürgen Habermas (1989). It can be defined as the *agora* where private people can gather to form a 'public'. Through clubs, associations, assemblies and media, citizens can freely discuss general interest matters and reach a consensus. Thus, media play an important part in the construction of a public sphere. As far as television is concerned, the profusion of channels does not necessarily provide more spaces to mediate democracy, since, as Peter Dahlgren comments, television is an industry whose main purpose is not so much 'public sphering' as profit-making (Dahlgren, 1995: 148). Hence the importance of paying attention to institutional factors, for instance in preventing audiovisual media from being totally controlled by private groups, thanks to regulating institutions, public policies and legal frameworks that guarantee pluralism and freedom of expression.

References

Anderson, B. (1983) *Imagined Communities*. London: Verso.
Benda, J. (1933) *Discours à la nation européenne*. Paris: Gallimard.
Benda, J. (1947) Conférence du 2 septembre 1946. In J. Benda, G. Bernanos, K. Jaspers *et al*. *L'esprit européen: conférences et entretiens des Rencontres internationales de Genève, 1946*. Paris: Oreste Zeluck.

Bourdieu, P. and Wacquant, L. (1998) Sur les ruses de la raison impérialiste. *Actes de la Recherche en Sciences Sociales* 121/122, 108–118.

Bourdieu, P. and Wacquant, L. (2000) La vulgate planétaire. *Le Monde Diplomatique*, April.

Calvet, L.-J. (2002) *Le marché aux langues: les effets linguistiques de la mondialisation.* Paris: Plon.

Certeau, M. de (1984) *The Practice of Everyday Life.* Berkeley: University of California Press.

Cheval, J.-J. (1996) Médias audiovisuels français et langues régionales minorisées. In A. Viaut (ed.) *Langues d'Aquitaine: dynamiques institutionnelles et patrimoine linguistique.* Bordeaux: Editions de la Maison des Sciences de l'Homme d'Aquitaine.

Conseil Supérieur de l'Audiovisuel (2003) *Bilan de la société nationale de programme France 3: année 2002.* Paris: CSA.

Constant, F. (2000) *Le multiculturalisme.* Paris: Flammarion (Dominos).

Crystal, D. (2000) *Language Death.* Cambridge: Cambridge University Press.

Dahlgren, P. (1995) *Television and the Public Sphere: Citizenship, Democracy and the Media.* London: Sage.

Giordan, H. (2002) La question des langues en Europe. In *The Assessment of European Multilingualism: Reviewing the European Year of Languages 2001*, lecture given at the Research Association for the Multilingual Societies, Tokyo, Japan.

Goban-Klas, T. (1989) Minority media. In Erik Barnouw (ed.) *International Encyclopedia of Communications* (vol. 3). Oxford: Oxford University Press.

Grimes, B.F. (2000) *Ethnologue: Languages of the World* (vol. 1). Dallas: SIL International.

Guyot, J. (2001) Une chaîne bretonne privée à l'ère du numérique. Quelques considérations socio-politiques sur la création de TV Breizh. *Mercator Media Forum* 5, 7–21. Cardiff: University of Wales Press.

Guyot, J. (2002) Intercultural challenge for French television. In N. Jankowski and O. Prehn (eds) *Community Media in the Information Age: Perspectives and Prospects.* Cresskill, NJ: Hampton Press Inc.

Guyot, J. (2004) Languages of minorities and the media: Research issues. *Mercator Media Forum* 7, 13–28.

Guyot, J., Ledo, M. and Michon, R. (2000) Production télévisée et identité culturelle en Bretagne, Galice et Pays de Galles/Produerezh skinwel hag identelezh sevenadurel e Breizh, Galiza ha Kembre, in *Klask* 6 (special issue).

Habermas, J. (1984) *The Theory of Communicative Action.* Cambridge: Polity Press.

Habermas, J. (1989) *The Structural Transformation of the Public Sphere.* Cambridge, MA: MIT Press.

Hobsbawm, E. (1990) *Nations and Nationalism since 1780: Programme, Myth and Reality.* Cambridge: Cambridge University Press.

Kymlicka, W. (1995) *Multinational Citizenship: A Liberal Theory of Minority Rights.* Oxford: Oxford University Press.

Libération (2003) TV Breizh moins bretonnante. Les programmes strictement régionaux revus à la baisse. 10 September.

Maalouf, A. (1998) *Les identités meurtrières.* Paris: Grasset.

Mattelart, A. (1994) *Mapping World Communication: War, Progress and Culture.* Minneapolis: University of Minnesota Press.

Mattelart, A. (ed.) (2005) *Sur la concentration dans les medias.* Paris: Liris.

Mercator Media (2004) On www at: http://www.aber.ac.uk/mercator

Moragas Spà, M. de, Garitaonadia, C. and López, B. (eds) (1999) *Television on Our Doorstep. Decentralisation Experiences in the European Union.* Luton: University of Luton Press.

Morley, D. and Robins, K. (1996) *Spaces of Identity: Global Media, Electronic Landscapes and Cultural Boundaries.* London: Routledge.

Semprini, A. (1997) *Le multiculturalisme.* Paris: PUF.

Tarde, G. (1989) *L'opinion et la foule.* Paris: PUF.

Taylor, Ch. (1992) *Multiculturalism and 'the Politics of Recognition'.* Princeton, NJ: Princeton University Press.

Wieviorka, M. (1993) *La démocratie à l'épreuve: Nationalisme, populisme, ethnicité.* Paris: La Découverte.

Chapter 4
The Media and Language Maintenance

MIKE CORMACK

In the increasing literature on minority language media little attempt has been made to tackle directly the issue that must be, for language activists at least, the central question: how can the mass media be used to support a minority language? Or, to put it another way, what is the media's role in language maintenance? For the media researcher, these imply another question: how can the impact of the media on language maintenance be studied? Most people working in minority language media have no doubt as to the usefulness of their work, but there is a paucity of empirical evidence. In their study of measures for minority language support, Grin and Moring have commented on this, pointing out that although the relevance of media to minority languages is generally accepted, 'the actual effect of specific media is still under-researched' and 'the specific cultural role of the different media (e.g. newspapers, radio, television, internet) is…not thoroughly known' (Grin & Moring, 2003: 117). In the European context, the minority languages that seem to have been most successful in their use of media (particularly television) – Catalan and Welsh – are also those in which a wide range of other institutional supports has been implemented for the language, making it very difficult to identify the specific impact of the media. This issue is at the heart of what follows. First, both possible good and bad effects of the media on minority language use are considered, in order to avoid a too facile assumption that the media can only be beneficial in such situations. Then conventional audience research is considered to see what it might contribute. Finally it is suggested that adopting an approach based on an ecology of language is most likely to be fruitful in this area, but this implies a rather different set of research questions than those hitherto considered in minority language audience research.

There are other arguments in favour of minority language media, quite apart from those concerned with language maintenance. Regardless of how media might be seen as helping or hindering the processes of language shift, minority language media provision can be supported from a human rights basis. Similarly an argument based in cultural ecology can be made in support of such media, regardless of the effects in any specific situation. (For more on these arguments, see Cormack, 2005, and, although not specifically concerned with the media, see also Crystal, 2000 and May, 2001.) In those countries in which there is some form of public service broadcasting, it can also be argued that this implies a much greater support for minorities than is currently seen in most countries. Minority language communities have other needs that media might satisfy, quite distinct from issues of language maintenance (although it would not be surprising if these various elements were, in fact, closely intertwined). Here, however, it is only the media's role in language maintenance that is to be considered.

Two factors make consideration of the role of the media critical. The first is that for most societies the media have become inescapable. This is obviously true for minority language groups within industrially developed societies, but is also increasingly true for less technologically advanced societies (as many of the examples in Browne, 1996, make clear). In other words, the media are going to be present and are going to be important, whatever language is used. The second factor is cost. The mass media, particularly television, are not cheap, and in areas in which finance for any kind of minority language support is in short supply (the standard situation for minority languages), the issue of whether to put a lot of money into broadcasting, for example, as opposed to putting it into education or community support initiatives, or even other branches of the media, becomes a central strategic decision, and one which may have important long-term consequences. It is not easy to assess such policy options, although François Grin has done important work in this area (see, for example, Grin, 2003a; Grin, 2003b; Grin & Vaillancourt, 1999), and the uncertainty about the outcomes of media policy exacerbates the problem.

The Media as Language Support

It might be thought that the media's role in supporting minority languages is obvious. It certainly seems to be so for many media practitioners involved in this area. However when the arguments for and against minority language media are put side by side, the answer does not appear to be so clear-cut. In favour of the media, it can be argued that they are central to the organisation of contemporary societies. It is through the media that members of a society (whether seen as citizens or as consumers) gain the knowledge that allows them to participate in complex social activities (such as politics or social development). This is related to the idea of the public sphere that has been much discussed within media studies (see, for example, Dahlgren, 1995), and clearly a community of speakers of the same language is implied by this concept. As I have argued elsewhere (Cormack, 1998: 43–45), it is difficult to see how a community can develop politically without some sense of a public sphere carried in the media, despite the criticisms that might be made of this concept (see, for example, in a minority language context, Hourigan, 2003: 47–50). Guyot's Chapter 3 in this book discusses further the question of minority language access to the public sphere.

A second point about the media helping minority languages is that media can meld people into a sense of a larger community. When Benedict Anderson developed his influential account of national identity as being based on a sense of an 'imagined community', he noted the importance to this process of the print media (Anderson, 1991). Anderson argued that national identity is '*imagined* because the members of even the smallest nation will never know most of their fellow-members, meet them, or even hear of them, yet in the minds of each lives the image of their communion' (Anderson, 1991: 6). Such imagining of the community is produced and reproduced in the media. Similarly, when Michael Billig considered how nationalism was reproduced and maintained on a daily basis in contemporary societies of all kinds, the role of the media was central to his analysis (Billig, 1995, particularly ch. 5). The relevance of such ideas to minority language groups is that the media within such a language can maintain and develop a sense of the language community's identity, strengthening its ability to stand up to stronger, neighbouring language communities. Iarfhlaith Watson has described how the Irish government attempted to use Irish language broadcasting to develop Irish national identity (Watson, 2003).

Another reason for thinking that the media can be a useful support for a minority language is that the media can function as a signifier that a community is fully modernised, capable of taking part in contemporary life. Since many minority languages have been labelled by dominant cultures as backward and rural, this is a significant issue. As Stephen Riggins has put it: 'Possession of the means of media production could be seen as a public validation of a minority's sophistication or modernity' (Riggins, 1992: 284). This is related to Stephen May's argument that 'legitimation and institutionalisation of a language are the key to its long-term survival in the modern world' (May, 2001: 163). Although May is not primarily concerned with the media, clearly both legitimation and institutionalisation are intimately bound up with a developed media system.

In addition to this, much media content is language-based, ranging from the print of newspapers and the spoken word on radio, through to the (usually) less language-intensive media of television and film. It seems natural to say that use of such media must help a minority language to stabilise its situation. Providing media in a language puts large amounts of language use into the public domain, whether in print, video and audio recordings, or multimedia formats. For languages that traditionally have had little media exposure, this is a significant achievement.

Finally, it should not be forgotten that the media can provide economic support and attractive employment. Given the fact that such languages are frequently in economically under-developed regions, this can be a significant factor. It also allows young people to have the kind of career they want without having to abandon their preferred language. In the European context, the examples of Wales, Catalonia and the Basque Country are well known. Stefan Moal has linked Brittany to this: 'Another outcome of the launching of TV-Breizh [the Breton-language television station] was the boost to all sectors of the Breton audio-visual industry. As a result, Breton teaching will at last lead to more careers than just those of...Breton teaching' (Moal, 2001: 41).

Moving from media writers to linguists, David Crystal has argued in favour of a strong role for the media, commenting that '[o]btaining access to the media (traditionally, the province of the dominant culture) is critical' if language death is to be prevented (Crystal, 2000: 130). He has also noted the importance of the status that the media can confer on a language: 'An endangered language will progress if its speakers increase their prestige within the dominant community' (Crystal, 2000: 130). It would seem, then, that a full and comprehensive range of media provision is essential for any minority language if it is to survive.

The Media as Language Threat

Against these views, however, several points can be made that suggest that the impact of the media on languages may not always be as beneficial as is sometimes thought. Joshua Fishman's sceptical comments on the media are well known, from the relatively minor role that he gave to the media in his original description of the stages of reversing language shift (Fishman, 1991: 395) through to his more recent comments on the 'mass-media fetish' of some language activists (Fishman, 2001: 482), and it is notable that in *Can Threatened Languages Be Saved?*, the collection of essays edited by him that considers language maintenance in a number of situations round the world, there is very little mention of the media in any of the 16 essays by other writers (Fishman, 2001).

Economics, while helping in some respects, can be a hindrance in others. The media tend to be organised on a large scale and the economics of the media push towards the largest possible audience, working against provision for a local or community audience, or even a regional one (as is being seen in the UK, with the merging of the regional commercial television companies and the accompanying dilution of regional provision). Gillian Doyle has spelt out the economies of scale that lead to this:

> In most sectors of the media, marginal costs tend to be low, and in some cases they are zero. Consequently, as more viewers tune in or more readers purchase a copy of the magazine, the average costs to the firm of supplying the product will be lowered. If average production costs go down as the scale of consumption of the firm's output increases, then economies of scale and higher profits will be enjoyed. (Doyle, 2002: 14)

With low marginal costs making it so easy to expand, and fierce competition in many media sectors, the push to ever-increasing numbers of readers/listeners/viewers is likely to be constant. This means that the more limited audiences of many minority language communities are likely to be seen as uneconomic. Even when minority media are provided, the pressure is likely to be to dilute the linguistic content (for example, by emphasising music or by making programmes that are bilingual in some way) in order to appeal to peripheral audiences (peripheral to the language concerned).

Quite apart from the organisation and economics of the media, formats and content are frequently international, rather than domestic, in origin. Much of television consists of formats that are familiar the world over and that have little connection with regional cultures. The spread of the 'Big Brother' format round the world, from its origin in the Netherlands, demonstrates this. And of course much of the content of popular television is not specific to the country in which it is broadcast. Hollywood films, Australian soap operas, music videos all make this clear. While these factors do not in themselves directly threaten minority languages (it would be easy to have minority language versions of 'Big Brother', and Hollywood films have been dubbed into many languages), the continuing spread and dominance of international and non-culturally specific media content is more likely to draw audiences to majority language media than to make them look to minority channels. Many minority language speakers are bilingual in the neighbouring majority language (this is particularly true of the older minority languages of Europe), resulting in an easy move to majority language media if the minority media are seen as unsatisfactory (for example, by having lower production values). In addition, if its distinctive culture is seen as an essential aspect of a minority language (a view that not every supporter of minority languages would agree with), then the use of media formats from other cultures is likely to work against the language's survival. International formats may pull the viewer into international culture, downgrading the value of the indigenous culture.

Against the argument that language-based media must inevitably help with language maintenance, it can be noted that much television content uses language in a fairly limited way, and even radio is usually limited to music content, often of an international style. Media styles and contents are frequently repeated from one country to another, and the uses of language are not necessarily the best for encouraging minority language use. Marshall McLuhan famously described television as a 'cool medium', that is, one which does not demand the same level of involvement as the 'hot media' of radio and print, with their concentration on a single sense (McLuhan, 1964). Even if McLuhan's assumptions can be questioned, there is a useful point to be made here, suggesting that while television may be necessary for any language community to demonstrate its participation in modernity, it may not be the best medium for encouraging language use. We should not make the mistake of thinking that because television seems to have been a major element working against minority languages, in the spread of dominant languages, particularly English, in the spread of 'americanisation', and in the internationalisation of popular culture, it can be therefore used just as easily to work in the favour of minorities.

Finally, it is not at all clear how much the presence of a minority language in the media actually encourages people to speak the language. This is particularly true of television and the Internet. One can imagine a scene in a bilingual home in which minority language programmes are watched, but are either not talked about, or are talked about in the dominant language (and see Moring's account of his research on bilingual Swedish/Finnish homes in his Chapter 2 in this book). Even the sense of identity and group solidarity that some see as being a possible product of minority language media may be different now. It may be that in the age of multi-channel broadcasting television fragments the audience, rather than brings it together, so that rather than assisting the identity of a minority language group, the media in fact further fragments the group. Few minority language communities, certainly in Europe, will be consumers of only media in the minority language. Most will also be watching dominant language media as well. Any calculation of minority language media impact must take this into account. In addition, it should not be assumed that the popularity of specific media content (such as a television programme) leads automatically to more use of the language in which the programme is made. It is not difficult to imagine a situation in which a very popular programme in a minority language is talked about most commonly in the majority language (music programmes aimed at teenagers may well fall into this category).

These points can be summed up by suggesting two propositions concerning minority language media use which, while often assumed, are – at best – unproven: (1) *A greater amount of media content in a minority language must help the survival of that language.* It is not at all clear in the case of television, for example. It is unlikely that television itself would bring more people to the language. It is also not clear that it makes people talk more to each other in the language, nor that it keeps children in the language – particularly the crucial (for language maintenance) mid-teens to mid-twenties category; (2) *A wider range of media in a minority language must help language survival.* Again, simply putting more of a minority language on the Internet, for example, is not in any clear way by itself likely to maintain speaking of that language. If different media are in effect in competition (by scheduling clashes, for example), or are duplicating content, then their impact is not likely to be cumulative. The point of all this is not that media are necessarily damaging to minority languages, but that we simply do not know enough about their impact in this type of situation.

New Media

Digital technology has now transformed the media at every level – production, distribution and consumption – making it appear to many that minority languages now have an opportunity that was denied to them in the days of spectrum scarcity and nationally organised media. Digitisation is, of course, a revolution that is still in its early stages. Precisely how it will develop – and how that development will affect minority languages – is far from clear. On the one hand there are optimistic views that emphasise the ease of use of new media, and the broadening of the spectrum of available media. Arnold and Plymire refer to Trahant's optimistic view of Internet use by Native Americans:

> Since the medium requires less capital outlay than does print media, Native groups might get their perspectives on political and social issues into circulation more easily. Second, tribes might use the sites to teach language and history, as do the Navajos and the Cherokees. Third, Trahant states that 'one of the oldest battles in the Native American press is over who controls information'. Print media may

give tribal governments or federal agencies the power of censorship, while the internet grants individuals a greater voice. Finally, individuals might use the net to communicate with one another, through newsgroups and e-mail discussion lists, to build the bonds of community across time and space. (Arnold & Plymire, 2000: 187–188)

I have written elsewhere of the possibilities for minority languages in the new media world of multiple channels, arguing that digital media open up a much wider range of opportunities, creating space for minority interests while at the same time reducing the power of the traditional national broadcasters (Cormack, 2000).

There is, however, a tension at the heart of new media use for minority languages: *any use by minority language communities of new media technologies, for either production or distribution, is likely to bring with it more majority language media.* The revolution that brought video workshops into some communities also flooded consumers with Hollywood films on video. Along with the chance of community access channels, cable television brought an increase in television channels overall. Digital broadcasting, while creating spaces for minority languages, has also massively multiplied the number of channels available in English and other dominant languages. The Internet allows any person and any community to create a website very easily, but everyone who has access to that, also has access to a vast – and steadily increasing – number of other websites. While the amount of minority language media content goes up, the percentage share of the minority language within the overall media offer goes down. Amezaga illustrates this general point when he notes the number of satellite channels available in the Basque Country – starting with 148 in English, 110 in Spanish, 104 in German, 88 in Arabic, 74 in Italian and 60 in French (Amezaga, 2004: 76). Of these, he notes that 87% were free to air. Any Basque speaker who gets satellite television in order to receive television channels in Basque, will also be the recipient of a large number of Spanish (and other) channels. No matter how good a minority language digital television channel might be, anyone who converts to digital reception to receive it becomes a potential receiver of many more channels in majority languages.

The Problem of Media Impact

If there are problems in deciding what kind of impact media have on language maintenance, then it might seem that audience research would provide an answer. After all, this is one aspect of the much larger problem of how the impact of the media can be studied. Although this is the oldest problem of media studies, and the most central, it still has no clear answer that commands general assent. Partly this is due to the very complex nature of media consumption. Typically we engage with several media each day, we do this in a variety of settings, and we look for different things from different kinds of media content. There is a wide range of possible reactions to media (immediate behavioural change, reinforcement of already-held attitudes, familiarisation with unusual content, etc., and not omitting the possibility of immediate forgetting), all of which can be assumed to have the potential to take place in all language settings, whether minority or not.

Even in relation to language maintenance, the media can function at various levels. The most basic level is simply the provision of a background against which language use can be developed. This level includes the development of vocabulary (what language planners refer to as corpus planning), the spreading of information about the language community, and the establishment of a communications framework. The second level is when the media provide opportunities and motivations for language use, for example, developing materials for educational use and providing material that gives rise to discussion. At the third level, the media actively promote language use directly. It is at this third level – arguably the most important when it comes to language maintenance – that the difficulties arise.

Using the media for language maintenance is using the media for direct and indirect behavioural effect and attitudinal confirmation or change. These are the most controversial aspects of media impact. However the media are not really designed for this kind of impact. Consider the BBC's famous trio of aims – to inform, to educate, to entertain (words that still appear in the BBC's Royal Charter). Any of these may influence behaviour but none is specifically aimed at this. There may well be examples of direct media effect on behaviour. However, despite much debate and controversy, the media's power to affect behaviour in such ways is, at best, unproven. This suggests that minority language media content may well have to be rather different from conventional media content if it is to be designed to change or maintain people's linguistic habits. It is also quite likely that such an aim might well conflict with the media's more familiar commercial role of providing entertainment (and if minority language media are not entertaining enough to attract a large audience, then no other impacts are possible).

In addition to this, it is important to understand how the minority language audience might interact with media. Muiris Ó Laoire, in a discussion of the relationship between language planning and broadcasting notes:

If language planning is examined at the micro-level of the individual family, then the issue becomes one of investigating the causes and conditions whereby an individual or an individual family changes, alters or modifies language within the home or other domains. (Ó Laoire, 2001: 63)

Based on such an awareness of the importance of the viewing context, Pertti Alasuutari has discussed what he calls the 'third generation' of audience research (the first two being reception research and ethnographic research) and has emphasised the need to study 'media culture', not just audience reactions:

> The objective is to get a grasp of our contemporary 'media culture', particularly as it can be seen in the role of the media in everyday life, both as a topic and as an activity structured by and structuring the discourses within which it is discussed. (Alasuutari, 1999: 6)

Audience reaction, then, is seen not just as an immediate (or even long-term) relationship with a programme, but is rather something that is constituted and negotiated between audience members, in the way they talk about media content, and use it among themselves. Seen in this light, it is not surprising that Sonia Livingstone has summed up the contemporary view of audience research as follows:

> After half a century of television audience research, we know that processes of media influence are far more indirect and complex than popularly thought. We know that not only does the social context in front of the screen frame the nature of the engagement with what is shown on the screen, but that in many ways which we can now elaborate, people are active in shaping their media culture. (Livingstone, 2004: 79)

This notion of a media culture may seem most applicable when the audience considered is that of metropolitan centres and their suburban peripheries (the unacknowledged but limited domain of conventional media studies and cultural studies) but in relation to minority language audiences (frequently found in non-urban regions), this factor becomes even more important since it centres on the issue of why bilingual audience members should choose to watch in one language rather than another. Linked to this is what Alasuutari terms 'the audience's notions of themselves as the "audience"' (Alasuutari, 1999: 7). It prompts the question of how a minority language audience sees itself in relation to the dominant language audience.

Taking these approaches into consideration allows researchers to look in a new light at the question of how the media might affect language maintenance. Instead of looking for quantitative results, or comparing audience figures with census returns, or asking opinions about specific media content, a much wider panorama of the impact of the media on language use opens up.

Rewriting the Question

All of this suggests that the question with which this chapter began – how can the mass media help minority languages? – needs to be reconsidered. It is based on problematic assumptions. First, the term 'media' is too broad. Although the interactions among different media today is blurring the traditional boundaries between television, radio, film and print, in terms of language use, these media, along with the newer digital media, are different enough to suggest that attention needs to be given to the different qualities of the different media – even in the still relatively rare situation of them all being experienced through the technology of the Internet. Second, it must be understood that language maintenance is an unusual task to give to the media. None of the media was designed to have such a direct and practical outcome. Indeed it is arguable that all media, from the printed book onwards, have worked, at least partly, to *replace* spoken language, rather than to encourage it. Asking the media to help in language maintenance is a bit like using an axe to dig a hole – it may be possible but it is certainly not what it was intended for. Third, we should not expect to find direct evidence of how successful or not media use has been in encouraging language use. The complexities involved in the social uses of language are simply to great to be simplified into a series of cause-and-effect relationships. Fourth, we need to be awake to the different impacts that media can have on different types of community, remembering that the kind of community that language activists are usually interested in is much smaller than the kind of community or audience that most media are interested in. Finally, the initial question has the fatal disadvantage of detaching media use from other aspects of social life. As the history of audience research has shown, the easiest way of producing wildly inaccurate statements of media effects is to isolate media use in this way.

Taking these factors into account, the initial question can be rewritten. In what ways can different media interact with other aspects of language use to contribute, directly or indirectly, to language maintenance in specific communities? This takes us away from attempting very general answers. It also emphasises the complexities of the issues. It should encourage us to look at very specific situations (remembering that the answers that may appear appropriate in one minority language community may not be the same as those in another language community), while being aware that the media consist of a range of different technologies with different capabilities, and which use language in different ways. But we also need to be well aware of the potential for harm to minority languages which some media have (as noted earlier). Just because television programmes or websites use a minority language, that does not mean that they are therefore necessarily useful for language maintenance. At the end of the day, to be useful in this way, media must encourage *actual* language use. They must encourage people to not give up the minority language and, further than that, actively encourage them to go out and speak the language. This is a new task for the media and its difficulty should not be under-estimated.

An Ecological Approach

One way of approaching these issues to adopt what Einar Haugen (in an essay originally published in 1972) has termed 'an ecology of language'. He defined this as 'the study of interactions between any given language and its environment' (Haugen, 2001: 57). The central factor in this ecology is, of course, the people who speak the language: 'The ecology of a language is determined primarily by the people who learn it, use it, and transmit it to others' (Haugen, 2001: 57). William F. Mackey applied this more directly to issues of language maintenance when he argued that 'the ecology of language shift is the study of interrelated sequences of causes and effects producing changes in the traditional language behaviour of one group under the influence of another, resulting in a switch in the language of one of the groups' (Mackey, 2001: 68). Mackey also noted that 'in studying the ecology of language shift, one cannot as a general rule single out any one cause for the retention or loss of an ethnic tongue. Causes generally are multiple and interrelated' (Mackey, 2001: 71). The implications for the study of the media's role will be clear: a straightforward cause-and-effect line between the media and language behaviour is likely to be a gross simplification and distortion. This approach to the question has several advantages. It can restore the complexity to the media situation. It can allow us to avoid an overly simplistic view of an 'audience' as a monolithic structure. It can emphasise that media use takes place in a complex behavioural environment. In addition to this there is, of course, what might be seen by some as a disadvantage – we must abandon the idea that a straightforward media–language link can be found. However, as noted in the previous section, there are good reasons for abandoning this on other grounds as well.

In developing his ecology of language, Haugen went on to list ten 'ecological' questions that researchers on a language should want to answer (Haugen, 2001: 65). Several of these are directly relevant to media use. What are the language's domains of use? What concurrent languages are employed by its users? What internal varieties does the language show? To what degree has its written form been standardised, i.e. unified and codified? What kind of institutional support has it won, either in government, education or private organisations, either to regulate its form or propagate it? What are the attitudes of its users towards the language in terms of intimacy and status, leading to personal identification?

Although criticisms can be made of the comprehensiveness of Haugen's list (see, for example, Edwards, 1995: 143), his points can function at least as a useful guide into this territory, and they suggest a number of questions that might be asked. Seeing media as one element in an ecology of language use points away from the idea of an audience confronting the media, and towards a model of a communicative community in which the various media interact with each other and with other forms of communication. The model, then, is not of media impacting on users, or of a two-way interaction between media and users, but rather of media and users being but two parts of a larger ecology. This model also fits very comfortably with the notion of 'media culture' already referred to.

An ecological approach to language implies a rather different research agenda concerning the media's role in language maintenance than that suggested by traditional audience research methods. It suggests that greater attention must be made to the specifics of media use and that a series of questions need to be considered if any specific language situation is to be understood. Some of these are questions that can be answered by observation and / or by in-depth interview:

- How do people use the media in their conversation and in other interactions?
- How are minority language media talked about by their users?
- What choices do they make about which language to use when talking about the media?
- How are choices about language use related to different types of media content?
- How do uses of different media overlap?
- How is popularity of media content related to language use?

Others can be answered by analysis of the media themselves:

- Who uses the language in the media?
- What domains are used by the language in the media?
- What differences are there in use of the language by different media?
- How does media use in the minority language link to media use in the relevant majority language?
- How do specific media interact with local, cultural and national identities?
- How is the language represented within neighbouring majority language media?

(Although this last point may seem to be a side issue for speakers of the language, it is an important aspect of how the language is seen by non-speakers, and hence relates to the overall status of the language). Still other questions involve study of both media and users:

- How do speakers of a minority language interact with the media in the dominant, hegemonic language?
- How do people participate in minority language media, for example by phone-ins, letters to the editor, studio audiences, even in competitions run by the media?
- Which users of the language participate most?

These questions can help us to construct an ecology of language use involving the media. Using the term 'ecology' serves to put the emphasis on the environment in which media use occurs, rather than concentrating too narrowly on the immediate media–audience interaction.

Making sense of the answers to these questions is not likely to be a straightforward matter and may well give rise to contradictory findings (as should be expected in any study of complex human behaviour). In addition, it may well be that answers that arise in one area may be very different from answers that arise in another. However such complexities should not count against this approach. Indeed part of the problem of traditional audience research has lain in the attempt to find simple answers to complex problems. Only in the consideration of such questions as those suggested above are we likely to get nearer to seeing the overall picture of minority language media and to get near an answer to the question of what it is about media use of a language that might encourage people to speak the language more. The emphasis here is not on media content as some kind of free-standing force, nor on media institutions and organisations as hegemonic powers, but rather on the space between the media and their users.

Such research can also serve as an evaluation of the media's role in language planning. As Ó Laoire notes:

Language planning itself requires systematic evaluation. This is true especially in the area of broadcast media. The evaluation is not only a measurement of success of the media product in terms of attracting audience and compiling TAM ratings, but is also an assessment of context, process and implementation within the framework of language planning itself. (Ó Laoire, 2001: 67)

If the media is to fulfil its potential as a factor in language planning, then the processes by which the media might encourage language acquisition need to be more fully understood than they are at present. The approach described here is the most appropriate to do this.

Conclusion

The argument in this chapter should not be misunderstood. It is not that minority languages should not have, for example, television channels. There are good reasons why they should, as noted at the start. Rather, it is that the role that media can play in the more direct forms of language maintenance – that is, actually encouraging people to use a language – should not be over-estimated. It is, in many respects, an unusual task to give to the media. Many features of the media work against this. Media seem most likely to encourage language use when they are strongly participative, strongly linked to communities (whether territorial or diasporic) of language speakers, and when they can give people a reason for adopting, or asserting, the identity of being a minority language speaker. However, at the moment, we simply do not know enough about how the media might encourage minority language use in a bilingual situation. New ways of researching this are needed, ways that can penetrate and make sense of the audience's interaction and use of media. An ecological approach seems best suited to do this, focusing on interactions amongst people, and the contexts in which these take place, rather than just on the media–audience nexus.

References

Alasuutari, P. (ed.) (1999) *Rethinking the Media Audience: The New Agenda*. London: Sage.
Amezaga, J. (2004) Linguistic space: Satellite television and languages around the world and in the European Union. *Mercator Media Forum* 7, 66–85.
Anderson, B. (1991) *Imagined Communities*. London: Verso.

Arnold, E.L. and Plymire, D.C. (2000) The Cherokee Indians and the Internet. In D. Gauntlett (ed.) *Web.Studies: Rewiring Media Studies for the Digital Age* (pp. 186–193). London: Arnold.

Billig, M. (1995) *Banal Nationalism*. London: Sage.

Browne, D. (1996) *Electronic Media and Indigenous Peoples: A Voice of Our Own?* Ames, IA: Iowa State University Press.

Cormack, M. (1998) Minority language media in Western Europe: Preliminary considerations. *European Journal of Communication* 13 (1), 33–52.

Cormack, M. (2000) Minority language media in a global age. *Mercator Media Forum* 4, 3–15.

Cormack, M. (2005) The cultural politics of minority language media. *International Journal of Media and Cultural Politics* 1 (1), 107–122.

Crystal, D. (2000) *Language Death*. Cambridge: Cambridge University Press.

Dahlgren, P. (1995) *Television and the Public Sphere: Citizenship, Democracy and the Media*. London: Sage.

Doyle, G. (2002) *Understanding Media Economics*. London: Sage.

Edwards, J. (1995) *Multilingualism*. London: Penguin Books.

Fishman, J. (1991) *Reversing Language Shift: Theoretical and Empirical Foundations of Assistance to Threatened Languages*. Clevedon: Multilingual Matters.

Fishman, J. (ed.) (2001) *Can Threatened Languages Be Saved? Reversing Language Shift Revisited: A 21st Century Perspective*. Clevedon: Multilingual Matters.

Grin, F. (2003a) *Language Policy Evaluation and the European Charter for Regional or Minority Languages*. Basingstoke: Palgrave Macmillan.

Grin, F. (2003b) From antagonism to convergence: Economics and linguistic diversity. In J.M. Kirk and D.O. O Baoill (eds) *Towards Our Goals in Broadcasting, the Press, the Performing Arts and the Economy: Minority Languages in Northern Ireland, the Republic of Ireland, and Scotland* (pp. 213–223). Belfast Studies in Language, Culture and Politics, 10. Belfast: Queen's University Belfast.

Grin, F. and Moring, T. (with Forter, D., Häggman, J., Ó Riagáin, D. and Strubell, M.) (2003) *Support for Minority Languages in Europe*. Final report on a project financed by the European Commission, Directorate Education and Culture. On www at: http://europa.eu.int/comm/education/policies/lang/langmin/support.pdf

Grin, F. and Vaillancourt, F. (1999) *The Cost-effectiveness Evaluation of Minority Language Policies: Case Studies on Wales, Ireland, and the Basque Country*. ECMI Monograph No. 2. Flensburg: ECMI.

Haugen, E. (2001) The ecology of language. In A. Fill and P. Mühlhäusler (eds) *The Ecolinguistics Reader* (pp. 57–66). London: Continuum.

Hourigan, N. (2003) *Escaping the Global Village: Media, Language and Protest*. Lanham, MD: Lexington Books.

Livingstone, S. (2004) The challenge of changing audiences, or, what is the audience researcher to do in the age of the Internet? *European Journal of Communication* 19 (1), 75–86.

Mackey, W.F. (2001) The ecology of language shift. In A. Fill and P. Mühlhäusler (eds) *The Ecolinguistics Reader* (pp. 67–74). London: Continuum.

McLuhan, M. (1964) *Understanding Media*. London: Routledge and Kegan Paul.

May, S. (2001) *Language and Minority Rights: Ethnicity, Nationalism and the Politics of Language*. London: Pearson Education.

Moal, S. (2001) Broadcast media in Breton: Dawn at last? In H. Kelly-Holmes (ed.) *Minority Language Broadcasting: Breton and Irish* (pp. 31–48). Clevedon: Multilingual Matters.

Ó Laoire, M. (2001) Language policy and the broadcast media: A response. In H. Kelly-Holmes (ed.) *Minority Language Broadcasting: Breton and Irish* (pp. 63–68). Clevedon: Multilingual Matters.

Riggins, S.H. (ed.) (1992) *Ethnic Minority Media: An International Perspective*. London: Sage.

Watson, I. (2003) *Broadcasting in Irish: Minority Language, Radio, Television and Identity*. Dublin: Four Courts Press.

Chapter 5
The Role of Networks in Minority Language Television Campaigns

NIAMH HOURIGAN

Some forms of minority language media such as radio and websites are relatively cheap to establish and thus have emerged organically from within minority language communities. Other forms of media, particularly television, are more expensive and the creation of minority language television services has required support from central or regional governments. The process of convincing authorities of the need for minority language television and winning the financial support necessary to set up these services has resulted in the emergence of several minority language television campaigns since the 1960s. In my book, *Escaping the Global Village* (Hourigan, 2003), six campaigns for minority language television services in Wales, Scotland, Ireland, Catalonia, Galicia and the Basque Country were examined. This analysis focused primarily on the activities of individual movements in demanding television services within national political contexts. In this chapter, a different dimension of the campaigns debate is explored, as the role of trans-national minority language movement networks in contributing to the success of three campaigns is examined in light of official and sustained European Union institutional support for the creation of these linkages.

This analysis focuses on the campaigns for minority language television services that emerged in Wales, Scotland and Ireland during the 1966–1996 period. Within the literature on minority language activism, minority language movements are generally characterised as having a local, regional or national focus because, by and large, regional and national administrations are the primary obstacles to the development of minority language infrastructure such as schools and media services (Hourigan, 2003; Johnston, 1991). However, European Union institutions such European Bureau for Lesser Used Languages (EBLUL) and the associated Mercator organisations have sought to create a European minority language trans-national network where there is routine collaboration, mutual learning and co-operation amongst minority language groups in order to achieve cultural and socio-economic policy change.

During the 1980s and 1990s, European Union minority language initiatives exerted top-down pressure to generate and support trans-national interaction and collaboration. Documentation from the EBLUL[1] states: 'Since its establishment in 1982, the European Bureau for Lesser Used Languages has been strengthening contacts and mutual co-operation between lesser used language communities. It has acted as a facilitator in their links and communications with European institutions.'[2] The aspiration to construct a European minority language network was integrated into the structure of the EBLUL as 'through its network of member state committees, EBLUL represents the regional and minority language communities of the European Union. It promotes their common interests at European and international level and acts as a channel of communication between them and European and international bodies.'[3] The associated Mercator group of organisations, which promotes media, education and legislative minority language initiatives, advocates a similar network approach, indicating that it aims to meet 'the growing need for an interchange of experiences and a fostering of co-operation between the linguistic communities within the European context'.[4]

The benefits of participation in a social movement network have been predominantly explained in terms of an increased capacity for mutual learning between movements, which allows individual organisations to benefit from the knowledge and experience gained by other groups of activists campaigning on similar issues in different political contexts (Diani & McAdam, 2003). The mechanism for mutual learning between language movements through communication and interaction is described as diffusion (Della Porta & Diani, 1999). EBLUL and Mercator literature indicates that these institutions view diffusion as a process that is facilitated from the top down, that is from official European Union institutions. This chapter re-orients this debate and adopt a bottom-up approach in order to examine whether grass-roots processes of diffusion between minority language movements were a significant factor in campaigns for television services in Ireland, Scotland and Wales during the 1966–1996 period.

The concept of diffusion has been imported into the social sciences from physics and is used to explain the transfer across time and space of particular cultural traits, information and ideas. McAdam and Rucht acknowledge 'protest makers do not have to reinvent the wheel at each place and in each conflict...they often find inspiration elsewhere in the ideas and tactics espoused and practised by other activists' (1993: 58). Welsh, Irish and Scots Gaelic activists would appear to be among the minority language groups most likely to experience diffusion because of the close geographical proximity of language movements. Della Porta and Diani comment that 'it is more likely that diffusion will take place between countries which are close together geographically. In fact, interaction will tend to be strongest between neighbouring countries' (1999: 247).

Aside from geographical proximity, there are a number of other factors suggesting that a process of diffusion would have occurred between these three campaign groups. Welsh, Irish and Scots Gaelic are all Celtic languages and thus share linguistic roots that could potentially support inter-community understandings. While the term Celtic language is primarily a lexicographical description, the Celtic language movements were able to access a pre-existing trans-national framework for contacts through pan-Celtic organisations such as The Celtic League[5] and the annual pan-Celtic festivals. Finally, groups involved in these campaigns were focusing on the same issue, television, and were trying to prove in each context that existing television services were neglecting minority language speakers and that new forms of minority language television service would be possible and viable.

Oliver and Myers (2003) assert that processes of direct diffusion between movements occur at the level of communication, influence and/or joint action. They argue:

A communication tie provides a basis for disseminating information that something has occurred. An influence tie provides a basis for one movement to affect the opinions or actions of another movement; influence requires communication but involves additional social processes beyond mere communication. Joint action may be considered an extreme case of influence, in which initially separate movements come to make joint decisions and act in concert. (2003: 176)

Processes of diffusion can also occur indirectly, through the dissemination of movement goals, ideologies and tactics through the mass media, which inspires conscious or unconscious imitation in other movements.

In this chapter, patterns of diffusion between Welsh, Irish and Scots Gaelic campaigners will be examined in order to determine whether they operated indirectly or directly at the level of communication, influence or joint action. Each campaign will be outlined in chronological order beginning with the Welsh campaign, which began in 1966, and ending with the Scots Gaelic campaign. Two key dimensions of each campaign will be reviewed. Firstly, the tactics employed by each campaign group in order to obstruct the operation of conventional media services and convince authorities of the need for minority language television will be examined in order to identify the diffusion of innovative forms of protest. Secondly, the ideological discourses employed by each campaign group will be examined in order to investigate how each campaign group borrowed from other Celtic campaigns in order to justify its demands for minority language television. The resulting models of diffusion between Celtic television campaigns groups will be reviewed in light of official European Union aspirations to create greater shared experiences, mutual understandings and co-operation between minority language groups within the European Union.

The Welsh Campaign

The Welsh were one of the first European linguistic minorities to become aware of the potentially damaging impact of broadcast media on the Welsh language. In 1927, the Welsh Board of Education stated that 'we regard the present policy of the British Broadcasting Corporation as the most serious menace to the life of the Welsh language' (Davies, 1994: 72).

The roots of the campaign for the Welsh television service, S4C, can be traced to a lecture given in 1962 by the writer Saunders Lewis, who prophesied the demise of the Welsh language. The attack was aimed at Plaid Cymru, the Welsh nationalist party. It was ignored however, until a number of students 'frustrated by Plaid Cymru's refusal to consider unconstitutional methods, were ready to respond to Saunders Lewis' challenge and devote themselves to a campaign on behalf of the Welsh language' (Stephens, 1976: 172). This resulted in the formation of the Welsh Language Society (WLS), which in 1966 began to campaign for a Welsh language television service. As the first Celtic television campaign, the WLS faced the difficult task of convincing the Westminster government of the legitimacy of their grievances concerning the invisibility of the Welsh language on television. Activists also had to develop a range of tactics that would draw government support and media attention without alienating the support of the broader population of Welsh language speakers.

In developing the case for a Welsh language television service, activists assembled a range of data concerning the lack of Welsh language programmes on existing broadcasting services. The lack of programming suitable for Welsh-speaking children was highlighted as a particular problem. Using cultural imperialist models, Welsh activists argued that the invisibility of the Welsh language community on television was eroding the size of the community and damaging the status and the viability of the language (Thomas, 1971: 90–93).

The broader ideological discourse that contextualised the television demand was linked to a nationalist agenda. In 1973, Cynog Davies highlighted the WLS's latent function 'to effect some kind of transformation in the Welsh psychology, to strengthen national consciousness, to inject new reality into nationalism by bringing to light through the language struggle, the hidden oppression in the relationship between Wales and England' (1973: 172). While in 1976, Meic Stephens stated:

> Every campaign of Cymdeithas yr Iaith Gymraeg (WLS) has in addition to the obvious aims of obtaining concessions in the public use of Welsh, a less immediate but equally central aim, which is to awaken a new spirit among the people. This is what Saunders Lewis meant when he spoke of using the language as a weapon. (1976: 183)

This radical ideological approach to the campaign led to the development of an equally radical range of tactics. In 1966, a petition demanding the new service was launched and following a march through Cardiff in 1968, it was submitted to the authorities. However, by 1971, it was clear that the sort of indirect action that had prevailed during the early stages of the campaign, was proving ineffective (Tomos, 1982: 40). As a result, the WLS launched their 'symbolic acts of damage' campaign. This involved a deliberate programme of destroying public property, particularly broadcasting equipment (bombs were often used), and then handing oneself in and admitting the crime. The rationale behind this campaign was articulated by Ffred Ffrancis, who stated 'it would be totally unjust to use personal violence against the body or personality of a broadcaster but it is totally just and in fact, it is the responsibility of a conscientious Welshman to damage the instrument that is used to violate people'.[6]

Another innovative tactic was developed in the early 1970s when members of the WLS began to deliberately refuse to pay their licence fees. By 1973, over 200 activists had defaulted on the charge and a number had been imprisoned as a result. The courtroom dramas resulting from these cases began to make an impression on the mass media and some speeches were fully reprinted in the press. The imprisonment of activists, who were mainly students, academics or professionals of various kinds created greater sympathy for the aims and objectives of the WLS. Direct action proved to be the more effective tactical approach and by, 1974, Pritchard-Jones insists that 'all political parties and most local and national bodies were in favour of having a Welsh channel' (1982: 28).

In response the campaign, the British government established the Crawford and Silberry committees to investigate the possibility of establishing a Welsh language TV channel. The process of waiting for the reports of these committees generated a lull in the Welsh campaign and during this period, close contacts were established with the Irish language movement which was just beginning to consider the television issue. The failure of either committee to produce any concrete results or proposals prompted a return to direct action in 1977 (Tomos, 1982: 41).

The ruling British Labour Party was facing a general election in 1979 and was dependent on political parties such as Plaid Cymru, Scottish Nationalist Party (SNP) as well as the nationalist Social and Democratic Labour Party (SDLP) and the Ulster Unionists in Northern Ireland. While direct action continued, forms of indirect action re-emerged as activists sought to create political alliances that would allow them to exploit the prevailing political instability. Before the 1979 election, both Labour and the Conservatives promised that legislation for the new channel would be put before parliament in the following year. In 1980 however, after her entry into government, Margaret Thatcher withdrew the television proposal. This move caused consternation among Welsh language activists. Gwynfor Evans, leader of Plaid Cymru threatened to go on hunger strike if proposals weren't restored to the government's legislative programme. The threat prompted a wave of renewed protest throughout Wales. Mother and toddler groups occupied the HTV premises, ordained ministers conducted their own protest, and scuffles broke out at the Eisteddfodd (Welsh language festival) when the Welsh secretary arrived. Under this pressure the Conservatives capitulated and Sianel Pedwar Cymru, the first Welsh television service was established in 1982 (Pritchard-Jones, 1982: 26–29; Tomos, 1982: 40–53).

The Irish Campaign

The activities of the WLS made a considerable impact on members of the Irish language movement and in particular, on members of Ireland's pre-eminent language organisation, Conradh na Gaeilge. From the 1960s, Conradh na Gaeilge had some form of media committee whose principal objective was to campaign for an increase in the amount of Irish language programming on the national broadcaster, RTÉ. However, as the television service (founded in 1963) was committed in broadcast law to support the Irish language, activists were initially hopeful that Irish would have a prominent position in RTÉ programming. By the early 1970s, this optimism was beginning to wane with increasing evidence that the amount of Irish on RTÉ was diminishing (Quill, 1993).

Formal contacts with Welsh activists through pan-Celtic organisations and informal contacts between activists in WLS and Conradh na Gaeilge stimulated Irish interest in forming a campaign for an Irish language television service. In 1975, Conradh na Gaeilge organised a conference on the broadcast media in Celtic countries. Members the WLS spoke at the conference about their campaign for a separate service. It is clear from contemporary activist reports that these speeches represent a key moment of diffusion in terms of communication and influence from Wales to Ireland (Ó Feinneadha, 1995: 10). The case made by Welsh activists concerning the futility of expecting state/national broadcasters to adequately serve lesser-used language speakers was very convincing and deeply affected younger members of the Irish language movement. Former Conradh president Ité Uí Chionnaith comments 'from then on, I have to admit that I was very strongly of the opinion that we needed a separate channel' (Mac Aonghusa, 1993: 375).

The 1975 conference not only convinced young Irish language activists that a separate channel for Irish language television programmes must be sought, but it also introduced Conradh na Gaeilge to the new set of tactics developed by the WLS. These tactics included climbing broadcast masts, sit-ins, invasion of studios, non-payment of licence fees, marches and petitions (Tomos, 1982: 37–59). Irish activists were impressed by the success of these tactics and anxious to incorporate this approach into their own television campaign. Student leader Ciarán Ó Feinneadha states how 'from that time forward, I have to confess that I was envious of the effectiveness of the Welsh campaign' (1995: 10). While Uí Chionnaith indicates the extent of Welsh influence on Irish television activists stating 'in the early days, the Welsh campaign would have been the driving force behind our efforts'.[7] Therefore, it is clear that within Oliver and Myer's model of diffusion, contacts between Welsh and Irish language groups during 1975–1976 led to communication and influence and contributed significantly to the emergence of a new campaign for Irish language television.

The range of tactics employed between 1975 and 1980 exemplifies this distinct Welsh influence on Irish activists. The year 1976 saw one student leader climb the broadcasting mast at RTÉ, thereby attracting considerable media attention. Members of Conradh na Gaeilge picketed RTÉ studios and Dublin's General Post Office, which was also the headquarters of those charged with collecting the television licence fee. Activists organised petitions, chained themselves to gates or the doors of state buildings. The tactic that Irish activists used most frequently throughout the first stage of the campaign was the refusal to pay television licence fees and was directly derived from the WLS tactical programme. Not only did activists refuse to pay their TV licence fee, but they also refused to pay fines imposed for non-payment. When brought to court, they would cite RTÉ Irish language policy as a reason for non-payment.[8]

It is also possible to detect the influence of Welsh groups in the ideological approach which Irish language activists adopted during the early stages of the campaign for a television service. Within Conradh na Gaeilge, the commitment to the Irish language had always been characterised as part of a broader cultural nationalism, an emphasis mirrored by the Irish state in the constitution. However, after the escalation of violence in Northern Ireland in the early 1970s, the legitimacy of this publicly enshrined nationalism and the associated project of reviving the Irish language became the subject of criticism. Conradh na Gaeilge activists were deeply troubled by this ideological change as it not only directly affected Irish language policy but also their own position as one of the most privileged social movements in Irish civil society.[9] By contextualising the early stages of the television campaign in terms of cultural nationalism, it is clear that Conradh na Gaeilge was directly challenging the Irish government. Within their campaign literature, activists asserted that the state was abandoning its historic commitment to the Irish language by allowing the state broadcaster to neglect the language and refusing to provide an alternative Irish language service. Despite this challenge, Watson notes that during this period successive Irish governments gradually began to contextualise Irish language issues in terms of minority rights[10] rather than cultural nationalism (1996: 170).

In contrast to the success of the Welsh campaign, the cultural nationalist ideology that underpinned the early stages of the Irish television campaign proved unappealing to a broader Irish population struggling to come to terms with the rise of militant nationalism in the North. By 1985, it was clear that Conradh na Gaeilge had not achieved the type of policy success that had been gained by the WLS. Perhaps as a result of the failure of tactics and ideologies diffused from the WLS to Ireland, the influence of Welsh activists on the Irish campaign began to diminish. Levels of Welsh activism had declined in overall terms after the establishment of S4C in 1982 and Conradh na Gaeilge activists now became aware of profound differences in the Welsh and Irish political context. The cultural nationalist discourse that was suitable in a context where Welsh nationalist sensibilities were relatively moderate became hugely problematic in Ireland where militant nationalists were espousing a nationalist ideology in order to justify bombing and maiming of innocent civilians. This key political difference would require the innovation of a new ideological approach and a tactical programme that would effectively sidestep the national question and thus, present a less complex and more appealing ideological argument to the Irish government and the broader Irish populace.

In 1985, newly elected Conradh na Gaeilge president Ité Uí Chionnaith decided to change the organisation's ideological approach to the television campaign and contextualise the demand for a television service in terms of a Bill of Rights for Irish speakers, which combined legal, educational and media rights. A number of new groups became involved in the campaign for Irish language television who also contextualised their demands in terms of minority rights including the Irish-medium schooling movement, Gaelscoileanna. The most significant group to enter the Irish language television campaign in the mid-1980s was the Gaeltacht television campaign group, Meitheal Oibre Teilifís na Gaeltachta. The group of Gaeltacht activists had no significant connection to the broader pan-Celtic movement and the growing prominence of Gaeltacht leaders in the television campaign ended any continuing Welsh influence. Gaeltacht groups contextualised their demands in terms of minority language rights, regionalism and the economic development of the periphery. This ideological discourse justifying the demand for Irish language television proved more attractive to government in the late 1980s, as Gaeltacht regions were economically underdeveloped and had a special designated status within the Irish constitution. Gaeltacht activists went to great lengths to prove that an Irish language television service based in the Gaeltacht could be a central pillar of the region's economic development. Activists even chartered a boat to the Faroe Islands to examine the island's local television service and wrote a subsequent report 'Take the Faroes for Example' outlining the economic potential of the audio-visual industry for Gaeltacht development. Meitheal Oibre activists advocated the establishment of a low-cost local television service for Gaeltacht regions that could be accessed by Irish speakers in other parts of the island through cable services. This innovative approach prompted the Irish government to allocate half a million pounds to the Irish language television project in 1987.

During the 1988–1990 period, significant divisions opened up between Conradh na Gaeilge activists who had been influenced by the Welsh approach and sought a service similar to S4C, and Gaeltacht groups who were more focused on regional development and were demanding a local Gaeltacht service. In 1990, a new umbrella organisation, FNT (Feachtas Náisiúnta Teilefíse),[11] attempted to unite both factions in the television campaign. This group put forward a compromise model of a national television service based in the Gaeltacht whose output was ideologically contextualised in terms of minority rights. In 1993, the Irish government set up two committees, which included campaign activists, to report on the feasibility of the new service and, in 1996, TnaG now TG4,[12] made its first broadcasts.

The Scots Gaelic Campaign

Patterns of diffusion from the Welsh and Irish campaigns to the Scots Gaelic campaign are more indirect. There are only a few examples of direct contact between campaigners, although it is clear that Scots Gaelic activists learned much by examining from afar the tactics and ideologies utilised by other Celtic language television campaign groups. The demand for increased Scots Gaelic broadcasting began in the mid-1980s and was prompted by the continuing decline of the Scots Gaelic-speaking community. It is evident that Scots Gaelic speakers experienced a sense of relative deprivation that contributed to the emergence of the campaign. Having viewed the achievements of Welsh-speakers in creating S4C, they began to ask themselves why Scots Gaelic was not entitled to similar levels of support and exposure in the broadcast media. In 1986, Catherine Dunn commented:

> The Welsh had a higher population base, but the linguistic rights of both languages should be the same. The main reason may lie in the aggressive stance adopted in Wales to fight for linguistic rights, and in fact that Gaelic speakers too often seem to accept in silent submission, the unfavoured position that is theirs. We must hope that the various organisations and public bodies with a commitment to Gaidhealtachd will cease to be silent and submissive, and help to bring to fruition an improved status in the media. (1986: 56)

Gaelic language activism had indeed, been relatively muted for most of the 20th century. The pre-eminent language organisation, An Comunn Gaidhealach (The Highland Association) tended to be more popular in the Lowland rather than Highland areas and 'secured only mild ameliorations of the position of Gaelic in the educational system, publishing and other media' (Hindley, 1990: 227). The movement was primarily an arts and culture organisation and though activists indicated in their movement literature in 1975 that adequate coverage of Gaelic in the media was one of their six stated aims, there is little evidence that any concrete action was undertaken in order to achieve this outcome.[13]

Attempts were made to radicalise Gaelic language activism in the early 1970s. Under the influence of the WLS, Comunn na Cànain Albannaich (The Scottish Language Society) was established in 1971. John MacLeod argues that young Scots Gaelic activists had become dissatisfied with An Comunn commenting: 'An Comunn, though worthy, has a decidedly dated image: tweedy, fusty, lots of harp-twanging ladies in sensible shoes' (1993: 11). Though not specifically media oriented, the new radical organisation was clearly also influenced by the tactical programme developed by the WLS and sought 'by methods of militant but non-violent civil disobedience to accelerate the polarisation of attitudes for and against Gaelic in the Highlands and Islands' (Stephens, 1976: 72). However, apart from a campaign to get the Post Office to accept Gaelic, which included blowing up post-boxes, the movement never received any popular support and quickly disintegrated.

Among some elements of the Scots Gaelic movement, there remained an appetite for the type of activism that characterised Welsh protest in the 1970s. At one conference, in the early 1970s, Derick Thomson stated: '[W]hen we know clearly what our policy is we should walk out on to the streets with it and walk into the district and regional councils and into committees, on to platforms and into the press. We should brand and boycott and shame people who advocate foreign policies in the Gaelic areas.'[14] Despite this call, the activities of the Gaelic language movement were rather tame in comparison to the confrontational tactics that characterised language activism in Ireland and Wales during this period. This approach changed in the early 1980s when, as John MacLeod comments

> weary of unsuccessful pestering for a more aggressive approach to arresting the Gaelic decline, there came schism. Younger hard-headed individuals broke away to form Comunn na Gàidhlig – CNAG – under the direction of the formidable Lewisman, John Angus MacKay, and began campaigning for Gaelic to enjoy the same status wrought for Welsh in Wales. (MacLeod, 1993: 11)

This new organisation spearheaded the campaign for the provision of Gaelic language television programmes. With a much smaller base of speakers, the Scots decided not to campaign for a separate channel. Activists felt that such a campaign would not enjoy popular support and funding for a separate channel would have been very difficult to win given the size of the community. This approach was also supported by management in Scotland's pre-existing terrestrial services. STV executive, Rhoda MacDonald commented: '[W]e don't have a big enough mass of speakers. It would be a ghetto channel. People would not opt to watch it' (1993: 14). The BBC and STV broadcasting services had already made inroads into Gaelic language broadcasting in the 1980s. Therefore, Gaelic language activists proposed that a fund be established to finance the production of Gaelic language programmes to be broadcast on Scotland's four existing terrestrial channels.

In contextualising their campaign, Scots Gaelic activists benefited from the achievements of the WLS in establishing the legitimacy of a demand for minority language television. However, activists could also point to the huge disparities between Welsh and Scots Gaelic in terms of official funding and support. Catherine Dunn comments:

> The main threats to Gaelic language and culture are posed by the influence of an English medium education and by English in the media. In Wales, sustained efforts to fight the erosive effect of both these powerful factors have produced widespread Welsh medium education and Sianel Pedwar Cymru. In Scotland we have come later to the struggle, and cannot begin to make comparisons with the present situation in Wales, either in our current level of achievement or in the wider recognition, in financial support as well as status, that the Welsh language enjoys. (1986: 53)

In posing a solution to their disadvantaged position relative to Welsh, Scots Gaelic activists highlighted the potential of the audio-visual industry to boost the economy of one of the most underdeveloped areas of the British periphery, the Highlands and Islands. The broadcasting benefits of this strategy to the Scots Gaelic community were described in terms of minority rights rather than nationalism. MacDonald states:

> Unlike Welsh and Irish, Gaelic is not tied to any political movement. You couldn't possibly support Plaid Cymru in Wales and not speak Welsh. We all know the political connections with the language in Ireland. Gaelic is not like that. The Scottish nationalists don't insist that Gaelic is their every day language. (1993: 13)

Although Scots Gaelic activists proposed a radically different approach to minority language broadcasting than the approach adopted by Welsh or Irish campaign groups, they were influenced by the successes and failures of other Celtic language broadcasting services. For instance, it became clear from an early stage of the campaign, that a Scots Gaelic soap opera would form a central dimension of the programmes funded by the new initiative given the success of the Welsh soap, *Pobal y Cwm*. Gus MacDonald, managing director of Scottish Television, took advice from the producers of S4C's two serials and commented in 1990:

> An artificially created community seems to continue the compelling appeal of all popular drama serials. It is the communion of a viewer, sometimes lonely, with the engrossing affairs of a community of life-like characters with whom they can identify. According to Welsh producers the creation of such an idealised community on screen is by far the best way to re-engage Gaels, lost to the lowlands, with their Gaelic heartland. (MacDonald, 1991: 30)

Therefore, communication and influence were part of the processes of diffusion between Welsh and Scots Gaelic community but occurred more at the level of broadcasting professionals than social movement activists. Although TG4 had yet to be established, Scots Gaelic broadcasters were also determined to learn from Ireland's Raidio na Gaeltachta, which was hamstrung in terms of output by a complete English language ban. Cormack notes: 'Most Scots Gaels have not taken this view, preferring to accept the reality of bilingualism' (1994: 123). Therefore, through processes of indirect diffusion, Scots Gaelic activists and broadcasters were able to learn from Celtic language broadcasting in Wales and Ireland.

Given this growing clarity about the type of output that would be supported by the new Gaelic Television Fund, the director of Comunn na Gàidhlig, John Angus MacKay, put a development plan to the Conservative British government stressing the value of investing in television and the audio-visual industry in the Scottish Gaidhealtachd. This move seems to have been inspired by an appreciation of a key political opportunity. The Tories were facing defeat in the upcoming general election. Of 70 Scottish seats at Westminister, the Conservatives held 9 and polls indicated that all these would be lost in the upcoming election. Secondly, the Conservative Scottish Secretary, Michael Forsyth had a close relationship with the prime minister and was very supportive of the project. MacKay recognised the potential within the situation and acted promptly. MacDonald notes: 'He employed the services of an economist called Cento Veljanovski who looked at the argument and presented it in a way that was attractive to a Conservative government' (1993: 14). MacDonald concludes that MacKay used 'an economic and cultural argument and was successful in persuading what was an essentially right wing government, opposed to handouts, into giving £9.5 million, an incredible amount of money, to provide 200 hours a year of Gaelic programming' (1993: 14). Margaret Thatcher approved MacKay's proposal and the Gaelic Television Fund, became part of series generous hand-outs to Scottish projects during this period. The CTG,[15] was established in 1990 with the programming resulting from the initiative spread over the four national channels. Following the Communications Act (2003), the name of the service was changed to Seirbheis nam Meadhanan Gàidhlig (Gaelic Media Service – GMS). The name change was recognition of a growing demand for increasing Gaelic programming in Scotland and the emergence of a new Gaelic media campaign – the campaign for a Gaelic digital service. Indirect diffusion of the achievements of Irish and Welsh language television after the establishment of TG4 in Ireland and S4C's digital channel, led to a renewed sense of deprivation among Gaelic media activists and it is possible that new discourses and tactics developed by this campaign group to demand a digital television service will be diffused not just to other Celtic language activists in Northern Ireland, Brittany and England but to minority language activists throughout the new enlarged European Union.

Diffusion within Celtic Television Campaigns

In terms of the mechanisms of direct diffusion identified by Oliver and Myers (2003), there is evidence of considerable communication and influence between Welsh and Irish television campaigners. Irish activists, who dominated the first half of the campaign, were drawn pre-dominantly from Conradh na Gaeilge and were deeply influenced by the tactics and the ideology of the WLS. A number of tactics including the withholding of licence fees, and the 'symbolic acts of damage' diffused directly from the tactical programme of Welsh activists. More significantly, the ideological discourse utilised by the WLS also influenced Irish activists. This is surprising considering that Irish at this time, was and remains the first language of the Irish nation-state with a government dedicated to its protection while Welsh activists were dealing with a less sympathetic Westminster government that had no formal commitment to the Welsh language and was deeply suspicious of its centrality within Welsh nationalism. However, as the Irish campaign progressed the unsuitability and unpopularity of the nationalist discourse became evident and Gaeltacht activists entering the campaign in the mid-1980s were quick to re-focus its ideology around the minority rights discourse favoured by the Irish government and the European Union.

There is less evidence of direct communication and influence between Scots Gaelic campaigners and other Celtic language activists. In formulating the proposal for the Gaelic Television Fund, Scots Gaelic campaigners had some contact with Welsh broadcasters however, indirect processes of diffusion provide a more accurate model of the relationship between Scots Gaelic and other Celtic campaign groups. Scots Gaelic activists primarily learned from afar, viewing the successes and failures of the other Celtic language services and adopting strategies suited to their own linguistic situation.

There is no evidence of joint action among any of the campaign groups involved in the minority language television campaigns in this survey. There would appear to be a number of concrete reasons why joint action did not take place. Firstly, there was a chronological time lapse between the start of the first campaign in Wales in 1966 and the subsequent Irish and

Scots Gaelic campaigns, which meant in many cases that opportunities for genuine joint action were relatively limited. Secondly, each campaign took place in a completely different political context. The Welsh campaign was primarily aimed at the Labour government of the late 1970s and sought to take advantage of the political instability of the time. Irish campaign groups had to cope with a succession of different Irish coalition governments who were all constitutionally committed to protecting the Irish language as the first language of the nation-state. The Scots Gaelic campaign was aimed at an established Tory government in the UK that, while having an electoral vulnerability in Scotland, was still almost guaranteed power within a broader UK context. Therefore, each campaign had to develop a strategy that was oriented to the specific dimensions of national political contexts.

Differences in broadcasting contexts also limited opportunities for joint action. Welsh, Scots Gaelic and Irish campaigners found that different models of television service were best suited to individual minority language communities. S4C was established under the auspices of independent broadcaster Channel 4 and operated as a publisher/broadcaster. The Irish service TnaG, subsequently TG4, was initially established under the auspices of the Irish national broadcaster RTÉ, though its headquarters was based in the Gaeltacht. Finally, the Scots Gaels campaigned for a fund to increased levels of production of Scots Gaelic programming, which was inserted into the programme output of existing terrestrial services.

Despite these factors, the central reason for the lack of joint action between Celtic media campaigners during this period was the absence of any meaningful trans-national policy-making structure that would have a direct and immediate impact on domestic media and language policy. While individual language movements borrowed tactics and ideological discourses from other movements, meaningful action was still focused on the nation-state and the national context rather than at the trans-national level. During the 1966–1996 period, the type of trans-national space in European minority language politics that would have made joint trans-national action between minority language media campaigners productive did not exist. The policies and institutions of the European Union had little relevance to campaigners in the 1970s though we can detect growing European Union influence in the shift to minority rights discourse by Irish and Scots Gaelic campaigners in the 1980s.

The Celtic language television campaigns ended in the mid-1990s with the establishment of the three services. In the intervening period, there has been a radical transformation in the structure of the European Union and a considerable increase in the influence which trans-national economic and political institutions have, on domestic media and language policy within European nation-states. The treaties of Maastricht and Nice as well as the proposed European Union constitution have provided the legislative basis for a European Union where cultural and media policy is increasingly determined at the trans-national level.

Since the General Agreement on Tariffs and Trade (GATT) negotiations in 1993/1994,[16] it has also become evidence that global economic institutions such as the International Monetary Fund and the World Trade Organisation regard European Union media policy (implemented at the national and trans-national level) as falling within the remit of global neo-liberal economic policy in which measures to promote cultural diversity that interfere with the operation of the market are viewed with some suspicion. Therefore, since the end of the Celtic television campaigns, a process of rapid political and economic trans-nationalisation has occurred. As a result, the need for the type of European trans-national minority language network advocated by the EBLUL has become much more urgent. Paradoxically, just as the focus of political opportunities has shifted to the trans-national level, the European Union has withdrawn its support for trans-national networks of minority language groups. In 2004, the EBLUL lost much of its funding. Hans Jörg Trenz (2005) asserts:

> Although the EBLUL tried to evade all possible conflicts with the Commission and the governments, its expanding activities in networking minorities all over Europe were watched with suspicion by some of the governments. In August 2004, the Commission unexpectedly withdrew its subsidies for the maintenance of the EBLUL organisational infrastructure. After the closure of the Brussels offices and the dismissal of the staff, the situation of European networking is still unclear but it can be expected that EBLUL will only be able to survive in larger and richer countries whereas the fragile infrastructure in Eastern Europe where national committees of EBLUL were established only recently, will collapse. (Trenz, 2005: 25)

Given the combined impact of these changes, the European Union and Europe's minority language movements need to develop much greater clarity about how they intend to interact in this emerging trans-national political context. For European Union institutions, the aspiration to create 'unity in diversity' needs to be examined in more depth, as there appears to be considerable fear in some quarters of unified minority groups demanding policy change at European Union level. For Europe's minority language groups, the time has arrived to explore the potential of establishing trans-national networks outside the formal structures of the EU.

A number of incipient networks such as the FUEN (Federal Union of European Nationalities)[17] already exist and it is clear that if Europe's minority language communities wish to maintain their prominence in the European Union and to retain their voice in European media policy, the creation of trans-national diffusion and collaboration networks will be central to successful political action.

Conclusion

The campaigns for Celtic language television services span a 30-year period where we can detect some diffusion of tactics and ideologies between minority language movements in the neighbouring countries of Wales, Ireland and Scotland. The contacts between Welsh and Irish language activists in particular, suggest that the basis of an incipient Celtic language movement network existed during this period. However, given that activists were still focused on changing the policies of national governments, the vast majority of movement resources and energies had to be invested into protest at the domestic level.

Although contacts with Scots Gaelic activists were less direct, the Scots Gaelic approach to the television issue exhibits considerable awareness of the experiences of other Celtic language movements and the achievements of other Celtic broadcasting services. We can conclude therefore, that while the potential for a trans-national minority language network existed during the period of these campaigns, there simply wasn't any pressing rationale for investing resources into creating such a network. In the intervening period, a series of rapid economic and political changes at the trans-national level has transformed the international political context and generated much more convincing reasons for Celtic language activists to invest time, energy and resources into the construction of a cohesive trans-national network where ideas, tactics and information can be diffused rapidly. Despite the withdrawal of European Union funding from network-supporting organisations such as EBLUL, Celtic language movements have a genuine opportunity to increase their influence at the trans-national level by forming cohesive alliances with other minority language organisations in Western and Eastern Europe in order provide a new unified voice for the protection and promotion of cultural diversity.

Notes

1. EBLUL, which was founded in 1982, is an independent non-governmental organisation that receives subsidy mainly for the European Commissions' Directorate General Education and Culture.

2. www.EBLUL.org
3. Ibid.
4. www.ciemen.mercator.org
5. The Celtic League was established in 1961 and emerged out of other less political pan-Celtic organisations, most notably the Celtic Congress. The League features representation from Irish, Welsh, Scots Gaelic, Breton, Manx and Cornish language speakers.
6. Quoted in Tomos (1982: 40).
7. Ité Uí Chionnaith. Interview with author, 4 December 1995, Dublin.
8. The 1976 Broadcasting Act provided some legal justification for their objections, as it directed RTÉ to have special regard for the elements that distinguish Irish culture and in particular, the Irish language.
9. Conradh na Gaeilge was founded in 1893 and was a key site of recruitment for Republican nationalism prior to the nationalist rebellion of 1916. When the Irish Free State was established in 1922, most of the senior members of the Cabinet had been members of Conradh na Gaeilge at some stage. As a result of the close alliance between government and the Irish language movement, Conradh na Gaeilge had a significant role in formulating Irish language policy in the Republic of Ireland until the mid-1960s. It also received state funding in 1965 to pay for the employment of two fulltime officers. For further discussion see Mac Aonghusa (1993).
10. Watson comments:
    It would clearly have been injudicious for political leaders to oppose Irish bearing in mind its popular support as a core element of Irish national identity (see CLÁR and ITÉ surveys) yet it seemed inappropriate to continue with the restoration of the language in the current political and ideological environment. Therefore, one could postulate that a gradual shift towards minority rights is the only possible solution: it is the accepted view in the EU and international circles and being founded on democratic principles it is an acceptable alternative in the current environment. (Watson, 1996: 170)
11. An Feachtas Náisiúnta Teilifíse translates as the National Television Campaign.
12. Changing the name of the Irish language television service from TnaG to TG4 forced national cable companies to recognise the service as Ireland's fourth national channel and place it in a more prominent position in cable services.
13. An Comunn Gaidhealach (1975).
14. Quoted in Stephens (1976, 75).
15. The name of the CTG was changed after the 1996 Broadcasting Act to CCG.
16. At the GATT negotiations during the 1993/1994, a key conflict emerged between the US and Europe concerning audio-visual policy. Morley and Robbins state:
    Whilst the United States was calling, in the name of free trade and the free circulations of ideas, for the scrapping of quota restrictions. European interests were resolved to preserve them in order, as they saw it, to defend the cultural specificity and integrity of European civilisation. (1995: 10)
17. FUEN was founded in 1949 and linked to the Council of Europe.

References

An Comunn Gaidhealach (1975) *A Policy for Gaelic*. Inverness: An Comunn Gaidhealach.
Cormack, M. (1994) Programming for cultural defence: The expansion of Gaelic television. *Scottish Affairs* 6, 114–131.
Davies, C. (1973) Cymdeithas yr Iaith Cymraeg. In M. Stephens (ed.) *Welsh Language Today* (pp. 161–189). Llandysul: Gomer Press.
Davies, J. (1994) *Broadcasting and the BBC in Wales*. Cardiff: University of Wales Press.
Della Porta, D. and Diani, M. (1999) *Social Movements: An Introduction*. Oxford: Blackwell.
Diani, M. and McAdam, D. (2003) *Social Movements and Networks*. Oxford: Oxford University Press.
Dunn, C. (1986) Mediating Gaelic. *Media Educational Journal* 6, 53–56.
Hindley, R. (1990) *The Death of the Irish Language*. London: Routledge.
Hourigan, N. (2003) *Escaping the Global Village: Media, Language and Protest*. Lanham, MD: Lexington Books.
Johnston, H. (1991) *Tales of Nationalism: Catalonia 1939–1979*. New Brunswick, NJ: Rutgers University Press.
McAdam, D. and Rucht, D. (1993) The cross-national diffusion of movement ideas. *The Annals of the AAPSS* 528, 56–74.
Mac Aonghusa, P. (1993) *Ar Son na Gaeilge: Conradh na Gaeilge 1893–1993*. Dublin: Conradh na Gaeilge.
MacDonald, G. (1991) *The Sabhál Mór Lecture*. Glasgow: Scottish Television.
MacDonald, R. (1993) Renaissance or preservation: Gaelic broadcasting. *Media Educational Journal* 14, 13–16.
MacLeod, J. (1993) Thoughts on Gaelic. *Media Educational Journal* 14, 17–20.
Morley, D and Robbins, K. (1995) *Spaces of Identity*. London: Routledge.
Ó Feinneadha, C. (1995) TnaG: An Ród a bhí romhainn. *Comhar* 4 (1), 10–15.
Oliver, P. and Myers, D. (2003) Networks, diffusion and cycles of collective action. In M. Diani and D. McAdam (eds) *Social Movements and Networks*. Oxford: Oxford University Press.
Pritchard-Jones, H. (1982) Wales gets its own TV. *Irish Broadcasting Review* 13, 26–31.
Quill, T. (1993) Television and the Irish language. *Irish Communications Review* 4, 6–17.
Stephens, M. (1976) *Linguistic Minorities in Western Europe*. Llandysul: Gomer Press.
Thomas, N. (1971) *The Welsh Extremist: A Culture in Crisis*. London: Victor Gollancz.
Tomos, A. (1982) Realising a dream. In S. Blanchard and D. Morley (eds) *What's This Channel Four: An Alternative Report* (pp. 37–53). London: Comedia.
Trenz, H.J. (2005) *Language Minorities in Europe: Dying Species or Forerunner of a Transnational Civil Society*. Working Paper 20. Arena: Centre for European Studies, University of Oslo.
Watson, I. (1996) The Irish language and television: National identity, preservation and minority rights. *British Journal of Sociology* 47 (2), 255–274.

Chapter 6
From Media to Multimedia: Workflows and Language in the Digital Economy

GLYN WILLIAMS

It is sometimes claimed that broadcasting has been both the demise and the salvation of minority language groups. It has been conceived as a threat that turns into an asset once the relevant states can be persuaded to offer a minority language media service. However, technology does not stand still and now that the media per se is virtually dead, we are entering a phase where the importance shifts to a concern with multimedia. In this chapter I would like to consider two aspects of the New Economy that are highly relevant for all members of minority language groups. Firstly, the nature of the economy itself and how it transforms the processes of production, obliging the development of new working environments and contexts. Secondly, how the transformation from industrial age economy to the New Economy is spatially selective with different activities being located in different kinds of regions. I argue that within the peripheral locations where many of Europe's minority language groups are located, the focus will be less on developing mainstream New Economy activities than on a transformation involving path dependency – the transformation of already existing industrial age activities into New Economy activities. In those locations that already have a strong minority language media presence this will involve the transformation from media to multimedia. However, the scope and reach of the transmission will now be global, and will engage many more sectors than the media sector pure and simple. However, before proceeding to the details of this development I would like to briefly consider how there have been parallel developments in the social sciences, developments that anyone reassessing the nature of the minority language media must take into account.

From Rationalism to Knowledge

Humanism opened the door for a focus on individualism, and led to the belief that humankind could control nature, thereby becoming the master of its own destiny. Enlightenment thought and the associated rationalism derived from it. Some claim that it is the current vogue for neo-liberalism that best encapsulates the concern of humanism with the individual's control over his/her own destiny. This is partly on account of how this meta-discourse[1] invokes the centrality of the individual in relation to the economic market. In contrast it is argued that Marx rejected any claim for the integrity of the individual, focusing rather upon the exploitation of one human group by another. If this is indeed the case then the current rejection of Marxism and its replacement by neo-liberalism as the driving meta-discourse of the relationship between the social and the economic order is indeed indicative.

There has been another intriguing development in the social sciences in recent years. It is sometimes claimed that the rejection of rationalism within post-structuralism implies a rejection of the entire edifice of humanism. Yet, assumptions inherent in post-structuralism have been of significant relevance for fairly orthodox social scientists. Both Giddens (1982) and Bhaskar (1986) argue that the normative social order does not involve the rational integration of the individual with the social norm but, rather, involves the normative order as vested in tacit knowledge. This derives from the severe critique of sociology that has derived from post-structuralism.

Sociology has re-evaluated the relationship between the individual, society and social practice in arguing for a reflexive modernisation that dissolves the traditional parameters of industrial society and associated collective consciousnesses (Beck, 1997). It is a capitalism without classes, but with individualised social inequalities within which social conflict takes new forms. The focus of activity shifts from the state to a global context. Similarly, critical social theory links the work of Giddens (1994) and Hayek (1988), in making claims for how individuals and social organisations account for the structures, mechanisms, powers, states and processes that underlie and generate individual action and social organisation. This involves an ontological[2] representation of people as knowledgeable rule followers. However, this knowledge is not explicit but relies upon tacit knowledge, with people embedded in constantly evolving systems of transcendental rules. The role of the state in establishing a normative order that is both explicit and functional in producing citizens whose allegiance to the state is a manifestation of identity formation, is replaced by a normative prescription that derives from a 'correct' theoretical representation of individual and social ontology.

It would appear that neo-liberalism is heavily integrated into the rationalism of orthodox social science, with individuals rationally integrating with the forces related to market principles. Within economics this involves the invisible hand of the market respecting the autonomy of the individual yet functioning so that it leads to a general agreement between members of a society.[3] Recent critiques have suggested that markets are not driven by this form of rational behaviour, and that most of our knowledge is tacit in nature. The transcendental nature of optimising behaviour recedes and is replaced by other means of determining the relationship between the individual and the economy. Several of those writing about the Knowledge Economy have been at pains to criticise the equilibrium and linear nature of neoclassical economic models.[4] The technological revolution is leading to a complete re-evaluation of economic theory.

Minority Language Groups and the New Economy

These developments should not be remote from how we understand the reproduction of language groups as social groups. Since the early 1970s it has been common currency to recognise that this largely depends upon the ability of the language group to find a foothold in the regional economy by insisting upon the use of the associated language in the relations and forces of production (Williams *et al.*, 1978). The notion of language prestige has been used to describe how such developments allow the individual minority language speaker to achieve social mobility through that language (Williams, 2005b). This is held to be a major motivating force for the production and reproduction of that language. In turn, it raises the question of the extent to which such language groups can enter the New Economy. It involves a reflection on the awareness that any group that fails to enter the New Economy is in grave danger of becoming the source of displaced labour for that economy (Castells, 1996: 260).

It is argued that the new technology breaks down the impact of space upon the core–periphery distinction. However, it is becoming increasingly clear that the death of distance argument is not sustained. Within Europe it is clear that there are two New Economy concentrations. Firstly, the hardware production core focusing on Helsinki and Stockholm, and secondly, the software belt which runs from Dublin through to Milan. Locations outside of these two concentrations are obliged to discover other means of entering the New Economy. New Economy peripheralism is defined by these concentrations.

Path dependency claims that the entry of any region or social group into the New Economy will involve New Economy activities that derive from earlier industrial age economic emphases. This could involve a range of possibilities including optoelectronics, biotechnology, multimedia etc. for any region. While all regions will encompass Knowledge Intensive Business Services that will allow regional business to engage with the principles of on-line service delivery, for several European regions the most appealing potential would appear to involve the transformation of regional broadcasting into multimedia activities and content production.

Indeed, it can be argued that the starting point for any contemporary discussion of minority language broadcasting is not merely the transformation from media to multimedia but how this fits in with the role of the new developments in the emerging economy. Unfortunately thus far an awareness of the potential of multimedia economic activities among the minority language groups extends little further than the production of digital programmes using analogue techniques and methods.

The media sector is being transformed into a digital economy that begins to encompass multimedia activities (Williams, 1999). Elsewhere, I argue for a post-structuralist emphasis upon discourse analysis as the foundation for any consideration of the tacit nature of knowledge (Williams, 2004, 2005a; Williams & Britt-Kenz, 2003). In this chapter I would like to focus attention upon how the new organisational structures of multimedia activities involve entirely new workflows that require a particular attention to the analysis of discourse. This has specific implications for minority language broadcasting.

First, however, I would like to show how there are two contexts within which the media sector is obliged to change. Firstly, there is the issue of convergence and how it merges previously separate sectors and activities; and secondly, there are the new ways of working associated with the development of knowledge as an asset. Economic activities are redefined as shown in Figure 6.1.

The convergence of ICT and media breaks down the barriers that have separated the worlds of broadcasting, publishing, communication and IT. New partnerships are required. The Infocom sector uses digital communication to create a content industry that uses hardware and software to distribute digitised information (see Figure 6.2).

The synthesis of many fields of expertise links with IT capabilities and stimulates content and services production. The content industry could be worth as much as 5% of EC GDP, becoming responsible for employing 4 million workers. Its annual growth rate could be up to 20%, creating up to a million new jobs between 2000 and 2005 (European Commission, 2000). There are already opportunities for the creation of new systems of entertainment that can reach a global market at relatively low cost. The key involves the link between product and process innovation (Williams & Britt-Kentz, 2003).

Knowledge and Work

Within the Knowledge Economy the process of work and the associated practices change. The emphasis in industrial age economy on information

Figure 6.1 Redefining economic activities
Source: Toivonen (2001: 75) (Modified by Britt-Kentz)

hoarding, command and control thinking, and departmental competition that escalates costs and subtracts value from goods and services yields to new ways of working.

Within the competition for markets, profits and growth organisations must be committed to information sharing, flexible processes, continuous improvement and new work styles. Collaboration, knowledge sharing and organising around customer-centred processes will be evident. This has profound implications for the media sector where 'the idea' is so central to programme production to the extent that secrecy is inherent to the industry.

The main components of industrial age business involved striving to manage physical assets and physical capacity while managing money as capital. Markets had to be identified and serviced, while the link between production and markets involved seeking locations close to transportation centres. Similarly, access to commodities and energy had to be guaranteed. Workflows were organised according to Taylorist principles

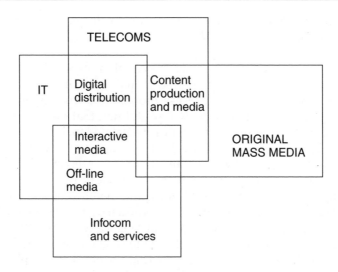

Figure 6.2 Infocom sector
Source: Toivonen (2001)

focusing upon the assembly line. Within the Knowledge Economy, knowledge becomes the source of capital, and the new technology becomes the means whereby information and collaboration is organised and accessed. The emphasis shifts to processes, knowledge and continuous improvement in increasing effectiveness and enhancing flexible work practices.

This change is driven, not merely by the new technology, but also by the assumptions associated with neo-liberalism. How the so-called 'information age' increased efficiency and reduced costs is now giving way to an awareness that this technological potential must be harnessed in a particular way. Technological change in itself does not really change anything, it is how the technology is used that determines the nature of change. It is a common mistake to believe that the information society and the New Economy are conditioned by ICT, that the precise nature of these two structures derives from technology. It is argued that the current round of restructuring realises the productivity potential contained in the mature industrial economy because of how the shift towards a technological paradigm based on IT has changed the scope and dynamics of the industrial economy, creating a global economy and fostering a new wave of competition between existing economic agents (Kelly, 1998). Globalisation is presented as the cause of the emergence of a new approach to economic development. While there is a grain of truth in these claims, what is driving the shape of the New Economy and the Information Society is neo-liberalism.

The entire process demands the creation of new business environments; a work environment that focuses on collaborative processes using shared resources; process models that encompass knowledge mixing and sharing; and the ICT scaffolding that can service these new processes. Communities of practice are claimed to be the means whereby these working processes are best organised (Wenger, 1997). These involve aggregates of workers in face to face interaction who learn from one another through the involvement in work practices – learning by doing. While what they learn is tacit, and thereby not easily expressed, it is crucial for the creation of new knowledge. Consequently, we are encountering a form of working that drastically changes the relations of production. Specifically, clerical and blue collar workers are transformed into knowledge workers. The industrial age economy emphasis on business processes based on the division of labour concepts are obliged to yield to team working. Since firms increasingly rely on IT to develop and deliver products and services, it becomes increasingly difficult for companies to compete simply on the basis of efficiency. They must become more effective. This is claimed to occur through collecting, sharing, disseminating and enhancing corporate knowledge that leads to better products and services, and customer-centric business processes. However, these pronouncements often tend to be made with little understanding of the nature of the Knowledge Economy and of how knowledge is generated.

Workflows

The most obvious reason for developing new workflows within the multimedia sector pertains to how the new activities merge previously disparate activities. Broadcasting activities must merge with those of publication or music production. Similarly, the product will be different and will require new marketing strategies. However, there are other, more compelling reasons for rethinking workflows.

Workflow pertains to how different tasks or features of the work process are organised in such a way that the production process is efficient and adequately managed. Within the industrial age economy work was organised, automated and managed from a functional context in order to maximise efficiency. This is replaced in the Knowledge Economy by the organisation of collaborative teams responsible for end to end process completion so that product-related and process-related knowledge flows across functional boundaries. This awareness obliges the shift from thinking in terms of the division of labour to conceptualising production teams, and from information hoarding to collaboration.

There is a sense in which the goal of trying to coordinate and structure the different components of workflows undermines the need for flexibility. Thus, how software that aims to codify and store business rules as the operational process changes, how process knowledge is modelled and integrated into software programmes, or how the knowledge base is codified and developed into shared knowledge must all allow space for flexibility, experimentation and innovation. Companies that are organised by process are few and far between. Given the uniqueness of all knowledge generating processes it is difficult to see how this can become a customised solution.

Nonetheless, it is futile to consider a Knowledge Economy based upon workflows that do not fully exploit the potential of ICT. Tools exist that allow the workflow process to be defined uniformally in the workflow computer system. Such programmes assign the work, pass it on and track its progress. There are numerous advantages that derive from this – work is not misplaced, it leads to labour saving, work is performed precisely by the best person and with specified priority, and two or more tasks can be performed concurrently with efficiency.

Workflows associated with multimedia activities are particularly delicate in that they constitute activities that were treated as separate in the industrial age economy. The shift from media to multimedia has been conceptualised by reference to the digital value chain wherein analogue archives are digitised, indexed through the use of metadata,[5] tagged and integrated into a digital archive which, in turn, is associated with a digital asset management system that allows these archives to be accessed remotely, viewed, cleared for rights, paid for and transported. Any new materials that are shot are indexed automatically and incorporated into the archive. This involves both edited materials and rushes. The archived assets are then capable of being recycled in the production of new content. The archive contains audio, visual and print materials.

This digitisation and archiving of media production makes it possible to search complete archives for materials that can be recycled in producing new content. Thus an archive on the Welsh in Patagonia could be searched for 'guanacos', and might well yield sufficient material to produce a new content item of say 30 minutes nature broadcast. Similarly, anyone wishing to create a drama documentary on the Welsh in Patagonia could use these materials as the backdrop for the drama, thereby eliminating the need to shoot in South America. These are highly orthodox uses of the potential of media archives and barely touch on the potential of multimedia activities.

It is sometimes claimed that the introduction of such a Digital Asset Management System within a broadcast organisation is not expected to lead to fundamental changes in workflow, even if significant changes in detail will occur. However, this is a narrow view, both of work and of the multimedia sector. It ignores the principles of working within the Knowledge Economy, and how it promotes the generation of knowledge. It also operates with a narrow understanding of how broadcasting changes within the context of convergence. It is a statement that focuses far too narrowly on the impact of technology. Unfortunately, there are many broadcasters who have failed to recognise the new possibilities of convergence, and who proceed to produce digital content with exactly the same methods and conceptions as they did for analogue broadcasting.

The obvious advantage of on-line systems is that data can be accessed from anywhere at any time. It is possible to open this access or to restrict it. This means that key information can be extracted to move with the workflow. An integrated Digital Asset Management System can allow users to access assets and metadata created during any production, from anywhere, any time. It is this that facilitates on-line collaborative working using shared resources. While this is an immense advantage, as we shall see, it does create problems by reference to the relevance of such work in the Knowledge Economy.

Any gains in the efficiency associated with distributed working groups can derive from eliminating redundant work processes, and from the improvement of the integrity of the collective information database. This only becomes possible if the Digital Asset Management System is integrated with the whole production workflow. It is tempting for the kinds of partnerships of museums, libraries, broadcasters etc. that are being developed in order to harness regional cultural content archives to think of their own Digital Asset Management System merely as the end of the story. This may well be the case in so far as how their public sector role defines their actions in terms of the provision of a public service that is free at the point of contact. It does little if the archive assets are to become the bases of regional content production economies.

If any newly created content and the associated metadata has to be fed into the archive and Digital Asset Management System at the point of creation, then the workflow has to be optimised in such a way that the metadata introduced into the system need only be written once within a continuing process of asset augmentation. This does involve paying attention to considerable detail, and also to 'imagining' where the event leads in terms of metadata.

The main issue that is claimed to hold up the transformation of asset management into the management of commercially exploitable assets is intellectual property rights. Current thinking involves moving from 'copyright' to 'copy left' in the sense that if the game is to move into its next phase 'owners' must become 'sharers'. This is in line with what we have already said about sharing within the Knowledge Economy. In theory the new content should be worth considerably more than the individual assets used to create it, and if content production is to be a team process it is from content sales that the profit from assets will accrue. Implementing this principle is much easier said than done. Nonetheless the intellectual property right is one of the three essential components of the Digital Asset Management System: (1) The asset management system linked to; (2) a machine control system that can synchronously transfer assets between the archive, production and transmission; and (3) the administration of intellectual property rights. Together they constitute the core component with which the elements of the working process will interact.

The content creation process begins in the orthodox way with the planning of the programme content. This is compatible with the convention of developing story lines except that the entire work team should now be involved in the process. Furthermore, programme content now has to be rethought in the sense that it involves far more in multimedia than in the production of a television or radio programme for transmission. This is combined with the scheduled assembly of all elements in acquisition, post-production, transmission, on-line publishing and associated discussions spaces. It is at this stage that the first metadata is created. It will, subsequently, be continuously enriched in the course of the actual content production process.

Any materials acquired from external production, external feeds or in-house productions are ingested into the system, being associated either to new objects or to already existing objects. The first annotation of the materials can be generated. Extraction tools now exist that allow this to operate automatically. It is sufficient to support basic queries and thereby the selection of suitable material. The editors access the entire Digital Asset Management System through metadata and the use of a structured search and query operation. At the same time the cataloguing department will work on the detailed description of content selected for long-term archiving. They will also check the quality of annotations created by automatic tools and, if necessary, they will correct them. The main task here involves searching for the intellectual property rights in order to update the intellectual property rights status of the stored content. This might be undertaken by a separate Licence Department.

In post-production the assembled content is transformed into the end product, whether this involves a programmes for transmission, a multimedia editorial or some other product. The outputs of the work must be reintroduced into the Digital Asset Management System and the archive, allowing anyone to reuse the materials in future work. For broadcasting production the transmission logs will be added by transmission control.

To a great extent the existing technical infrastructure within a broadcasting organisation will constitute the decisive component for the definition of workflows since it defines how assets and metadata will be generated and transported through the production chain. It is essential to rethink this infrastructure by reference to the goals of the Knowledge Economy, and especially those goals associated with team working and operating as a community of practice. This does not mean that the same elements of the architecture will not reappear. Thus, for example, the assets will be digitised in full resolution by a suitable encoder and will be recorded on a server. Similarly, production quality assets, key frames and preview copies are stored permanently in near on-line mass data storage e.g. a tape robot. The web server provides the graphical user interface to all the workstations connected through the local area network.

The digitising process involves creating assets of different qualities – high-resolution copies are recorded on a video server, while low-resolution Internet copies are made for preview purposes. If resale is an objective then the low-quality items will be offered for viewing and the high-quality assets exported on payment. Special algorithms can automatically extract information about the assets – edit points, key frames, speakers, faces and key words. Also intelligent tools based on semantic description standards allow augmenting information that has previously been extracted automatically. At this stage manual logging is of particular importance, being the first manually generated information in the production process. It is here that the collaborative process is crucial. It requires in-depth knowledge of documentation, and an intimate knowledge of the requirements of editors and teams that will work on the materials. Thus the editor, the cataloguers and archivists and any other asset users and manipulators should work as a team. In this sense, job descriptions change from those of analogue production.

This leads to a detailed search and query request that is usually submitted by the editor. Again I would emphasise that this should involve team work. Single hits are evaluated by accessing metadata, key frames and preview video and audio. Any selected material are automatically transferred from the Digital Asset Management System to the editing station for final editing and programme conformation. This is followed by using technical, legal and contextual criteria for conforming the edit results and the end result is routed to the playout server for transmission after which the programme is transferred back to the archive.

What is evident is that team work for multimedia is essential, and that new job profiles are required. This derives partly from the need to create a closed loop for metadata generation along the production chain, together with the possibility of transferring content automatically from system to system on the one hand, and on account of the advantages that derive from knowledge generation on the other. It does mean that specific jobs give way to multi-skilling, and that responsibility and accountability become team functions. In a sense all workers must also be 'media managers', carrying the main responsibility for ensuring that specific content required in different phases of production are reliably available whenever and wherever needed.

Let us assume that a topical multimedia system such as one focusing upon rugby involves a number of different components – the live broadcast that may involve broadband access, the archive of old matches, the magazine, the match analysis process, coaching, club fixtures, club information and web site etc. All of these relate to a particular audience. Furthermore, they are all automated. The magazine is no longer a paper product, but will draw upon customary match reports that are supplemented by clips of the match drawn from the archive, which also serves as the materials for specific forms of match analysis and coaching developments.

The other end of the process involves marketing. Where, in the industrial age economy, there was a tendency for the production process to be driven by the manufacturer or creator who mysteriously sought to gauge the market, within the New Economy, the market drives production. Furthermore, that market is global and must be seen as global. Unfortunately, the notion of a digital value chain does not entirely divorce itself from Fordist principles of operation. The notion was introduce by Porter (1985) as an elaboration of the idea of Value Added Partnerships, focusing upon business activities rather than upon the functional structure. The relationship involved the individual company and its associated supply chain. It remained very much a linear notion. It is rapidly being replaced by the notion of a valuenet which, in turn, evolves into a digital economy business web (b-web) (Bovet & Martha, 2000).

Within the b-web, a large network of players whose traditional roles as primary and support activities become diffused, operate both collaboratively and compete. Primary actors, more than ever, become dependent on support actors, and these support actors may even guide the process, especially where the necessary competence is scarce and substitutes for them do not exist. This is particularly true of peripheral labour markets that now achieve a new competitiveness within the global economy. The end result is that b-nets become customer-focused and wide open to cooperation. They must be highly sensitive to changes in customer markets and rival markets.

Thus, the b-net is a particular system of suppliers, distributors, commercial service providers, infrastructure providers and customers that use the Internet for their primary business communications and transactions. However, the principles of the Knowledge Economy insist that these different components be seen as a single community. In contrast to the industrial age economy there is an enhanced integration of roles, and a redefinition of roles. The central ingredient is the creation of a system that is capable of innovation and competence transfer. They demand a new way of thinking and political decision-making, and regional financial resource allocation.

Workflows now come to encompass end to end systems that define the nature and extent of the collaborative team. Every component of the system must have a voice in the definition and operationalisation of the tools and tasks of the others. The on-line editor must be capable of defining the metadata for the asset archive, the person creating the metadata must recognise the use that will be made of the archive and its contents by everyone else in the system. The entire system must be driven by principles of mutual trust and collaboration using the shared resources. Furthermore, this must all operate on-line. While there are examples of regional cultural institutions such as museums, libraries or broadcasters coming together to create a common archive, it is clear that they do so as separate entities that buy into a system. Their internal organisation remains unchanged and are therefore incapable of forging a new institutional, collaborative entity. There is also resistance to the use of the digital assets by regional content creators. However, the main hindrance to the development of new content industries is that no single region has sufficient diversity of digital assets to enter content production for the global market on its own.

Online Communities of Practice

If no single region has sufficient diversity of assets to go alone then it becomes essential to develop on-line working environments where partners from different cultures can operate across languages in sharing resources and developing content. This is no easy task. The essential starting point must be the Digital Asset Management System. Evidently, the archive becomes a shared entity that will include materials from across all collaborating regions. This means that numerous agreements must be put in place if this collaborative archive is to work effectively and efficiently. Firstly, the terms on which the assets can be accessed and used must be agreed. This includes intellectual property rights issues. Secondly, the metadata must be created in conjunction, and they must be capable of operating across the regional languages. The various interfaces must be available in all languages. That is, steps must be taken to ensure that any regional language should not be presented with an obstacle to participation within the Digital Asset Management System.

This leads to a consideration of how shared documents and materials can be worked upon. XML enables all web authors to create their own tags or hidden labels that annotate web pages or sections of text on a page. This facilitates the creation of an arbitrary structure for documents without saying what the structure means. A customised logical structure for each document or set of documents is created independently of the display medium or content. Rules, organised into 'style sheets', can then be applied in order to reformulate the work automatically for various devices. This can be taken a step further by defining the XML style sheets by reference to a multilingual environment that allows for the maintenance and recovery of information in any of the supported languages from a single set of pages. This provides the tools for multilingual processing, even if more needs to be done by reference to the effectiveness of such systems for multilingual content management. Thus XML provides a basic format for structured documents without any particular semantics. However, it can be used to write an RDF which encodes meaning in sets of triples, each set being not dissimilar to the subject, verb and object of an elementary sentence. This allows a basis for processing of metadata and interoperability between applications that exchange machine-understandable information on the web. The RDF/XML syntax does provide considerable flexibility in the syntactic expression of the data model, and it is also possible to specify consistency constraints that should be followed by these data models. Furthermore, intelligent tools based on semantic description standards allow augmenting information that has previously been extracted automatically.

Ontologies define a set of categories that a computer can manipulate in classifying information, thereby establishing the set of metadata that a computer can manipulate in classifying information. The metadata structures any given body of assets. Apart from standard ontologies such as the Dublin Core it is also possible to create specific ontologies from standard terminologies. Once an ontology has been developed for a domain area it is made available via RDF files so that the code used in a web page may be defined by pointing to it. It is also possible to provide a repository for data definitions that can be retrieved.

Collaborative environment tools enable a local work model to be transformed into a distributed form. One such development involves Basic Support for Cooperative Work (BSCW), which facilitates collaboration through shared work spaces that support document upload, event notification, group management etc. It is accessed through a web browser. It maintains information about the main events related to documents – creation, modification, reallocation, deletion etc.

This should be aligned with a document tracking capability within the collaborative environment.

Shared workspaces are necessary because the Internet offers insufficient opportunities for joint working by spatially distributed teams from heterogeneous computer environments, BSCW makes it possible to transform the Internet from a primarily passive information repository into an active cooperative tool. The BSCW shared workspace system expands the internet's search and information download functions with more sophisticated tools without additional user software. It also processes multilingual user interfaces. It also provides the repository for econtent as it is generated. Clearly, the working environment must be structured in such a way that it can accommodate the fundamental principles that enable knowledge generation and management. This, in turn, must be designed by reference to the relevant workflow. Much of this revolves around developing the kind of collaborative environments that enhance access to shared meaning, which is the key element by reference to the inherent characteristics of institutionalised practices or tacit knowledge. It is this shared meaning which allows the 'taken for granted' to operate in such a way that it does not require specific expression. It has a relationship to both a specific activities workflow and to language. It is the link between these two elements that will determine an effective collaborative working environment using shared resources.

Language, Meaning and Knowledge

If, as is maintained, no single region has sufficient diversity of cultural resources to develop content alone, then trans-regional collaboration becomes essential. This includes operating through collaborative working on-line, using shared resources. Clearly this must involve the development of human language technologies that facilitate operating a trans-regional workflow across language and culture. We focus directly upon cross-cultural knowledge creation and knowledge transfer. Indeed, it can be argued that it is at the interface of languages as meaning systems that one identifies the crux of innovation.

The most obvious problem by reference to developing trans-regional digital value chains, which include the production capacity end of the chain, is the need for on-line working to be able to proceed seamlessly. As has already been stated, this involves paying attention to how the semantic web is used to respond to the workflow. However, this issue is merely one aspect of the production process. Reference to the new ways of working within the Knowledge Economy makes it clear that the central principle of such work is the ability to link social capital to the generation of knowledge within operational networks. This is claimed to rely on trust, mutual respect and related principles. These elements are claimed to derive from strong interactional ties that involve working as communities of practitioners. To develop on-line working across cultures without recourse to the technology that can translate meaning – by reference to both culture and language – is an enormous undertaking.

As a theory of organisations, Taylorism systematically destroyed meaning at work, with the organisation assuming the responsibility for the creation of meaning for people at work in order to enhance production. In contrast, the relevance and value of knowledge generation for effectiveness within global markets becomes a central feature of the Knowledge Economy. As we have implied, knowledge is tacit in nature and is not, therefore, subject to rational manipulation by already pre-formed subjects. This creates a fundamental dilemma for social scientists, and especially linguists, whose entire edifice is constructed around rationalism.

The task to hand requires more than the simple translation of text or voice. Translating language is easy, translating meaning is profound. Translation must focus on meaning, since knowledge is closely related to the social construction of meaning. It must also facilitate the team working referred to above in such a way that the entire team can operate as a community of practice. Unfortunately, syntax is essentially a political problematic deriving as it does from how language planning relates to standardisation and the formalisation of language. Similarly, most human language technology draws upon syntax and focuses upon the formalisation of language. It does allow the recognition of translation as a formal exercise, but fails once we begin to recognise the relationship between knowledge as a tacit system, and how knowledge relates to the construction of meaning. This is because the meanings are relatively fixed and ignore the essential ambiguity of language.

It is hardly surprising therefore that the boundaries between translation, interpreting and multilingual communication are becoming blurred.
It also means that multidimensional language competencies, including
technology and project management skills, are necessary in confronting
new challenges. The integration of intralingual, interlingual and inter-
semiotic translation with new technology is beginning to transform one-
dimensional translation tasks into multidimensional communication
scenarios. This brings together a number of disparate fields. Semiotics
confronts interlingual translation where anthropology questions the
translatability of cultures, involving both translatability between different
languages and cultures, and between different discursive formations.
This, in turn links to the emphasis on power, representation and translatability. The emergence of human translation science, with its emphasis on
applied and contrastive linguistics, gave way to a paradigm based on
historico-descriptive studies that tended to be literature based. This philo-
logical emphasis in turn led to a functional translation school and, ultimately to a pragmatic orientation. I argue that if tacit knowledge is to be
engaged, this pragmatic approach must yield to one which focuses upon
discourse analysis. The central message here is that language is essentially
ambiguous and, if meaning is so central to knowledge, then creativity
must lie in this ambiguity. When we move away from syntax, without
completely dismissing its relevance, towards a linguistic analysis that
begins from striving to understand language as how social relations are
constructed into language, we recognise how meaning is differently
constructed across languages. This only partly relates to different cultural
systems and has a great deal to do with language as a manifestation of
culture. Discourse views language process as social process so that the
language/social distinction disappears. It is language production that
puts the social structure in place, while also incorporating the individual
into that structure.

There is an obvious link between multimedia technologies and the
form, content and mode of translation. Certainly language technology and
knowledge representation, electronic textuality and multimodal translation scenarios are intrinsically related to translation subfields such as LSP
communication, interlingual translation and audiovisual translation.
What is involved in all such relationships is a relatively simple structure
involving a source material, which might be knowledge or text, being
'transferred' to another material, that is, another knowledge or system or
text. What is difficult is that modern translation tasks cut across the interlingual, intralingual and polysemiotic categorisations in that they involve
knowledge management and text, linear to non-linear structures

involving hypertext, spoken to written, and auditory to visual etc. How these fields are deployed largely depends upon how language is understood. The tendency for it to focus upon the rationalism of pragmatic studies is giving way to the post-structural focus upon meaning as socially constructed. Not only does this lead to questioning the existence of an original, but it also confronts the belief in equivalence or fidelity.

Evidently, these observations apply to all languages, and to the relationship of all language groups to how their language is codified within Human Language Technology (HLT). Work on state languages within HLT has been in progress for numerous years. The picture is quite different from the European minority languages. The amount of HLT that is available for these languages is limited, and there is an urgent need to develop the basis whereby the interactional basis of the New Economy can be implemented using these various minority languages. As the programmes are elaborated, the cost of such development declines, but there is an urgent need to develop the programmers and other technologists who can work in the various regional languages.

Conclusion

It should be evident that transforming the media industry into a multimedia industry premised upon the principles of the Knowledge Economy is an enormous task. It is further complicated by reference to the relationship between the multimedia sector and content production. Above I have sought to outline what may be involved in this development. It is a development that is particularly appealing to regional languages and cultures in regions striving to enter the New Economy on their own terms. Yet it demands the kinds of collaboration within and across regions that are hampered by a number of factors, not least of which are a lack of understanding of the issues to be confronted, and the rooting of developmental thinking in the basic principles, structures and functions of industrial age economy. If minority languages are to survive the shift from industrial age economy to the New Economy they must be ready and willing to embrace the new conception of work and production. For some minority language groups the most obvious route of entry into the New Economy involves the shift from media to multimedia. These groups must be sufficiently self-confident to take the lead in the new industry, to break new ground in forging new kinds of multimedia products. Above I have tried to outline some of the issues involved in the transformation. These are the very issues that those involved in minority language broadcasting must integrate into their operations.

Notes

1. The notion of meta-discourse treats theory as a subjective discourse rather than as objective truth or reality.
2. Ontology pertains to an understanding of 'being in the abstract'.
3. For a discussion of neo-liberalism and language planning see Williams and Morris (2000).
4. This is discussed in some detail in Williams (2003).
5. Content metadata is the equivalent of library indexing systems for books.

References

Beck, U. (1997) *The Reinvention of Politics*. Oxford: Polity.
Bhaskar, R. (1986) *Scientific Realism and Human Emancipation*. London: Verso.
Bovet, D. and Martha, J. (2000) *Value Nets: Breaking the Supply Chain to Reveal Hidden Profits*. New York: Wiley.
Castells, M. (1996) *The Rise of the Network Society*. Oxford: Blackwell.
European Commission (2000) *The New Economy of the Global Information Society: Implications for Growth, Work and Employment*. Luxembourg: IST Programme.
Giddens, A. (1982) *Profiles and Critiques in Social Theory*. London: Macmillan.
Giddens, A. (1994) Living in a post-traditional society. In U. Beck, A. Giddens and S. Lash (eds) *Reflexive Modernisation* (pp. 56–109). Cambridge: Polity.
Hayek, F. (1988) *The Fatal Conceit: The Errors of Socialism*. London: Routledge.
Kelly (1998) *New Rules for the New Economy*. London: Fourth Estate.
Porter, M. (1985) *Competitive Advantage: Creating and Sustaining Superior Performance*. New York: Free Press.
Toivonen, M. (2001) *Growth and Significance of Knowledge Intensive Business Systems (KIBS)*. Helsinki: Uudenman.
Wenger, E. (1997) *Communities of Practice: Learning, Meaning and Identity*. Cambridge: Cambridge University Press.
Williams, G. (1999) *French Discourse Analysis: The Method of Post-structuralism*. London: Routledge.
Williams, G. (2003) *Final Report of the TEDIP Project*. Luxembourg: IST Programme.
Williams, G. (2004) Multimedia, minority languages and the New Economy. *Noves SL, Journal of Sociolinguistics* Winter 2005.
Williams, G. (2005a) Regional innovation systems, communities of practice and discourse analysis: Three themes in search of knowledge. *Sociolinguistica* 19, 168–184.
Williams, G. (2005b) *Sustaining Language Diversity in Europe: Evidence from the Euromosaic Project*. London: Palgrave.
Williams, G. and Britt-Kentz, M. (2003) Technology and economic development in the periphery. *Tripodos* 14, 101–119.
Williams, G. and Morris, D. (2000) *Language Planning and Language Use: Welsh in a Global Age*. Cardiff: University of Wales Press.
Williams, G., Roberts, E. and Isaac, R. (1978) Language and social mobility. In G. Williams (ed.) *Social and Cultural Change in Contemporary Wales*. London: Routledge and Kegan Paul.

Chapter 7

Speaking Up: A Brief History of Minority Languages and the Electronic Media¹ Worldwide

DONALD R. BROWNE

It is one of the ironies of history that radio – the first electronic medium to provide the possibility of *mass* communication – rose to prominence during a period when the languages of indigenous peoples and other minority groups were under serious threat of extinction. Radio's development during the first three decades of the 20th century coincided with attempts on the part of 'majority culture' educators, governments² and industry to wean or force minority language speakers away from the use of their native tongues, sometimes with the active collaboration of those speakers themselves. Such languages were regarded variously as impediments to personal progress, industrial growth, integration with the majority culture and loyalty to the national government. The irony is that radio is ideally suited to assisting in the preservation, 'modernisation' and demystification of minority languages. As an oral medium of communication, it can serve as a channel for minority language songs, poetry, comedy and other cultural vehicles, as well as furnishing an 'oral newspaper' for the speakers of those languages.

Why did those who were interested in preserving minority languages not succeed in establishing a presence in this new medium of communication until much later in time? What factors led to its eventual development? What have groups done with various electronic media outlets when there finally were opportunities to use them? And what does the future appear to hold for such services?³ These are the central considerations of the brief history that follows.

In the Beginning

The period of experimentation with radio as a transmitter of the human voice ran from shortly after the turn of the 20th century until the early to mid-1920s. Because we have little documentation from that period – radio was considered an amateur activity where the spoken word was concerned, and amateurs tend to be far more interested in doing rather than in writing about their activities – it is possible that there were experiments in which minority languages were utilised. If so, it seems likely that their appearance would have been a rarity: those speaking minority languages often were discouraged from using them, especially in public forums.

Once radio began to develop as an instrument of mass communication, there was in fact a linguistic minority presence in the electronic media in a few nations. In the United States of the 1920s, a few local stations in cities where émigrés (largely from Europe) were most numerous broadcast a weekly 'Polish [or other language] Hour' (Migala, 1982). It usually featured music from the 'homeland,' perhaps a live performance by a local German (or other language) choir/band/soloist; and often a community calendar, all of it held together by an Italian- (or other language) speaking host (or, rarely, hostess). Smaller stations in particular hoped to fill out their schedules, and French-American and other émigré societies might pay for the airtime. Indigenous peoples and other long-term-resident populations generally fared less well. Opportunities for airtime were few, and usually were limited to occasional appearances by African-American musicians or Native American storytellers. There is no record of any linguistic minority-operated radio station until the late 1940s.

By the 1930s, several stations in major northern cities (e.g., New York City, Chicago) were providing blocks of airtime for linguistic minority listeners. Usually these were programme slots leased by individuals who then sold advertising on their shows. Spanish language radio was one of the largest users of leased time, thanks to the rapid growth of the Spanish-speaking population. In general, it offered little aside from popular music, most of it in Spanish and recorded by Latin American artists (A. Rodriguez, 1999; C. Rodriguez, 2001). Native Americans occasionally appeared as 'cultural guests'. A Native American-produced programme appeared in 1941, when University of Oklahoma radio station WNAD initiated a weekly programme hosted by a Sauk/Fox individual who highlighted the accomplishments of Native Americans but also provided their perspectives on such issues as treaty negotiations with the US government. (Indians for Indians, 1943). Apparently he spoke in English only.

In all of those instances, the predominantly commercial nature of US radio served to discourage linguistic minority participation. By the late 1920s, stations were relying increasingly on the sale of airtime for advertising commercial products as the favoured means of meeting their operating expenses. Advertisers thought in terms of majority culture audiences, and few were interested in reaching those small segments of the population that might listen to programmes in their own languages.

That also made it difficult for any would-be minority language radio service to secure the financial support of banks and other lending institutions. The prevailing climate of assimilation made such a service even less attractive, as did the widespread practice of discouraging and even forbidding use of minority languages in schools.

Most other countries offered even fewer examples of linguistic minority broadcasting during the 1920s and 1930s. In general, they too were bits and pieces of 'minority culture'. Countries still followed assimilationist policies, and linguistic minorities usually could expect little more than occasional appearances as cultural exotica on the airwaves. This was true for all types of radio services, whether national or local and whether supported by advertising revenue, annual licence fees, or government appropriations. The BBC began limited broadcasts in Welsh and in Scots Gaelic in 1923. Some programmes featured music, others the spoken word, and there were a few attempts to offer instruction in Welsh.[4] Norway's public service broadcaster, Norsk Rikskringkasting (NRK), introduced occasional broadcasts in Sami in 1934, but did not provide them as part of the regular programme schedule until 1946 (Heatta, 1984). Sami in Sweden and Finland began to receive similar service from their public broadcasting institutions in 1948.

Iraq's national radio service initiated Kurdish language programming in 1939. In the ensuing years, other states with Kurdish minorities – Iran, Turkey and Syria – followed suit, but such services often were discontinued and recommenced, depending on the state of relations between the Kurds and the national governments. That led to numerous instances of clandestine (unlicenced) broadcasting by various Kurdish political factions. (The relative stabilisation of the Kurdish region in northern Iraq following the 1991 Gulf War encouraged the creation of a host of broadcast services, some of them easily receivable by Kurds living in neighbouring nations.)

The Second World War

By the early 1940s, the presence of African-Americans, Hispanic-Americans and Native Americans in the US military, along with increases in the migration of substantial numbers of minorities to northern US industrial centres (Cleveland, Detroit), led the national radio networks to broadcast individual programmes and short series about ethnic minority contributions to the war effort (Savage, 1999). Also, numbers of radio stations carrying foreign language programmes grew during the 1930s, and reached over 250 by the end of the decade, although that dropped below 200 by the end of 1940; most were in European languages, with Italian, Polish, Spanish, Yiddish and German leading the list (Federal Communications Commission, 1940).

The presence of foreign language broadcasts in wartime highlighted a potential problem that would arise not just during the Second World War, but also in peacetime: how to ensure that such broadcasts would not be used *against* a state. Even before the United States entered the war, there were reports that some of the domestically produced German- and Italian-language programmes expressed support for the German and Italian governments. Theodore Grame notes 'rumours' that some members of the US Congress were considering legislation abolishing all foreign language radio stations and newspapers, although none was formally introduced (Grame, 1980: 125–126). Once the US had entered the war, the US Office of War Information's Foreign Language Division and the Federal Communications Commission (FCC) began to coordinate their efforts in order to pressure station managers to remove 'suspect' minority language programme hosts, even when the evidence to support such an action was weak (Holten, 2002: 81–83). The Foreign Language Division also produced, and strongly encouraged foreign language stations to produce, foreign language programmes supporting the US war effort and criti-cising the Axis powers, which it then distributed to still other stations as part of a 'campaign for ethnic unity' (Holten, 2002: 75–80).

In some countries, the war led to new linguistic minority broadcast services, such as the creation in 1942 by the New Zealand Broadcasting Service of a five minute weekly newscast in Maori, in recognition of the part played by Maori in the New Zealand military forces and often featuring interviews with Maori troops (Lemke, 1995). But most industri-alised states had minuscule linguistic minority communities, and the war had little effect on their media invisibility. Even in the United Kingdom, where linguistic minority broadcasting had begun in the 1920s, the war did nothing to substantially increase broadcasts in those languages. In fact, Davies indicates that Welsh language broadcasts were under serious threat of being abolished, and perhaps were spared because a report (unsubstantiated) noted that the Germans had begun to broadcast in Welsh (Davies, 1994: 127). Davies also states that, much as in the United States, such linguistic minority broadcasting was under suspicion. In the initial stages of the war, the BBC controller of home broadcasting wanted Welsh language programmes to be monitored carefully to ensure that 'they did not make for national disunity' and argued unsuccessfully that BBC headquarters should be provided in advance with translations of all Welsh broadcasts (Davies, 1994: 133). Davies contends (1994: 133) that there was 'a widespread belief [at headquarters] that they [Welsh language programmes] were inherently subversive'.[5]

The Postwar Period and Ethnic Minority Ownership in the US

Wartime broadcasts featuring linguistic minorities often ceased at war's end, although some continued: the Maori radio newscasts ran until 1972. Also, the occasional one-time radio programmes or short series continued to appear in the immediate postwar years. Television, seen by relatively few individuals before or after the Second World War, began to develop as a truly mass medium in some industrialised countries by the early 1950s. It followed the pattern set by radio, in that it was owned, operated by and programmed for the white majority. Few shows included linguistic minority performers and lifestyles. When they were present, they usually were portrayed as servants, 'sidekicks', or comic figures, such as the US television figures Tonto (Native American) in 'The Lone Ranger', Kato (Philippine-American?) in 'The Green Hornet', or Pancho (Hispanic-American) in 'The Cisco Kid'. They rarely spoke in their own languages, and often displayed something well short of fluency in English.

The postwar years also saw the beginning of linguistic minority owned and operated (O&O) electronic media services in the US. The first such service appeared in 1946 – an amplitude modulation (AM) radio station purchased by a Hispanic-American (Meyer, 2001). Minority ownership increased with the re-introduction of frequency-modulated or ultra high frequency (FM or UHF) radio broadcasting just after the Second World War. Few potential owners cared to take the risks associated with the new medium, since few people owned FM receivers. That made it fairly easy to acquire an FM broadcast licence, and many of the linguistic minority O&O stations that followed were on the FM band, particularly if they were licensed for low power operation.

Until the 1970s, US linguistic minority O&Os remained relatively few in number. Aside from the unwillingness of banks to make loans to 'risky' ventures, especially when specific linguistic minority groups were not all that sizable in most US cities (size of audience *did* matter to potential investors), there was the dominance of the commercial model: It was difficult to sell investors on a venture that did not have the experienced administrators and reasonably large and affluent audiences that would attract advertisers. Since very few surveys (and none by 'reputable' organisations) revealed anything about the size and/or purchasing habits of linguistic minorities, there was little evidence that would give investors the requisite confidence to back such stations.

The European Public Service Tradition

In most other countries, the possibility of obtaining a licence to broadcast was not simply difficult, it was impossible. Most European states licensed broadcast services as public service broadcasting (PSB) monopolies. The BBC had such a monopoly until 1954, when Parliament passed legislation authorising the creation of a commercially supported television service. The BBC's income came from annual licence fees paid by households owning radio and television sets, while the Independent Television (ITV) companies (14 in all, with no other commercial competition) derived theirs from advertising. The BBC did not broadcast its first television programme in Welsh until 1953, and by 1957 was producing a single 30-minute programme in Welsh per week. When the ITV company Granada Television began to produce one-hour Welsh programmes twice a week in 1957, the BBC was taken by surprise. The 1958 inauguration of another ITV company, Television Wales and West, brought yet more Welsh language television, and led Alun Oldfield-Davies, who had served as head administrator for the BBC in Wales since 1945, to press BBC headquarters for funding of increased television programming in Welsh (Davies, 1994: 218–219).

As its empire shrank, Great Britain experienced growth in its non-indigenous minority population (those other than Welsh, Scots and Northern Irish) following the Second World War. However, the BBC did little to serve the more recently arrived ethnic and linguistic minority audiences until 1967, when BBC local radio was inaugurated. Since many of the new local stations were located in or near major urban areas where South Asians, Caribbean Islanders and other non-indigenous minorities were most numerous, some of them began to provide airtime for programmes highlighting the various cultures, largely through their popular music. There also were programmes that served as sources of assistance and advice for members of those ethnic communities. As local commercial radio stations began to come on air through the Independent Local Radio (ILR) system in 1973, some of them followed the BBC's lead. In neither case was service to ethnic communities mandatory, and few stations offered more than one or two hours per week for such programmes, usually scheduled during the less popular hours and days. Also, while minorities were involved in producing the programmes (some in English, some in the languages of the ethnic groups), they were subject to BBC and ILR control in terms of programme content.

Most of the other European PSB monopolies were slower than the BBC had been to serve their respective countries' linguistic minorities, e.g.

Breton in France, Frisian in the Netherlands. They generally remained unilingual until the 1970s. Ireland's national PSB, Raidio Telefís Éireann (RTÉ), created an Irish language radio network for the west coast in 1970: Raidió na Gaeltachta (RnaG). Teachers concerned about the diminishing number of Irish speakers strongly supported it. They felt that a full-time radio service devoted to the language would help to reinforce and expand its use (Browne, 1992; Ó Glaisne, 1982). Most European countries did not have national and local commercial services until the 1980s or even 1990s, and few afforded opportunities for linguistic minority broadcasters. But another form of broadcasting had begun to emerge by the late 1940s, providing airtime for linguistic and ethnic minority groups large and small, as well as many non-ethnic minority groups. In an oft-used phrase, it became a 'voice for the voiceless'.

Community Radio and Linguistic Minority Involvement

The US FCC began to license low power (10 watt) community radio stations in 1948. KPFA-FM Pacifica Radio in San Francisco, California, came on air in 1949 and soon began to broadcast programmes in which Communists, 'beat' poets such as Allan Ginsberg, and ethnic minorities including the 'radical' Black Panthers, spoke, often for the first time over radio, usually in English but occasionally in Spanish. However, the development of community radio in the United States and Canada was glacially slow until the 1970s, when the civil rights demonstrations and anti-Vietnam War protests of the 1960s became a catalyst for a substantial increase in electronic media activity undertaken by linguistic minorities. That activity also was helped by start-up training and other US Government grants, as well as by the rapidly decreasing cost of studio equipment and a general spirit of citizen activism (leading to increased volunteer participation in the operation of such services) that marked the 1970s.

While there was no requirement that a US community station commit airtime to broadcasts by and/or for linguistic minorities, most stations did and still do provide some airtime for the purpose. Many offer a wide assortment of programmes, some of them in minority languages. Since community radio stations have had to operate on a non-commercial basis, they have often relied on donated (used) equipment and unpaid volunteers for everything but management and engineering (themselves low-wage positions at such stations). Still, most have remained on air, and also have served as training grounds for many individuals, including linguistic minorities, who have distinguished themselves in the field of broadcasting.

The FCC's adoption of preference policies designed to assist ethnic minorities in acquiring broadcast licences aided the expansion in linguistic and ethnic minority broadcast activity in the 1970s (Browne, 2005: ch. 3). Those policies made it more likely that linguistic and ethnic minorities would receive licences for both community and commercial broadcast services. Dozens of stations (largely radio) owned and operated by African-Americans, Hispanic-Americans, Native Americans, Inuit and others, came on air during the 1970s and 1980s. The US Corporation for Public Broadcasting's Minority Station Improvement Project Grant, and the National Telecommunications and Information Administration's Minority Station Start-Up Program also offered various forms of financial assistance. Interestingly, stations receiving their licences through preference policies were not *required* to serve linguistic and ethnic minority audiences, although almost all of them did.

Community broadcasting in other parts of the world blossomed during roughly the same period, and for some of the same reasons: anti-Vietnam War protests, civil rights activism, and demands for 'voices of our own'. The Canadian, Australian and New Zealand experiences form the closest parallels with the US experience. That is not surprising, since those nations had featured strong commercial broadcasting sectors for several decades, and the community broadcasting sector of each took on an aura of anti-commercialism. Furthermore, civil rights demonstrations and anti-Vietnam War protests were prominent in all three countries.

Each of the countries provided funding earmarked for specific minority services, namely those by and for Native Americans and Inuit in Canada,[6] Aboriginal Australians, and New Zealand's Maori. In addition, Australia created a special licensing category for community radio stations dedicated *solely* to ethnic minority broadcasting. While they were not required to offer programmes in the languages of ethnic groups, they did and continue to do so. (Australia remains the only nation in the world with such a category.)

In the late 1970s the Australian government also authorised the development of a temporary national radio service exclusively for linguistic and ethnic minority groups. It was intended to reach such group members in their own languages with information about a new government health programme. It turned out to be useful in still other ways, the linguistic and ethnic minority groups themselves fought for its survival, and it became a permanent organisation: the Special Broadcasting Service (SBS). SBS remains one of very few national broadcast services for a broad range of linguistic and ethnic minorities, with dozens of minority languages in radio and on TV, and is far and away the largest such service anywhere

(Browne, 2005: ch. 3; Davies, 1998; Jakubowicz & Newell, 1995). Germany's nationally distributed (by satellite) multilingual Funkhaus Europa (Cologne), in cooperation with Radio MultiKulti (Berlin), offers several languages, most of them European, and only over radio (Browne, 2004; Vertovec, 1996; Voss, 2001a, 2001b; Zambonini, 2002).

Although Australia developed outlets for linguistic minorities earlier than did most other countries, there were groups that took matters into their own hands, and broadcast illegally. The Aboriginal communities of Yuendumu and Arabella (Northern Territory) set up unauthorised satellite reception systems in 1985 to bring in television signals from other parts of the country, but also to add some of their own videotaped productions, which they had begun to make a few years earlier. While this constituted self-expression, it also led to some disagreement over who in the communities had the right to show what, and to whom (Michaels, 1986: 50–78, 88–89). In 1988, the first licensed Aboriginal-operated TV service came on air from Alice Springs, but limited financial support restricts its Aboriginal language programming to a few hours weekly (Molnar & Meadows, 2001: 54–59).

New Zealand took a quite radical approach to the question of who was to be served by a licence fee-supported public broadcaster. Decades of pressure from Maori (Browne, 1996: ch. 5), who claimed that they, too, paid licence fees, but received little programming featuring their culture or in their language,[7] brought change. Parliament passed the Broadcasting Act of 1989, under which a newly created agency, the Broadcasting Commission, would disburse some of the licence fee money for the specific purpose of 'promoting Maori language and culture [through broadcasting]'. The financial support provided – several million dollars a year – permitted the development of roughly two dozen Maori tribal radio stations (Government of New Zealand, 1989: 2). Broadcasts in Maori ran second – often a distant second – to broadcasts in English on most of the stations. That caused some Maori leaders to argue that tribal radio stations receiving such financial support should be required to provide at least a majority of their programming in Maori, and the new (March 2004) Maori television service has just such a requirement. Community access radio stations were licensed starting in the 1980s, and are scattered across the country; virtually all have linguistic minority broadcasts, mainly in Maori and in South Pacific languages. Three radio stations are operated by and for South Pacific Islanders, one of them broadcasting almost exclusively in Samoan. Annual government appropriations help to support those services.

Creating Other Outlets

Other countries took somewhat different approaches to the introduction or expansion of linguistic minority broadcasting. While one might contend that the protests, demonstrations and 'power to the people' movements influenced government policy in the US, Australia, Canada and New Zealand, it is more difficult to sustain that argument for Europe. Sweden, Finland and Norway, for example, had featured PSB monopolies since the 1930s. Their services for linguistic minorities were limited to small amounts of Sami radio programming (Horn, 1999; Olson, 1984), and in the case of Sweden and Finland, larger amounts of radio programming for their Finnish- and Swedish-speaking minorities. When Sweden and Norway opened up their systems in the late 1970s, it was pressure from non-Lutheran religious organisations, rather than linguistic minorities, that played the major role in winning parliamentary approval for the creation of a state-supported set of low power transmitters that would serve as access radio channels (Tomlinson, 1994). Both the parliaments and those religious bodies were quite surprised to discover that linguistic and ethnic minorities in the larger cities and in some university towns soon were among the heaviest users of the new *närradio* ('nearby-radio') services. Those in Oslo, Stockholm, Gothenberg and Malmo all feature major involvement in *närradio* on the part of Iranians, Kurds and others.

In Great Britain, the 1970s saw a number of extra-legal challenges to the system. Non-indigenous linguistic and ethnic minorities were among the challengers, but they had to do so largely by operating *unlicensed* radio services as 'land-based pirates', which meant that they were frequent targets of the authorities.[8] Many of the stations provided South Asian, Caribbean and African listeners with full-time services, often in their own languages. Such groups continued to press for the creation of a community broadcasting sector. It looked as if one was about to be created in 1986, but opposition from within the Conservative government halted the effort, in part due to suspicion that linguistic minorities might use their 'linguistic invisibility' to criticise the government. Finally, in the early 1990s, interested parties were permitted to apply for limited power radio licences, and Caribbean, South Asian and other ethnic stations, as well as many others, took to the airwaves legally, often using their own languages. In 2002, the British government authorised an experiment with access radio. Fifteen low power FM (UHF) stations were licensed to broadcast for a year. Several of them devote much or all of their airtime to serving ethnic minorities, many broadcasting in their own languages

(Everitt, 2003). The experimental designation was dropped in 2004, and the category now has full legal status.

Some West German public radio stations had provided broadcasts in the languages (Italian, Serbian, Croatian, Spanish) of Germany's so-called 'guest workers' by the early 1960s, usually for 15 or fewer minutes per day, and not necessarily on all days (Voss, 2001b). Zweites Deutsches Fernsehen (the second national channel) began to offer a weekly television magazine programme, Nachbarn ('Neighbours') in the mid-1960s, in the same languages. Unlicensed radio services appeared in the 1970s, most of them short-lived and few with airtime for linguistic minority groups. The growth of cable in the 1980s stimulated the development of cable access radio and television in northern *Länder* (states), and many ethnic minority groups used those services. Southern *Länder* followed a different path by licensing independent, non-commercial radio stations as *Freies Radios* ('Free Radio') starting in the late 1980s. Stations in the larger cities such as Munich and Stuttgart often have made blocks of airtime available to linguistic minorities.

France began to create opportunities for broadcasting in some of the regional languages (Breton, Alsatian, Provencal etc.) in the mid-1970s, when the French PSB's regional TV service, FR3, developed a new legal framework which specified that FR3 'contributes to the expression of the main regional languages spoken on the metropolitan territory'. However, even by 1998 there were only 265 hours of television programming *per year* in the six regional languages. Alsatian with 68 hours and Breton with 66 led the list (Guyot, 2002: 242). France began to develop PSB regional radio in the late 1970s, and the conservative government promised to build the system that would create a larger place for regional languages (there already had been broadcasts in Breton, Alsatian and Provençal). It also stated that it would consider liberalising the licensing of alternative (to the PSB) radio and television services. The opposition Socialist Party had promised to end the public service broadcasting monopoly if it won the 1981 national election, and it did.

Initially, the Socialist-led government attempted to restrict the licensing of new radio stations to non-commercial licence-seekers, which included numerous linguistic and ethnic minorities, but that restriction was lifted within two years, and commercial licensees soon became predominant (Browne, 1999: 98–101, 129–131). Even so, various linguistic and ethnic minority groups managed to obtain a foothold (El Atia & Kibbee, 2001: 32; for Breton, see Guyot, 2002: 231–245). Some of the stations operated by North African Arabs living in France developed into a small-scale national Arabic-language network, Radio Beur, based in Paris. Numerous community radio stations broadcast in one or more of the French minority languages. For example, Radio Pays in Paris carries programming in seven of them. Frequence Paris Plurielle offers 'bilingual' material in Chinese, Farsi, Kurdish, Turkish, Serbo-Croat and others.

Italy, which also had a public service monopoly system, found itself in the position of having to license 'pirate' radio stations (most of them operated by trade unions and student groups) in the late 1970s simply because the existing broadcast law did not provide a legal basis for prohibiting them. Relatively few served linguistic and ethnic minorities, although Milan's Radio Popolare did and still does.

Spain under Franco maintained a PSB monopoly and forbade most forms of self-expression – and certainly linguistic self-expression, which was prohibited as a public activity – on the part of the country's regions (Basque,[9] Catalan, Galician and others). After Franco's death in 1975, national elections brought the Socialist Party to power. The regions soon received more autonomy, which included having their own broadcast facilities in their own languages. Catalan and Basque services appeared on radio by 1977, and on television by 1983 (Moragas Spà & Corominas, 1992: 186–193; Rodriguez, 2001).

The Netherlands, with its rapidly growing ethnic minority population, had begun to provide very limited amounts of airtime for ethnic minority languages (e.g., Moluccan) in 1966, through its public radio service (NOS). The public television service (also NOS) began in 1976 to carry even more limited amounts of ethnic minority material. The government also permitted experiments with local and regional cable television during the 1970s, but they featured little ethnic minority involvement. However, pressure from émigrés for local radio and television services mounted in the early 1980s. In 1983 an Amsterdam cable television channel began to carry a service specifically for such groups: *Migranttelevisie* ('Migrant Television'). It featured a mix of programmes, some imported from the minority homelands but others produced by minorities living in the city.[10] In 1985, the city government and other organisations helped to establish a cable radio and television access service. SALTO (Stichting Amsterdamse Lokale Televisie/Radio Omroep) was open to any and all interested parties, linguistic minorities included.[11] During the same period, local and regional radio spread to other parts of the country; many of the new services were transmitted through cable as well as over the air, and often featured programmes made by linguistic (e.g. Frisian or Frysk) and ethnic minority groups (Browne, 1999: 202–204; Gooskens, 1992).

The Soviet Union and the People's Republic of China (PRC) both supported linguistic minority broadcasting within their republics or regions, in Ukrainian, Armenian, Dai, Uighur and many others.[12] However, the broadcast time devoted to those languages was far outstripped by broadcasts in Russian and in Mandarin, and a speaker of Georgian or of Amoy who happened to live anywhere else in the country generally would search the airwaves in vain for any trace of her or his language. In other words, for the most part these were linguistic *majority* languages within the areas where they were broadcast, but unavailable elsewhere. The Soviet Union and the PRC appeared to have three policy objectives: to reach illiterate people; to 'keep the locals happy'; to reinforce the notion that both countries featured 'unity with diversity'. The PRC continues to follow such a policy, while most of the former Soviet republics have maintained and even expanded their language services, and the commercial stations in the republics broadcast in the major national languages; some provide programming in more localised languages, as well.[13]

Community Radio in the 'Third World'

The current of activism on behalf of social change helped motivate members of religious groups, particularly Roman Catholic priests in Latin America, to use radio to assist and even empower many of the indigenous groups in Mexico, Central America and South America. 'Liberation theology' and other teachings by individuals such as Paolo Freire inspired numerous priests to create local radio services for Mayan, Incan, Aztec and other indigenous populations, usually with broadcasts in their own languages and often with 'the locals' themselves as programme producers. Mexico's Instituto Nacional Indigenista (INI) and Ministry of Education had operated a shortwave radio service from 1958 until 1963 for the purpose of teaching Spanish to indigenous peoples. In 1979 it began a multi-station indigenous radio network whose principal languages were Aztec or Mayan (Ramos & Diez, 2003; Vargas, 1995: ch. 4).[14] In 1985 the Mexican *state* government of Hidalgo began to support a radio station already serving indigenous audiences, and assisted in developing a seven-station system for Hidalgo's indigenous peoples. However, much of the programming was in Spanish, with restricted amounts of airtime in Nahuatl, Hnahnu and other languages (Peppino Barele, 1989: 64–74).

Elsewhere in Latin America, there were other Roman Catholic-supported linguistic minority radio services at the community level. One of them, Radio San Gabriel in Bolivia, began broadcasting in Aymara shortly after its foundation in 1956, largely because it discovered that it had to do so in order to teach Spanish to the Aymara speakers (Aguilar, 1992: 21–26). Other religious organisations became active, as well. Various evangelical and other groups (e.g. Baha'i; see Hein, 1988) established stations to assist indigenous populations in expressing themselves in their own languages. While empowerment of those populations was a frequent goal, so was religious proselytisation, either to combat Communist influence or to win converts over from the Catholic Church. Substantial numbers of local Aymara and Quechua (a group of languages and dialects) radio stations appeared in Bolivia during the 1970s, and eventually the Quechua stations formed their own network, which began to be transmitted by satellite in 1990, and has grown to include Quechua stations in Ecuador and Peru (Luykx, 2001).

Community radio was slower to develop in Africa, but by the late 1980s a few stations had begun to broadcast, generally with the financial support of outside governments and organisations rather than their own national governments. Two Italian non-governmental organisations, Gao and Terranuova, supported the creation in 1988 of a local radio station in Kayes, Mali. It was founded largely because the local population considered itself neglected by Mali's national broadcast service, and wished to express itself in its own languages. Because the funding sources were both external and uncertain, the station often found itself financially insecure, but also learned to rely more on local support (Berque, 1992: 122–131). The Liberian Rural Communications Network, founded in 1986, brought local radio service, exclusively in local languages, to the northern counties in Liberia (Kweekeh, 1987). It featured strong local participation, but the outbreak of civil war in 1989 saw its three stations destroyed or taken over by warring factions.

By the end of the 1990s, many more African states had community radio services, and in nearly every instance they provided services in local languages, which the national services generally carried in brief intervals or not at all. The South African Broadcasting Corporation (SABC) broadcasts in all 11 of South Africa's official languages, but lacks the resources to fulfil its constitutional obligation in that regard, which would mean considerably more airtime on SABC-TV for the indigenous African languages and less for English and Afrikaans (SABC can't go for broke, 2002). However, SABC operates eight separate radio stations offering full schedules of programming in the official languages, as well as an English language service for South Asians and two community radio stations carrying Khoisan ('Bushman') languages. Several dozen community radio stations not connected with SABC emerged during the 1990s, and many of them carry the more commonly spoken local African languages. Radio

ALX serves the township of Alexandra in *all* of the official languages, although the shortage of speakers for a few of them makes it difficult to sustain such broad service (Browne, 2005: *passim*; Siemering, 1998).

External Broadcasting and Linguistic Minorities

Using external radio services to reach audiences in other countries with broadcasts in their own languages usually means attracting listeners who may not think of themselves as linguistic minorities. However, there have been several instances where that is precisely what they were in terms of the amount of domestically produced radio material available in those languages. The practice began shortly before the Second World War, but on a small scale. Since those services usually were directed to minority audiences in 'enemy-occupied' countries, it was difficult to recruit linguistically expert staff. Nevertheless, Nazi Germany broadcast to India (then under British rule) in Hindi; Japan broadcast to South Asia in Hindi, Urdu, Bengali and Tamil; and Italy broadcast to Palestine (also under British rule) in Arabic. There is little evidence indicating how effective those broadcasts (opposing British rule) may have been, but they helped to spur the British Foreign Office to support BBC external broadcasting in languages other than English (Browne, 1983).

The practice became quite widespread starting in the 1950s, in part because some of the Communist states began to support independence movements in Africa and Asia at that time. A few of the former colonies and protectorates, such as India, Indonesia and Egypt, had achieved independence by the early 1950s. However, most had not, and in many of them the European colonial powers either had not introduced radio broadcasting in the indigenous languages or provided little airtime for them. In essence, the indigenous peoples were treated as linguistic minorities. Radio Moscow, Radio Havana and Radio Peking (later, Beijing) provided broadcast services in various African and Asian languages such as Swahili, Bambara, Tamil and Zulu, and often employed political exiles fluent in those languages and living in Moscow or Peking to produce some of the programmes.[15] Radio Cairo followed suit when Egypt under President Nasser began to identify itself as an African nation in the mid-1950s – political exiles formed the core of Shona, Ndebele, Fulani, Zulu and other minority language services to Africa. In all cases, the basic message was liberation from British, French or other European rulers (Browne, 1982).

The Union of South Africa in part was reacting to external broadcasts when it developed an unusual radio service for Black South Africans in

1964.[16] Radio Bantu featured programmes in seven different Bantu languages – Zulu, Xhosa, and others – as well as English and Afrikaans. Unlike the Soviet and Chinese linguistic minority services, Black South Africans could receive broadcasts in their particular languages in areas other than the tribal regions and so-called Black homelands.[17] It also could be heard in some of the Black townships housing the miners, garbage collectors and others filling various undesirable or dangerous jobs in the cities. The service was available on FM (UHF) only, to discourage the target audience from listening to broadcasts from the external services (almost never on FM) of surrounding countries, most of them with anti-apartheid Black governments. Tanzania, Southern Rhodesia (now Zimbabwe) and other neighbouring states also made their radio studios and transmitters available to individuals and groups belonging to or allied with the outlawed (in the Union) African National Congress, which in 1967 developed an anti-apartheid radio service – Radio Freedom. It broadcast in the same languages as did Radio Bantu, but could not be picked up by FM receivers, so it distributed audiocassettes of some of its material to reach FM-only households, as well as to circumvent the Union's jamming of its broadcasts from nearby countries (Phelan, 1985; Tomaselli *et al.*, 1985).

Black African nations often provided external services in the languages of neighbouring countries, whether under colonial rule or independent. The Republic of Guinea, which became independent of French rule in 1958, soon initiated broadcast services for Equatorial Guinea (a Spanish colony), Sierra Leone and the Gambia (British colonies), but also to Senegal following its independence from France in 1960 (Browne, 1963: 113–122). Political exiles again provided the necessary indigenous languages, with differing messages for the present colonies ('Get rid of your colonial rulers') and for the former colony ('Get rid of your present rulers, who serve only as the stooges of the colonial rulers').

There is little evidence that external services directed to indigenous minorities have had much success in fomenting rebellion. They often serve to encourage the development or expansion of indigenous language services within the target areas, and a few, such as Radio Freedom, helped to sustain the hope for an indigenous government. The effectiveness of such external services often has been compromised by poor reception quality in target areas, limited amounts of airtime in each indigenous language, and, for the more ideological services (Communist, Christian), messages couched in highly doctrinaire language that either is unclear or uninteresting to the intended audience. However, if an external service happens to be the only one providing a specific language, it may improve its chances of attracting listeners.

Linguistic Minorities, Cable and Satellite

With certain exceptions (Canadian and US Inuit; Hispanic-American; Welsh; Basque, Catalan; Galician), television services operated by linguistic minorities did not appear until the 1990s (Alia, 1999; Frachon & Vargaftig, 1995; Montalvo, 2004; Moragas Spà & Garitaonandia, 1995; Rodriguez, 2001).[18] The medium simply was too expensive. Linguistic minorities usually had to content themselves with access cable services:[19] channels through which the citizenry could express itself. Cable companies began to provide such service in the US in the mid-1960s, and also were to provide training and equipment to users, at low cost or even free of charge. Many individuals and groups, including linguistic minorities, took advantage of the opportunity.[20]

Cable television was slower to spread in most other countries. Many did not require that cable companies provide access channels or training programmes, but cable operators often discovered that doing so helped to increase the cable subscriber base. Participation by linguistic minorities usually was an unexpected by-product rather than a calculated move to attract them as subscribers. Some German cities have developed impressive access channel radio and television operations (*Offener Kanale*), financed in part through a surcharge on the monthly cable bill. They are heavily used by minorities living in the larger cities, particularly in Hamburg and Berlin.

Still, there are many countries with very low cable subscriber rates. Italy, for example, has a rate of less than 10% as of 2004, and cable access is largely undeveloped there.[21] Spain, Portugal, Greece and the Balkan States are in much the same situation, as are Australia and New Zealand. Japan had a rate of over 50% as of 2003, but just slightly over half of those subscribers could receive anything more than terrestrial stations. In any case, there are few cable access services, and even fewer possibilities for linguistic minority electronic media participation in that highly homogeneous country.[22]

Cable radio may be available for an additional fee through cable television systems, but usually does not attract anything like the number of cable television subscribers, so audiences for it tend to be small and to include relatively low percentages of linguistic minority subscribers, perhaps because of the fees. Linguistic minorities do present programmes through cable radio, and are particularly prominent in the Netherlands. No nation requires provision of access cable radio or television time or production assistance specifically for linguistic minorities.

Satellite television reaches sizable numbers of subscribers in a few countries – the United States, Germany, Great Britain, Japan – but most satellite services currently do not relay locally originated programming, so there is no opportunity for cable access channels to find additional outlets through satellites. However, satellites *have* been keys to success for the nationally and internationally distributed linguistic minority services that have come into existence or have expanded during the past decade or so. American Indian Radio on Satellite (AIROS), BBC Asian Network (UK, radio), the Aboriginal Peoples' Television Network (APTN, Canada), Broadcasting for Remote Aboriginal Communities Scheme (BRACS, Australia), Univision and Telemundo (Hispanic-American), Maori television (New Zealand), TG4 (Ireland), Scots Gaelic television and others owe their existence as national services to the availability of satellite channels.[23]

Most linguistic minority listeners or viewers receive such services through cable, although some services – AIROS, for example – serve primarily as relays to feed individual terrestrial radio stations.[24] The annual cost of leasing a satellite channel is high enough that only operations with sizable target audiences (thus, good commercial potential) or financial support from the government, sponsors or their parent corporations such as the BBC in the case of the BBC Asian Network can afford them, which often tends to exclude the smaller ethnic groups.

Summarising History

Clearly the number and variety of linguistic minority electronic media services has increased greatly over the past 20 years. Several factors account for their slow initial growth:

(1)   Minority languages suffered from what at best might be termed benign neglect and at worst passive and active opposition during the 1920s and 1930s.

(2)   Minorities seeking to establish electronic media services in their languages during earlier periods often lacked financial support for radio stations, much less television stations.

(3)   While the Second World War saw increased attention to linguistic minorities, much of that was curtailed or disappeared at war's end. However, it also helped to create small cadres of linguistic minority broadcasters who often worked within the established broadcast services; some managed to broaden their experience and even to argue successfully for increased hours in their languages or to help found linguistic minority services.

(4)   The various tides of change sweeping through the 1960s and early 1970s in many industrialised nations created a climate in which 'power to the people' movements encouraged individuals and

groups to speak through the media in their own voices, including their own languages.

(5) The spread of cable and of direct broadcasting by satellite offered still other outlets for linguistic minorities. That coincided with larger-scale movements of many minority population groups, whose members often subscribed to satellite-delivered services from their ancestral homelands,[25] helping them maintain close contact with their roots.

The Future

The growth of linguistic minority expression through the electronic media has provided opportunities to strengthen and to spread the use of their languages, to counteract stereotyped mainstream media images, to address their 'media invisibility', to create a greater sense of self-pride, and to link up with their compatriots in other parts of the world. Most linguistic minority services are not well-financed, but some have created programmes that rival in quality what is presented by mainstream media. Some attempts to encourage acquisition or improvement of fluency in minority languages have been quite innovative (Browne, 2005: 157–158). Language 'purists' may oppose such attempts, and one of the more demanding aspects of operating a linguistic minority media service is maintaining a balance between those insisting on strict standards of correctness and those favouring a more 'relaxed' approach to language usage.

The sheer abundance of media availability, at least in the industrialised world, has made it more difficult for minority services to attract attention. Many of the linguistic minority services that I have visited seem unaware of the growing importance of promotional advertising in this era of media proliferation, yet it would seem to be vital to their long-term survival.

As émigré groups in particular become settled and begin to raise families, linguistic minority media have an excellent opportunity to play an important role in reinforcing use of the languages on the part of the younger generation. Some are creating engaging programmes for children, teenagers and even adults that encourage them along those lines (Browne, 2005: 163–166). Sadly, many linguistic minority services offer little or no programming of that sort. Also, educators and media staff too often seem unaware of, or even opposed to finding ways in which they might collaborate to emphasise the relevance of minority languages for young people.

Hopefully, more governments will see the wisdom of assisting linguistic minority media services, as some already have done. Commercial services are unlikely to feature a wide variety of linguistic minority experiences and viewpoints, and minority non-commercial services often need help. Newly arrived minority groups, often poor and unfamiliar with technology, may be in particular need of assistance in expressing themselves. The suspicion with which linguistic minority services sometimes have been treated appears to be receding, although some still feel that minority languages are an impediment to economic and social progress. Yet it should be evident by now that individuals, and society as a whole, are enriched by linguistic diversity, especially in an increasingly mobile and interdependent world.

Notes

1. My account does not include the Internet or audio- and videocassettes. See also Browne (2004); Cisler (1998), Girard (2003), *Hommes et Migrations* (2002) and Moseley *et al.* (2001) for various accounts of minority languages on the Internet and on cassette.
2. For example, Lazreg (1990: 45–47) notes that Algerian President Ahmed Ben Bella halted broadcasts in Kabyle, or Tamazight ('Berber') shortly after Algeria gained its independence in 1963, probably to discourage separatist tendencies. Eventually the service was restored, and had become a 19-hour-per-day operation by the early 1990s.
3. Cormack (1998) notes major points to be considered when assessing possible roles of minority language media.
4. Davies (1994) has a very detailed account of the first several decades of BBC Welsh radio; McDowell (1992) provides similar information on BBC Scots Gaelic broadcasts; Withers (1984: 249) notes that a BBC (Scots) Gaelic Department was created in 1935, and produced 35 minutes *per week* in the language. Instruction in Scots Gaelic was *not* encouraged by the BBC, and when in 1931 the BBC regional director for Scotland suggested to BBC head-quarters in London that such broadcasts might be worth considering, he was told by the BBC director of programmes that 'I personally disagree with the idea, as I should have thought that it was better not to do anything that would stimulate the spread of "native" languages at a time when we are doing all we can for the English language' (quoted in McBride, 1995: 38).
5. Australia also proved to be suspicious of broadcasts in foreign languages, even though such services did not appear there until after the Second World War. With the emigration of many Europeans, some of the commercial radio stations began to offer small slices of air time for programmes in their own languages. In 1953, the government imposed a limit of no more than 2.5% transmission time on such broadcasts, which also had to be translated into English; that restriction lasted until 1974 (SBS, 1979: 10).
6. Canada's Northern Native Broadcast Access Program (NNBAP) was particularly generous by the standards of the times. From 1983 to 1987 it provided approximately CAN$40 million for the support of Inuit broadcast activity (Stiles and associates, 1985: 24–25). It furnished another CAN$140 million between 1988 and 2003. Annual funding levels began to drop in 1989, and have been level (*c.* CAN$8 million p.a.) over the period 1997–2003. Still, it continues

to serve as a major source of financial support for Canadian Aboriginal and Inuit electronic media services. The Northern Development Program (NDP) helps to offset the costs of leasing, operating and maintaining the satellite distribution system that interlinks the services. Over the period 1989–2003, it furnished c. CAN$35.5 million, with annual support level at CAN$2.1 million over the period 1998–2003 (Whiteduck & Consilium, 2003). See Alia (1999) and Roth (1995) for a detailed account of Inuit broadcasting activity.

7. The New Zealand Broadcasting Corporation did provide limited amounts of Maori language programming on radio, and even lesser amounts on television.

8. Hind and Moss (1985) note several linguistic and ethnic minority-operated pirate services, such as the Dread Broadcasting Corporation (Jamaican).

9. In 1946, a group of Basques began operating a largely Spanish, but part Basque, language service directed to the Basque region in Spain. At first, the broadcasts came from southwestern France, where Basque speakers already lived just across the border from their Spanish Basque kin. A Spanish government protest led to the French government led to the closing down of that service in 1954. In 1965, it relocated to Venezuela and continued the service on shortwave until the initiation of Basque language radio within Spain in 1977. See Soley and Nichols (1987: 158–159).

10. Personal interviews with Gerard Reteig and Richard Troelstra, Migranttelevisie, Amsterdam, September 1995.

11. Personal visits to SALTO, September 1995 and April 2001.

12. There are no extended accounts of ethnic minority broadcast services in the Soviet Union, although Mickiewicz (1988: 6–7) notes their existence. See also Rising voices (1991: 203–215). For the PRC, see UNESCO (1986: 88–91).

13. Moscow radio station Krasny Most offers several of the languages of other former Soviet republics (e.g. Armenia), in recognition of the fact that there are many Armenian, Kazakh and other speakers living in the city (Solovyova, 1999).

14. Gumicio-Dagron (2001) has several chapters on Catholic Church-supported local stations. See also Carmen Marquez (1993) and Vargas (1995) for details on such services.

15. In certain instances – Radio Havana, Radio Peking – the target audiences were indigenous peoples such as Quechua and Aymara speakers in South America, but that was rare.

16. Tomaselli et al. (1985: 39) note that the SABC had provided a service in Zulu, Sotho and Xhosa during the Second World War, delivered over telephone lines to 'compounds, hostels and institutions' in all cities and major towns. It ceased operation in 1945, but SABC began a 'Bantu programme' in the 1950s, over medium wave and for 'a couple of hours daily only'. Eventually, it was discovered that some of the black announcers had been broadcasting 'anti-Government propaganda', and the SABC tightened control over the service by installing white supervisors who could speak the various Bantu languages (Tomaselli et al., 1985: 94–95).

17. In fact, Wilkins and Strydom (1979: 1) indicate that the Broederband (a politically powerful Afrikaaner group of hard-core racial separatists) thought of Radio Bantu as a way of ensuring that Blacks would remain in their segregated 'homelands'. For more information on Radio Bantu, see Phelan (1987); and Tomaselli et al. (1985: 89–103).

18. KYUK-TV, serving the isolated and largely Inuit town of Barrow on Alaska's North Slope, was an early exception (1973). It carried limited amounts of locally produced programming, often in Inuit languages.

19. Another outlet sometimes available to linguistic minorities in the US is the provision of airtime on local public television stations, especially in those instances where a station has two TV channels at its disposal. As of 2004, the Minneapolis/St Paul, Minnesota public TV stations, KTCA and KTCI, carried six minority produced series, all weekly or less often and ranging from Hmong to Arabic. The former was entirely in Hmong, the latter largely in English (Tillotson, 2004). The Hmong series also had been translated into English for a number of years, so that mainstream audiences could learn something about the community, but support for the translated version ended, leaving only the Hmong language version. (The practice was revived when the emigration of thousands of Hmong to the Twin Cities in mid-2004 led to the broadcast on 25 July of a set of programmes intended to help that group make the transition to their new lives; English subtitles were provided to help the mainstream population understand what the group would face.)

20. Starting in 1972, the FCC required that cable systems serving cities with 3500 or more subscribers provide similar access services; it later dropped that requirement, but many US cable companies continue to provide access channels.

21. The Italian PSB for the Autonomous Province of South Tirol, Rundfunkanstalt Sudtirol (RAS) provides extensive radio and TV service in German, but it does not offer public access, and much of its programming is in the form of relays of material broadcast by the Austrian, German and Swiss PSBs.

22. Broadcast activities of the more than 600,000 Koreans living in Japan are limited to blocks of airtime on local commercial radio stations in Tokyo, Osaka and Fukuoka, and to 'mini-FM' (very low power) radio stations in such cities. The Ainu, Japan's indigenous people, have small amounts of airtime on a commercial radio station in Hokkaido, and also have a tape distribution service. Both outlets are used primarily to preserve the Ainu language (DeChicchis, 1995: 114–115; Kristof, 1996; Sterngold, 1992).

23. Cormack (1995) describes the discussion (at times heated) over Scots Gaelic television policy.

24. The AIROS-distributed daily discussion programme 'Native America Calling' also uses the satellite, along with the Internet (www.nativeamericacalling.org) to allow listeners to join in on the discussions, usually in English.

25. A wide variety of Turkish television services is available to subscribers in Germany and the Netherlands. Whether such services help or hinder linguistic minorities operating within 'mainstream' culture is a much-debated issue (Browne, 1999a). A similar service available to Arabic speakers – Al Manar, operated by Hezbollah out of Lebanon – has become highly controversial in France. Some of its programming features strongly anti-Semitic material, and the French government, frustrated by Al Manar's refusal to abide by an agreement that it would refrain from carrying such material, obtained a ruling in mid-December 2004 from the Council of State that banned the French satellite Eutelsat from carrying it. Ironically, the Paris-based company GlobeCast, a subsidiary of France Telecom, continues to distribute Al Manar to various parts of the world. See Carvajal (2004) and Sciolino (2004).

References

Aguilar, E. (1992) Radio San Gabriel: The voice of the Aymara people. In H. Mowlana and M. Frondorf (eds) *The Media as a Forum for Community Building* (pp. 21–26). Washington, DC: Paul H. Nitze School of Advanced International Studies Program on Social Change and Development.

Alia, V. (1999) *Un/Covering the North: News, Media and Aboriginal People.* Vancouver: University of British Columbia (UBC) Press.

Berque, P. (1992) The hard lesson of autonomy: Kayes rural radio. In B. Girard (ed.) *A Passion for Radio* (pp. 122–131). Montreal: Black Rose Books.

Browne, D. (1963) Radio Guinea: A voice of independent Africa. *Journal of Broadcasting* 7 (2), 113–122.

Browne, D. (1982) *International Radio Broadcasting.* New York: Praeger.

Browne, D. (1983) Going international. *Journalism Quarterly* 60 (3), 423–430.

Browne, D. (1992) Raidio na Gaeltacha. *European Journal of Communication.* 7 (3), 415–433.

Browne, D. (1996) *Electronic Media and Indigenous Peoples: A Voice of Our Own?* Ames, IA: Iowa State University Press.

Browne, D. (1999a) The snail's shell: Electronic media and emigrant communities. *Communications* 24 (1), 61–84.

Browne, D. (1999) *Electronic Media and Industrialized Nations.* Ames, IA: Iowa State University Press.

Browne, D. (2005) *Ethnic Minorities, Electronic Media and the Public Sphere.* Cresskill, NJ: Hampton Press.

Carmen Marquez, L. del (1993) The uses of radio by ethnic minorities in Mexico: A study of a participatory project. Ph.D. thesis, University of Texas at Austin.

Carvajal, D. (2004) French court orders a ban on Hezbollah-run TV channel. *New York Times*, 14 December, A 12.

Cisler, S. (ed.) (1998) The Internet and indigenous groups. Special issue of *Cultural Survival Quarterly* 21 (4).

Cormack, M. (1995) Broadcasting and the politics of cultural diversity: The Gaelic television debate in Scotland. *European Journal of Cultural Policy* 2 (1), 43–54.

Cormack, M. (1998) Minority language media in Western Europe: Preliminary considerations. *European Journal of Communication* 13 (1), 33–52.

Davies, C.L. (1998) Multicultural broadcasting in Australia: Policies, institutions and programming, 1975–1995. Ph.D. thesis, University of Queensland.

Davies, J. (1994) *Broadcasting and the BBC in Wales.* Cardiff: University of Wales Press.

DeChicchis, J. (1995) Current state of the Ainu language. *Journal of Multilingual and Multicultural Development* 16 (1/2).

El Atia, S. and Kibbee, D. (2001) Language protection and cultural policy in France. In C. Moseley, N. Ostler and H. Ouzzate (eds) *Endangered Languages and the Media. Proceedings of the Fifth FEL Conference* (pp. 29–33). Bath: Foundation for Endangered Languages.

Everitt, A. (2003) *New Voices: An Evaluation of 15 Access Radio Projects.* London: Radio Authority.

Federal Communications Commission (1940) *Analyses and Tabulation of the Returns of the Commission's Questionnaire Concerning Broadcasts By Licensees in Languages Other Than English.* Washington, DC: FCC.

Frachon, C. and Vargaftig, M. (eds) (1995) *European Television*. London: John Libbey.

Girard, B. (ed.) (2003) *The One to Watch: Radio, New ICTs and Interactivity*. Rome: Food and Agriculture Organization.

Gooskens, I. (1992) Experimenting with minority television in Amsterdam. In N. Jankowski, O. Prehn and J. Stappers (eds) *The People's Voice* (pp. 225–234). London: John Libbey.

Government of New Zealand (1989) *Broadcasting Act of 1989*. Wellington: Government Printer.

Grame, T. (1980) *Ethnic Broadcasting in the United States*. Washington, DC: American Folklife Center, Library of Congress. Publication 4.

Gumicio-Dagron, A. (2001) *Making Waves*. New York: Rockefeller Foundation.

Guyot, J. (2002) An intercultural challenge for French regional television. In N. Jankowski (ed.) *Community Media in the Information Age*. Cresskill, NJ: Hampton Press.

Heatta, O.M. (1984) NRK's Samisk Sendinger, 1946–1984. MA thesis, University of Tromso.

Hein, K. (1988) *Radio Baha'i Ecuador*. Oxford: G. Ronald.

Hind, J. and Moss, S. (1985) *Rebel Radio: The Full Story of British Pirate Radio*. London: Pluto Press.

Holten, G. (2002) *Radio Goes to War: The Cultural Politics of Propaganda During World War II*. Berkeley, CA: University of California Press.

Hommes et Migrations (Nov.–Dec. 2002). Issue No. 1240.

Horn, F. (ed.) (1999) *Sami and Greenlandic Media (Juridica Lapponica 22)*. Rovaniemi: The Northern Institute for Environmental and Minority Law, University of Lapland.

Indians for Indians (1943) *Time* 41 (31 May), 40.

Jakubowicz, A. and Newell, K. (1995) Which world? Whose (who's) home? Special Broadcasting in the Australian communication alphabet. In J. Craik (ed.) *Public Voices, Private Interests: Australia's Media Policy*. St Leonard's: Allen & Unwin.

Kristof, N. (1996) Japan's forgotten people are trying to be heard. *New York Times*, 5 October, p. A6.

Kweekeh, F. (1987) Radio for rural development in Liberia. *InterMedia* 15 (2), 27–29.

Lazreg, M. (1990) Media and cultural dependency in Algeria. *Studies of Broadcasting* (NHK Japan) 26, 45–47.

Lemke, C. (1995) Maori involvement in sound recording and broadcasting, 1919–1958. MA thesis, University of Auckland.

Luykx, A. (2001) Across the Andean airwaves: Satellite radio broadcasting in Quechua. In C. Moseley, N. Ostler and H. Ouzzate (eds) *Endangered Languages and the Media. Proceedings of the Fifth FEL Conference* (pp. 15–19). Bath: Foundation for Endangered Languages.

McBride, S. (1995) Scottish Gaelic and Welsh language broadcasting in the United Kingdom. MA thesis, School of Journalism and Mass Communication, University of North Carolina at Chapel Hill.

McDowell, W. (1992) *The History of BBC Broadcasting in Scotland, 1923–1983*. Edinburgh: Edinburgh University Press.

Meyer, V. (2001) From segmented to fragmented: Latino media in San Antonio, Texas. *Journalism and Mass Communication Quarterly* 78 (2), 291–306.

Michaels, E. (1986) *The Aboriginal Invention of Television in Central Australia, 1982–1986.* Canberra: Australian Institute of Aboriginal Studies.

Mickiewicz, E. (1988) *Split Signals.* New York: Oxford University Press.

Migala, J. (1982) *Polish Radio Broadcasting in the United States.* Boulder, CO: East European Monographs No. 216 (distributed by Columbia University Press).

Molnar, H. and Meadows, M. (2001) *Songlines to Satellites: Indigenous Communication in Australia, the South Pacific and Canada.* Annandale: Pluto Press.

Montalvo, D. (2004) *Must Si TV: The evolution of Spanish-language television in the United States.* Paper presented at Annual Convention of the Broadcast Education Association, Las Vegas, Nevada.

Moragas Spà, M. and Corominas, M. (1992) Media and democratic participation in local communication. In N. Jankowski, O. Prehn and J. Stappers (eds) *The People's Voice.* London: John Libbey.

Moragas Spà, M. de and Garitaonandia, C. (eds) (1995) *Decentralization in the Global Era: Television in the Regions, Nationalities and Small Countries of the European Union.* London: John Libbey.

Moseley, C., Ostler, N. and Ouzzate, H. (eds) (2001) *Endangered Languages and the Media. Proceedings of the Fifth FEL Conference.* Bath: Foundation for Endangered Languages.

Ó Glaisne, R. (1982) *Raidio na Gaeltachta.* Indreadbhan: Clo Chois Fharraige.

Olson, S. (1984) Devolution and indigenous mass media: The role of media in Inupiat and Sami nation-building. Ph.D. thesis, Northwestern University.

Peppino Barele, A.M. (1989) *Las Ondas Dormidas: Cronica Hidalguense de una Pasion Radiofonica.* Azcapotzalco: Universidad Autonome Metropolitana, Division de Ciencias Sociales y Humanidades.

Phelan, J. (1985) *Apartheid Media.* Westport, CT: Lawrence Hill.

Ramos, J.M. and Diez, A. (2003) Blending old and new technologies: Mexico's indigenous radio service messages. In B. Girard (ed.) *The One to Watch: Radio, New ICTs and Interactivity* (pp. 180–190). Rome: Food and Agriculture Organization.

Rising voices: Minorities and the future of Soviet and American television (1991) *Media Studies Journal* 5 (4), 203–215.

Rodriguez, A. (1999) *Making Latino News: Race, Language, Class.* Thousand Oaks, CA: Sage.

Rodriguez, C. (2001) *Fissures in the Mediascape: An International Study of Citizen's Media.* Cresskill, NJ: Hampton Press.

Roth, L. (1995) *Something New in the Air.* Montreal: McGill-Queen's University Press.

SABC can't go for broke (2002). *Cape Times,* 18 September, 6.

Savage, B. (1999) *Broadcasting Freedom: Radio, War and the Politics of Race.* Chapel Hill, NC: University of North Carolina Press.

SBS (Special Broadcasting Service) (1979) *Ethnic Broadcasting in Australia.* Sydney: SBS (mimeo).

Sciolino, E. (2004) A new French headache: When is hate on TV illegal? *New York Times,* 9 December, A3.

Siemering, B. (1998) *Community Radio Stations in South Africa: Six Case Studies.* Newlands: Open Society Foundation for South Africa.

Soley, L. and Nichols, J. (1987) *Clandestine Radio Broadcasting.* New York: Praeger.

Solovyova, J. (1999) Russia: Multiethnic radio. *Transitions.* On www at: www.ijt.cz.

Sterngold, J. (1992) This man has dream [*sic*]. It's un-Japanese. *New York Times*, 19 August, p. A4.

Stiles, Mark and associates (1985) *Broadcasting and Canada's Aboriginal Peoples*. Report to the Task Force on Broadcast Policy. Ottawa: Canadian Radio-Television and Telecommunications Commission.

Tillotson, K. (2004) Ethnic TV. *Minneapolis Star Tribune*, 8 January, E3.

Tomaselli, R., Tomaselli, K. and Muller, J. (1985) *Broadcasting in South Africa*. New York: St Martins Press.

Tomlinson, T. (1994) The development of local and religious radio in Norway and Sweden. Ph.D. thesis, University of Minnesota.

UNESCO (1986) *Mass Media and the Minorities*. Paris: UNESCO.

Vargas, L. (1995) *Social Uses and Radio Practices*. Boulder, CO: Westview Press.

Vertovec, S. (1996) Berlin Multikulti: Germany, 'foreigners' and 'world openness'. *New Community* 22 (3), 381–399.

Voss, F. (2001a) Personal interview, Berlin.

Voss, F. (2001b) Radio Multikuturell: Beitraege des Hoerfunks zur Foerderung multikultureller Vielfalt, *ARD Jahrbuch*. Hamburg: Hans Bredow Institut.

Whiteduck Resources Inc. and Consilium (2003) *Northern Native Broadcast Access Program (NNBAP) & Northern Distribution Program (NDP) Evaluation*. Ottawa: Department of Canadian Heritage.

Wilkins, I. and Strydom, H. (1979) *The Broederbond*. New York: Paddington Press.

Withers, C. (1984) *Gaelic in Scotland, 1698–1991*. Edinburgh: John Donald Publishers.

Zambonini, G. (2002). Personal interview, Cologne.

Chapter 8
Minority Languages and the Internet: New Threats, New Opportunities

DANIEL CUNLIFFE

One of Crystal's six postulates for a theory of language revitalisation is that 'an endangered language will progress if its speakers can make use of electronic technology' (Crystal, 2000: 141). Whilst *electronic technology* encompasses a variety of media, including radio and television, more recent Internet-based media are claimed to have a particularly important role to play in the future of minority languages (Buszard-Welcher, 2001). In fact there will often be more minority language material produced on the Internet than in traditional print or audio-visual forms (UNESCO, 2004a). Despite this, Internet-based media has a somewhat ambiguous status with regards to traditional mass media (Morris & Ogan, 1996). For example, the European Charter for Regional or Minority Languages, Article 11 – Media, makes explicit recommendations with reference to television, radio and newspapers but makes no mention of the Internet, or whether these media services can be Internet based.

Any discussion of Internet media, in terms of production or consumption, must be grounded in the realities of access and use. Access to the Internet is far from universal and far down the list of priorities for many communities. Where figures are available, they show huge discrepancies in the numbers of Internet users across the globe, as indicated in Table 8.1.

Table 8.1 Regional variation in Internet use and PC distribution

Region	Internet users per 10,000 inhabitants			PCs per 100 inhabitants
	Average	*Maximum*	*Minimum*	
Africa	147.93	Seychelles 1452.10	Dem. Rep. Congo 9.50	1.38
Americas	2592.71	USA 5513.77	Haiti 96.41	28.95
Asia	674.25	Korea (Rep.) 6034.20	Myanmar 5.64	4.45
Europe	2373.19	Iceland 6747.40	Albania 97.63	21.44
Oceania	3763.99	New Zealand 5262.37	Solomon Islands 49.51	42.40

Source: Based on ITY (2003)

133

There are many dimensions to the 'digital divide' both between nations and within nations, which go beyond simple issues of access and cost (Cawkell, 2001). As digital exclusion tends to follow existing patterns of social exclusion, where minority language communities are already socially excluded, they are also likely to be digitally excluded. There may also be digital divides within communities. There is evidence that in some minority language communities, website production is dominated by young, educated males (UNESCO, 2004a).

Even where there is appropriate access, it is not clear if the Internet will be beneficial or detrimental to the survival of minority languages. Whilst the Internet offers new opportunities for minority language use, it is currently dominated by majority languages in much the same way as are traditional media. A minority language presence is required to meet the needs and aspirations of its online community. However, a successful online community requires both media producers and consumers. The question of whether minority language Internet provision is activist led or is driven by actual consumer demand is an interesting one, but one which is difficult to answer (UNESCO, 2004a).

The benefits of a presence on the Internet may go beyond language use (Eisenlohr, 2004). It may provide a way to challenge perceptions of particular minority languages as being old-fashioned, rural or of low social status. Through association with new media and technology, a minority language can assert its role as a contemporary, living tool.

Internet Media

While it is usual to talk simply of 'the world wide web' or 'the Internet', Internet media offer a variety of different communicative possibilities.

Websites are probably the most common form of Internet-based media. Websites are typically text based, though they often contain images and less commonly animation, sound and video. Web pages and websites can be linked together by hyperlinks, which allow the user to navigate from one to another at the click of a mouse button. Content on the site is controlled by the individual or organisation that owns the site. The user (or 'visitor') is usually purely a consumer of content (e.g. news) or a user of services (e.g. making purchases). Websites on a common theme are sometimes linked together to form a *web ring*. Links are provided so that users can move from one site in the ring to another, jump to a random site on the ring, or choose from an index of sites on the ring. *Portals* are thematic indexes to the Internet, which are another way of providing links to a set of websites that form a related community.

Wikis are communal websites. Members of the community are able to add, modify and delete content on the site. In this way the distinction between user and owner is broken down, arguably leading to a more democratic form of content control.

Blogs or *weblogs* are again similar to websites, however the form of a blog is typically that of a journal or diary, with regular dated entries on a particular theme or themes. Generally a blog is the product of a single owner, though in some cases there may be co-owners or the opportunity for users to respond.

Chat rooms allow members of a community to communicate in real-time using text and occasionally graphics. The content in chat rooms tends not to be archived and is therefore transitory in nature. Chat rooms can be owned by a host who may control community membership.

Bulletin boards (also known as discussion groups, news groups, message forums and a variety of similar names) allow non-real-time, text-based communication. Messages are posted, can be read and can be replied to. Different bulletin boards have specific themes and messages may be vetted by a moderator (manager) to ensure that they are appropriate. Bulletin boards often provide a searchable archive of previous messages. *Email lists* are similar to bulletin boards, except that messages are delivered to the community via email rather than being made available on a central site. Email lists also tend to be archived.

Generally websites, web rings and portals are considered to create *passive communities*, as the majority of users are media consumers. Wikis, chat rooms, bulletin boards and email lists can be considered *active communities* as users have the option of becoming producers as well as consumers. Blogs may fall into either category depending on whether or not users are able to contribute.

There are other forms of communication supported by the Internet, such as instant messaging, which provides real-time person-to-person chat, and video conferencing. There are also other forms of computer-based media that do not use the Internet, such as CD-ROMs. Whilst these technologies are all relevant to minority languages, they fall beyond the scope of this chapter. There are many differences between traditional media forms and Internet media that make Internet media particularly attractive to minority languages and minority communities generally. Typically the Internet is not heavily regulated by the state, people are generally free to establish an Internet presence on whatever topic and in whatever language they choose. Where regulation prevents the expression of particular views, it is usually possible to base this presence in another jurisdiction. The lack of regulation of the Internet raises questions as to its credibility as a source of information. However in some contexts it may be seen as more credible than a mass media that is controlled by the state or by commercial interests (e.g. Wood, 1999: 153).

The establishment of an Internet presence is a far less complicated process than the establishment of, for instance, a television channel. As the state typically does not control or licence the Internet, it is not necessary to show that there is public demand or to campaign for the establishment of an Internet presence. A presence can be established by a motivated individual at a relatively low cost, with a minimum technical knowledge and with access to only basic computer equipment. Internet media may therefore provide an alternative that avoids some of the concerns relating to state support associated with other forms of minority language media (Riggins, 1992: 4).

Once it has been established, it can be accessed by any individual who has use of the Internet (though some states do restrict access to certain parts of the Internet or certain types of content). This low entry threshold offers minority language communities the opportunity to be *producers* of media rather than merely *consumers* of majority language mass media. However, simply establishing a presence on the Internet does not guarantee that it will attract users. One of main failings of the Internet is the difficulty in finding information. Registering the site with portals and search engines (particularly those dedicated to a particular language or community, e.g. Cymru ar y We) and exchanging links with like-minded sites are effective ways of establishing a coherent minority language presence online. Another possibility is to provide minority language versions of existing popular sites (where permitted) or to introduce minority language content into existing sites. For example, Wikipedia, the popular collaboratively authored online encyclopaedia, has versions in a number of minority languages including Occitan, Breton and Welsh. Users have introduced Welsh tags into Flickr, which then act as keywords to describe and facilitate searching for photos.

An Internet presence can be used to deliver content in similar ways to traditional media forms. There are numerous Internet radio stations, newspapers and other publishing ventures. Full Internet-based television is currently still under development, but short, generally low quality video clips are provided on some sites (for example, euskaraz.tv provides five themed channels all through the medium of Basque). The Internet can be seen as a cheap alternative to traditional media (though one which might undermine calls for these media in a minority language) and may also be used to demonstrate that a demand for minority language media exists. However, the real potential of the Internet lies not in the replication of traditional media and the formation of passive communities of minority language media consumers, but in the formation of active communities of collaborative minority language producers. These active communities provide not only the opportunity for people to produce material in their minority language, but also to engage with their community online.

Minority Languages on the Internet

The English language and Western values were predominant during the development of the Internet. Much of the underlying 'philosophy' and technology of the present Internet is still rooted in these cultural and linguistic origins.

Language dominance

In the past, one of the most obvious manifestations of this legacy was the inability to represent non-Latin characters on the Internet. Whilst more modern standards are able to represent a much wider range of characters, the extent to which these standards are supported varies greatly between different software packages and different versions of the same package (Pargman & Palme, 2004). Often minority language communities will only have access to older technology, which is less able to support their language. In many cases, users will not wait for the development of technology capable of supporting their language or for technology that does support their language to become affordable, but will instead adapt their language to suit the available technology. The *Romanisation* of a number of languages has been reported, for example Egyptian Arabic (Warschauer *et al.*, 2002) and Greek (Koutsogiannis & Mitsikopoulou, 2003). Here users of the language have developed unofficial phonetic representations of their language using standard Latin characters, sometimes supplemented by numerical or other characters. This allows them to use older technology that does not support their language in its native form. People's desire to use the technology can drive them to find solutions (albeit unsatisfactory ones) that overcome the technical barriers to using their language online.

Historically the Internet has been dominated by the USA in terms of infrastructure, users and content providers. Exact measurement of Internet content and of users is difficult and any such measurements must be treated with a fair degree of caution. In recent years the proportion of the online population who are native English speakers has waned and was estimated to be just over one-third in 2004 (Global Reach, 2004). Despite the continuing diversification of online languages, these estimates suggest that almost 95% of users were native speakers of just 11 languages (English, Chinese, Japanese, Spanish, German, Korean, French, Portuguese, Italian, Russian and Dutch).

Estimates for online populations of minority language speakers are hard to come by and figures for minority languages and stateless nations are often simply included within those of the appropriate state. The figures that are produced for language use online are often commercially motivated and minority languages typically only represent small markets. The Global Reach (2004) figures include an estimate of 3.4 million native Catalan speakers online, but no figures for native Welsh speakers (which is a much smaller language community). Where figures are available, the basis on which they have been estimated is often overly simplistic, for instance being based on the proportion of minority language speakers within a state. Estimates like this fail to recognise differences in use between minority and majority language communities or between different regions within a state. Radoll (2004) reports that computer and Internet use by Aboriginal people in Australia is less than half that of non-indigenous Australians. The difference is far greater in remote regions of Australia where only 1% of Aboriginal people have Internet access compared to 23% of non-indigenous Australians. A report produced in 2002 showed that number of adults using the Internet and email for personal use in Wales was approximately half that of the UK average (Egg, 2002). Figures for 2004/2005 produced by Beaufort Research Limited for the Welsh Consumer Council (cited in Thomas & Lewis, 2006) suggest that Internet use in Wales has plateaued at around 44% of the population, while the UK average continues to rise. In some areas of Wales the proportion of people with Internet access in their home was actually lower in 2005 than it was in 2002. However, little difference is reported between Internet use among Welsh speakers and non-Welsh speakers.

The Internet brings languages and speakers into contact in a very direct way, unlike traditional media, and it is not just minority languages that feel threatened by English language dominance of the Internet. English remains the de facto lingua franca of the online world. In 2002 it was estimated that just over 70% of website content was in English and that 55% of websites originated from the USA (OCLC, 2002). English is often used when different language communities meet online, even when none of them speak it as a first language (Durham, 2003). Despite this, where sufficient online content exists, national languages appear robust in resisting English. However, where content does not exist there may be increased use of English by non-native speakers in both consumption (e.g. reading websites) and production (e.g. email), thereby contributing to language shift (Kelly-Holmes, 2004). The concept of languages being 'information rich' and 'information poor' with regard to online content and services is an important aspect of the digital divide for minority languages. Even when minority language content is available on the Internet, the software used to access or create that content is often in English or the majority language, implicitly reinforcing the dominant status of these languages.

The linguistic diversity of the world is poorly reflected on the Internet and estimates suggest that 90% of the world's languages are simply not represented (UNESCO, 2004b). Again estimates of minority language content are fragmentary and should be treated with caution. Estimates from 2000 (Vilaweb, cited in Pastore, 2000) suggested that 0.14% of web pages were in Catalan and 0.01% in Basque, but gave no figures for Welsh even though the language has slightly more speakers than Basque and a healthy online presence. Langer (2001) suggests that between 1999 and 2001 the number of web pages (per speaker) in Basque almost doubled, in Catalan more than doubled, in Galician increased by almost four times and in Welsh by almost five times. The bare figures give little insight into the content and purpose of the pages or how much they are actually used. The absence of detailed figures and analysis of online minority language presence makes it difficult to define what constitutes a successful online presence and what the stages are in achieving such a presence.

Etiquette and policies

In addition to the quantitative dominance of English and other majority languages, it is important to recognise that social aspects of dominance are found on the Internet, as in the real world. There are indications that the imbalance in the relative power and authority of majority and minority languages is maintained on the Internet, particularly when language communities meet. The use of a minority language online is often perceived as a political statement, particularly where minority language speakers speak the majority language as well (Fernandez, 2001). The use of the majority language or English may be seen as being apolitical and neutral, even where that language has formerly been the language of colonisation (Wright, 1996).

Other arguments against minority language use are based on issues of courtesy and netiquette (the informal 'rules' of Internet etiquette), suggesting that it is rude or even against the spirit of the Internet to use a language that not everyone understands. Ostler (1999) quotes a message posted to the Teachers of Celtic Languages email list by the moderators:

'Please show the courtesy to subscribers to this mailing list who do not speak a specific or any Celtic language – include a short summary in English of your posting.' The issue of translation as a form of courtesy imposes an additional burden on those who wish to use their minority language and encourages bilingual users to use only the majority language. Posting only in the majority language is never seen as discourteous.

Explicit exclusion of minority languages also occurs, arguably as a result of the lack of regulation of the Internet. Ostler (1999) gives the example of a message posted by the manager of the Peace in Ireland message board: 'This board is designed for English speakers and Gaelic postings are not allowed [...] posts in Gaelic [even with an English translation] will be removed without further recourse to the person who posted it.' A similar case is reported by Atkinson and Powell (1996) where a message board that had previously welcomed Welsh language use, reversed the policy when the board management was taken over by a non-Welsh speaker who was unable to moderate Welsh language messages. Following complaints by both Welsh speaking and non-Welsh speaking users and intervention by the Welsh Language Board, a bilingual moderator was appointed.

Issues of ownership of the media and control over language use do not disappear on the Internet, but there is far greater opportunity for users to create alternative places to use their language. In the context of bulletin boards, Fernandez (2001: 35) suggests that 'positive action' in the form of setting a minority language only policy is necessary in order to have any real online exchange in a minority language. This approach may be appropriate for strong minority language communities with sufficient numbers of online speakers, or when the topic is only of relevance to minority language speakers. However, where minority language speakers are competent bilinguals, segregation between the majority and minority languages raises concerns. If the majority language community has more participants or more active participants, this may encourage minority language speakers to give up their use of the minority language and move to the majority language. The separation of languages in this way may also be seen as legitimising the exclusion of minority languages, and will reduce the visibility of the minority language to both speakers and non-speakers. An alternative to linguistic segregation is to create environments that support online communities using more than one language. This might be achieved through the provision of translation facilities, either automatically (Climent et al., 2003) or manually (Cunliffe & Harries, 2005) depending on the characteristics of the community and the availability of automatic translation facilities (Thomas et al., 2001).

Cultural integrity

The transformation of a language to the Internet will typically decontextualise the language from its traditional cultural and physical context. It is one thing to bring a language to the Internet and quite another to bring a culture. Genres of traditional forms of communication and constraints on delivery may not sit easily with those provided in an electronic environment (Hinton, 2001). However, Wood (1999: 158) suggests that certain rhetorical possibilities inherent in Internet media may actually be better suited to traditional cultural practices and forms of expression than print and broadcast media.

The Internet is still predominantly a textual medium, so where a language has no written form, a limited literary tradition or low levels of literacy, the Internet may further marginalise minority languages (Kelly-Holmes, 2004). The multimedia capabilities of the Internet offer some possibilities for languages in these situations and in particular provide languages without a written form an alternative to reduction to text. However, even though audio can capture an oration and video can capture movements, gestures and facial expressions, these multimedia forms are a reduction from a live telling or performance and can be seen as an erosion of the true form of the language.

One of the underlying 'philosophies' of the Internet is that of freedom of knowledge. This attitude towards control over knowledge is often at odds with cultural values. It is easy to assume that these will typically be 'traditional' cultures, but it is important to recognise that even in 'modern' Western cultures there will be certain types of control applied to the possession or misrepresentation of knowledge, for instance under privacy, defamation, obscenity or blasphemy laws. Traditional cultures may have similar controls (though these are rarely protected by law), for instance concerning who may possess certain knowledge, or how and when that knowledge may be used (Monroe, 2002). Making knowledge available on the Internet may remove these controls and undermine a culture's social structures. It also raises the possibility of the misappropriation or misuse of a culture's knowledge by outsiders. Whilst intellectual property rights do apply on the Internet, they are difficult and expensive to enforce, and they often do not fit well with non-Western concepts of 'ownership' where cultural artefacts and knowledge may be owned collectively (Burk, 2004). There is also the possibility that in the process of digitising cultural property it may become commercialised (perhaps to pay for hardware, digitisation or for maintaining an archive) and that the originating community may subsequently become excluded, for instance due to cost or limited access (Smith, 1997).

Related to the issue of ownership is the issue of authenticity. While users may often have concerns about the identity and qualifications of Internet authors, a particular concern for minority communities is that of misrepresentation. One form of misrepresentation is when stereotypical, misleading or incorrect information is provided about a minority culture. One of the reasons that a minority community may choose to have an Internet presence is to assert its own cultural identity rather than have its online identity shaped by others (Martin, 1995). A second form is when someone purports to be a member of a minority community and then exploits that fake identity or fake 'indigenous knowledge' (Anderson, 2003; Martin, 1995; Monroe, 2002). Even when this is detected, it can be difficult to get it stopped. Martin (1995) reports that Native American protestors were barred from a chat room when they tried to prevent the chat room's host pedalling fake Native American spirituality and passing himself off as a Native American. When the chat room and its host were eventually replaced, the hosts of the replacement Native American Chat Room were also apparently not Native Americans (though they did not claim to be) again raising issues of authenticity and control over cultural identity.

Perhaps a less obvious issue of identity is the extent to which domain names (such as '.uk' or '.com') embody a particular world view. The generic top level domains, such as '.com' were originally intended to (implicitly) denote sites from the USA while other states were meant to use an explicit identifier, such as '.uk'. State identifiers are problematic for stateless nations and sub-national regions (Steinberg & McDowell, 2003). The '.uk' country code for example, explicitly identifies the United Kingdom as a state, whilst the individual nations (England, Northern Ireland, Scotland and Wales) have no official domain names even within the '.uk' domain. However, in New Zealand the '.nz' country code has a sub-domain '.iwi.nz' which is explicitly reserved for the Maori tribes (Smith, 1997) and in the USA the '.nsn.us' domain has been established for Native American tribal sites (Anderson, 2003). More recently, ICANN (the Internet Corporation for Assigned Names and Numbers), has approved the creation of a new top level domain '.cat' for the Catalan linguistic and cultural community (Gerrand, 2006). While this may provide a useful precedent for other minority languages with large numbers of speakers, it is unlikely that smaller minority languages will meet ICANN's criteria.

Internationalisation, Localisation and Indigenous Production

When faced with issues of language diversity, the typical approach taken by software and web developers has been to *internationalise* or *localise* existing products or content. According to Nielsen (2000: 315), internationalisation refers to the use of a single design regardless of language or culture, while localisation refers to the creation of different version for different locales. Internationalisation thus retains the original language (typically the majority language or English) but in a simpler form that can be understood by non-native speakers, and culturally specific references are removed, forming a 'culturally neutral' product. Localisation involves the creation of a local version, including translation of content and the introduction of local culturally specific references and design elements. Nielsen also notes that, for the web, internationalisation tends to be the preferred approach as there may be insufficient users to justify a localised version.

Where a minority language exists alongside a dominant majority language the commercial argument for minority language services, content and software is often hard to make. Majority language provision will typically meet the needs of the majority of users, including minority language speakers who will tend to have some majority language skills. In the absence of significant commercial benefit or legal obligation, arguments for minority language provision often have to be made on social grounds. However, many organisations will not have any social or ethical commitment to a minority language. Even where there is some commitment or obligation to make minority language provision, there will often be a lack of additional resources required to develop the provision. This can result in partial or poorly implemented minority language provision, or simple translations of majority language provision. A translation-based approach to minority language provision may fail to recognise cultural differences, such as in the conceptual categories used to understand the world, in social organisation or in the genres available. Bunte and Franklin (2001), for instance, describe the translation of a tribal constitution from English into Paiute where, in addition to the development of appropriate terminology, it was necessary to map the hierarchical organisation of English language legal documents to the linear narrative form used in formal Paiute discourse. Software generally reflects cultural conventions and social practices of the place in which it is developed. Even when software has been localised, it is often only a very superficial process, changing the surface elements, but not considering the underlying assumptions that are built into the way the program operates. Abdelnour-Nocera and Hall (2004) suggest that a more sophisticated consideration of localisation is necessary in order to recognise the importance of cultural differences between the producers and users of software which may make localised software unusable. However, even a more sophisticated form of localisation is likely to be based on translation, rendering the minority language purely a language of consumption rather than a language of production and innovation (Cronin, 1998).

Where the necessary skills exist within a language community, there is the possibility for *indigenous production* of both content and software as an alternative to internationalisation or localisation. In this approach the minority language community creates from scratch or localises content and software itself. Meddal, for example, provide a wide range of software in Welsh. Other Welsh language initiatives include bulletin board facilities, maes-e, and an email service, Sgwarnog. Indigenous production has the benefit that it can better suit the needs of the minority culture, creating or adapting content and software that accord with the needs and cultural practices of that community. The motivation behind indigenous production is often a commitment to the language community rather than commercial interests. However, the lack of a commercial return will sometimes mean that the production process is slow, or that the end product is not of the same quality as a commercial product.

The Role of the Internet for Minority Languages

As resources for the development of minority language provision are often limited, it is important to consider the range of possibilities provided by the Internet and the balance between resource expenditure and benefit. The Internet can potentially play a number of different roles for a minority language community. The appropriateness and importance of any particular role will vary, depending on the local context. Some of the roles will be more relevant for organisations, while others can be achieved by motivated individuals.

Where there are few or no speakers of a language, a web-based archive of documents and recordings can be created. For example, the Formosan Language Archive contains annotated texts with audio, geographic information and bibliographical databases (Zeitoun et al., 2003). This is a useful resource if it is decided to re-establish a language. Many documents or recordings may already exist in other collections, digitisation and indexing will provide a more accessible and usable, unified resource. A web ring could be used to link existing online resources. Community facilities could be added so that those interested or involved in the creation of the archive can share information. Such an archive could be extended to include a wider range of cultural artefacts, thereby recording more of the context of the language, preserving and possibly showcasing the wider aspects of a minority culture.

There is also a role for the Internet in language learning. This could be in the form of web-based materials in both text and audio-visual form. A simple example of this for Nawat can be found online (Ward & van Genabith, 2003). A more sophisticated site could also make use of chat rooms or bulletin boards to support learners and to provide them with opportunities to practise the language or to interact with tutors. Facilities such as these have played a role in the revitalisation of Hawaiian (Warschauer, 1998). Interactivity could also be used to reinforce the learning and provide assessment. The BBC Wales Learn Welsh site provides a variety of resources, including lessons, a dictionary, spelling and grammar checkers, games, a message board and more besides. Clwb Malu Cachu, which uses chat rooms, blogs and email lists in addition to providing a range of resources and tips for Welsh learners, is a good example of what a dedicated and sufficiently skilled individual can achieve.

An online community can be created for those faced with physical isolation from other speakers of the minority language. Even where speakers exist, the opportunities for using the language may be limited. Through the use of chat rooms, message forums and blogs, new opportunities for language use can be created, even if they are limited to textual forms. An example of a successful minority language bulletin board is maes-e in which a large number of Welsh speakers discuss a range of topics from the Welsh language and politics through to sport and computers. Morfablog covers a range of topics but in blog form. Whilst a precise definition of 'community' is difficult and questions remain as to relative merits and drawbacks of real-world and virtual communities, the potential benefits for minority language communities appear to go beyond simply providing opportunities for language use. Mitra (1996) reports on the use of the Internet to create new senses of community where traditional identities have been disrupted by migration and immigration. Similar points, based on the significance of community in Wales, are made by Mackay and Powell (1998) and with regard to the Welsh diaspora by Parsons (2000).

The Internet can also be used to bring a minority culture to the attention of a wider audience and to mobilise activism at a national or international level (Tekwani, 2003). For example, Cymdeithas yr Iaith Gymraeg and Cymuned are organisations that use the Internet as part of their campaigns in support of the Welsh language. It is also possible to bring minority language communities together to share their experiences and information, for instance, Eurolang is an online press agency for news relating to minority language issues.

Where a minority language is in a relatively healthy state, the aim should be to normalise the use of that language online and to extend the domains of minority language use. This involves providing a range of services and information through the minority language that are viable alternatives to majority language services and information providers. For instance, the Welsh Books Council runs an online bookshop, gwales, the site not only allows users to swap between Welsh and English whilst using the site, it also allows registered users to set their language preferences for using the site and for receiving email correspondence relating to the orders they place. This form of presence can serve to *facilitate* or *promote* minority language use. It can *facilitate* the use of a minority language simply by making information available in that language. A site of this type will passively support minority language use by providing quality minority language content and by adopting a design that reflects likely patterns of use by minority language speakers. However, it can go further than this and actively *promote* the use of a minority language by providing both information and language support. In addition to facilitating use of a minority language, a site of this type will include content and adopt a design that actively promotes, encourages and supports the use of the minority language. For example, the BBC Wales Vocab/Geirfa facility is a tool that provides English translations of Welsh words on the BBC Cymru website.

Although there are numerous possibilities, it is not clear how a minority language can make best use of the technologies available and which are the most effective in maintaining and revitalising minority languages. When putting minority language content onto the Internet, should the aim be for quantity, quality or cultural significance, should it focus on the historical or the contemporary, should it be a language archive or an online community? Many of the initiatives may be individual ventures developed in a piecemeal fashion, others may have substantial backing from the community or state. Ideally these Internet-based initiatives should be coordinated, not just with each other, but with other initiatives, as part of an integrated language plan.

Conclusion

The origins of the Internet and its early adoption by majority languages and in particular English have led to a dominance that poses a threat to minority languages. These dominant languages tend to have additional advantages in terms of infrastructure, economic power, and state commitment to the creation of e-societies. The widespread use of English in the real world, as a first and second language, and its dominant position, even among majority languages on the Internet, has established it as the lingua franca of the Internet.

Minority cultures and languages should not be viewed simply as victims of the Internet or as passive recipients of Internet technology, services and content. Instead it should be recognised that they have the potential to be active shapers of this technology, able to create their own tools, adapt existing tools to the local needs and to create culturally authentic, indigenous Internet media. A culture interacts with a technology and that interaction changes both the culture and the technology. The Internet does not necessarily need to be viewed as being in opposition to traditional cultures, values or minority languages. A real opportunity exists for those languages that have the resources and the determination to make the transition to the Internet.

Researching the effects of the Internet on minority languages is difficult and it is not yet clear how best to utilise the Internet to maintain or revitalise minority languages. It appears obvious that many minority languages will never make a successful transition to the Internet and that some may consciously choose not to in order to preserve their language and culture. For others the Internet will remain an irrelevance due to lack of appropriate access or more pressing social needs. In some cases the Internet will lead to online language shift and even strong national languages with large numbers of speakers may find themselves to be minority languages on the Internet. The extent to which this will affect the real-world use of these languages remains to be seen.

References

Abdelnour-Nocera, J.L. and Hall, P. (2004) Global software, local voices: The social construction of usefulness of ERP systems. In F. Sudweeks and C. Ess (eds) *Proceedings of the 4th International Conference on Cultural Attitudes towards Technology and Communication (CATaC 2004)*, Karlstad, Sweden, June/July (pp. 29–42). Murdoch: Murdoch University.

Anderson, C.G. (2003) American Indian tribal websites: A review and comparison. *The Electronic Library* 21 (5), 450–455.

Atkinson, K. and Powell, T. (1996) Welsh-language ban in 'Wales'. *Planet* 116, 81–84.

Bunte, P. and Franklin, R. (2001) Language revitalisation on the San Juan Paiute community and the role of a Paiute constitution. In L. Hinton and K. Hale (eds) *The Green Book of Language Revitalisation in Practice* (pp. 255–262). London: Academic Press.

Burk, D.L. (2004) Privacy and property in the global datasphere: International dominance of off-the-shelf models for information control. In F. Sudweeks and C. Ess (eds) *Proceedings of the 4th International Conference on Cultural Attitudes towards Technology and Communication (CATaC 2004), Karlstad, Sweden, June/July* (pp. 363–373). Murdoch: Murdoch University.

Buszard-Welcher, L. (2001) Can the web help save my language? In L. Hinton and K. Hale (eds) *The Green Book of Language Revitalisation in Practice* (pp. 331–345). London: Academic Press.

Cawkell, T. (2001) Sociotechnology: The digital divide. *Journal of Information Science* 27 (1), 55–60.

Climent, S., Moré, J., Oliver, A. *et al.* (2003) Bilingual newsgroups in Catalonia: A challenge for machine translation. *Journal of Computer Mediated Communication* 9 (1). On www at: http://jcmc.indiana.edu/vol9/issue1/climent.html

Cronin, M. (1998) The cracked looking glass of servants: Translation and minority languages. *Translator: Studies in Intercultural Communication* 4, 145–162.

Crystal, D. (2000) *Language Death*. Cambridge: Cambridge University Press.

Cunliffe, D. and Harries, R. (2005) Promoting minority-language use in a bilingual online community. *The New Review of Hypermedia and Multimedia* 11 (2), 157–179.

Durham, M. (2003) Language choice on a Swiss mailing list. *Journal of Computer Mediated Communication* 9 (1). On www at: http://jcmc.indiana.edu/vol9/issue1/durham.html

Egg (2002) *Embracing Technology: The Egg Report.* On www at: http://www.mori.com/polls/2002/pdf/egg-feb.pdf

Eisenlohr, P. (2004) Language revitalisation and new technologies: Cultures of electronic mediation and the refiguring of communities. *Annual Review of Anthropology* 33, 21–45.

Fernandez, L. (2001) Patterns of linguistic discrimination in internet discussion forums. *Mercator Media Forum* 5, 22–41.

Gerrand, P. (2006) Cultural diversity in cyberspace: The Catalan campaign to win the new .cat top level domain. *First Monday* 11 (1). On www at: http://www.firstmonday.org/issues/issue11_1/gerrand/index.html

Global Reach (2004) *Global internet statistics (by language).* On www at: http://global-reach.biz/globstats/

Hinton, L. (2001) New writing systems. In L. Hinton and K. Hale (eds) *The Green Book of Language Revitalisation in Practice* (pp. 239–250). London: Academic Press.

ITU (International Telecommunication Union) (2003) *Internet Indicators: Hosts, Users and Number of PCs.* On www at: http://www.itu.int/ITU-D/ict/statistics at glance/Internet03.pdf

Kelly-Holmes, H. (2004) An analysis of the language repertoires of students in higher education and their language choices on the internet (Ukraine, Poland, Macedonia, Italy, France, Tanzania, Oman and Indonesia). *International Journal on Multicultural Societies* 6 (1), 52–75. On www at: www.unesco.org/shs/ijms/vol6/issue1/art3

Koutsogiannis, D. and Mitsikopoulou, B. (2003) Greeklish and Greekness: Trends and discourses of 'glocalness'. *Journal of Computer Mediated Communication* 9 (1). On www at: http://jcmc.indiana.edu/vol9/issue1/kouts_mits.html

Langer, S. (2001) Natural languages and the world wide web. In *Bulag. Revue Annuelle* (pp. 89–100). France: Presses Universitaires Franc-Comtoises. On www at: http://www.cis.uni-muenchen.de/people/langer/veroeffentlichungen/bulag.pdf

Mackay, H. and Powell, T. (1998) Connecting Wales: The internet and national identity. In B.D. Loader (ed.) *Cyberspace Divide: Equality, Agency and Policy in the Information Society* (pp. 203–216). London: Routledge.

Martin, G. (1995) Internet Indian wars. *Wired* 3 (12). On www at: http://www.wired.com/wired/archive/3.12/martin_pr.html

Mitra, A. (1996) Nations and the internet: The case of a national newsgroup, 'soc.culture.indian'. *Convergence* 2 (1), 44–75.

Monroe, B. (2002) The internet in Indian country. *Computers and Composition* 19, 285–296.

Morris, M. and Ogan, C. (1996) The internet as mass medium. *Journal of Computer-Mediated Communication* 1 (4). On www at: http://jcmc.indiana.edu/vol1/issue4/morris.html

Nielsen, J. (2000) *Designing Web Usability*. Indianapolis: New Riders.

OCLC (Online Computer Library Center) (2002) *Country and Language Statistics*. On www at: http://www.oclc.org/research/projects/archive/wcp/stats/intnl.htm

Ostler, N. (1999) Fighting words: As the world gets smaller, minority languages struggle to stake their claim. *Language International* 11 (2), 38–39, 45.

Pargman, D. and Palme, J. (2004) Linguistic standardisation on the Internet. In F. Sudweeks and C. Ess (eds) *Proceedings of the 4th International Conference on Cultural Attitudes towards Technology and Communication (CATaC 2004), Karlstad, Sweden, June/July* (pp. 385–388). Murdoch: Murdoch University.

Parsons, W. (2000) Becoming a diaspora: The Welsh experience from Beulah Land to cyber-Cymru. In A.J. Kershen (ed.) *Language, Labour and Migration* (pp. 92–117). Aldershot: Ashgate Publishing Ltd.

Pastore, M. (2000) *Web Pages by Language*. On www at http://www.clickz.com/stats/big_picture/demographics/article.php/408521

Radoll, P.J. (2004) Protecting copyrights on the Internet: A cultural perspective from indigenous Australia. In F. Sudweeks and C. Ess (eds) *Proceedings of the 4th International Conference on Cultural Attitudes towards Technology and Communication (CATaC 2004), Karlstad, Sweden, June/July* (pp. 339–348). Murdoch: Murdoch University.

Riggins, S.H. (ed.) (1992) *Ethnic Minority Media: An International Perspective*. London: Sage.

Smith, A.G. (1997) Fishing with new nets: Maori internet information resources and implications of the Internet for indigenous peoples. In *Proceedings of the 7th Annual Conference of the Internet Society* (INET '97), *Kuala Lumpur, Malaysia*. On www at: http://www.isoc.org/inet97/proceedings/E1/E1_1.HTM

Steinberg, P.E. and McDowell, S.D. (2003) Mutiny on the bandwidth: The semiotics of statehood in the internet domain name registries of Pitcairn Island and Niue. *New Media & Society* 5 (1), 47–67.

Tekwani, S. (2003) The Tamil diaspora, Tamil militancy, and the Internet. In K.C. Ho, R. Kluver and K.C.C. Yang (eds) *Asia.com: Asia Encounters the Internet* (pp. 175–192). New York: Routledge Curzon.

Thomas, J. and Lewis, J. (2006) 'Coming out of a mid-life crisis'?: The past, present and future audiences for Welsh Language Broadcasting. *Cyfrwng* 3, 7–40.

Thomas, N., King, A. and Jones, E.H.G. (2001) Machine translation and the Internet. *Mercator Media Forum* 5, 84–98.
UNESCO (2004a) *UNESCO Sponsored Research Finds WWW Fracturing into Language Communities*. On www at: http://portal.unesco.org/ci/en/ev.php-URL_ID=17439&URL_DO=DO_TOPIC&URL_SECTION=201.html
UNESCO (2004b) *Endangered Languages*. On www at: http://portal.unesco.org/culture/en/ev.php-URL_ID=8270&URL_DO=DO_TOPIC&URL_SECTION=201.html
Ward, M. and van Genabith, J. (2003) CALL for endangered languages: Challenges and rewards. *Computer Assisted Language Learning* 16 (2/3), 233–258.
Warschauer, M. (1998) Technology and indigenous language revitalisation: Analysing the experience of Hawai'i. *The Canadian Modern Language Review/La Revue Canadienne des Langues Vivante* 55 (1), 139–159.
Warschauer, M., Said, G. and Zohry, A. (2002) Language choice online: Globalisation and identity in Egypt. *Journal of Computer-Mediated Communication* 7 (4). On www at: http://jcmc.indiana.edu/vol7/issue4/warschauer.html
Wood, H. (1999) *Displacing Natives: The Rhetorical Production of Hawai'i*. Lanham, MD: Rowman and Littlefield Publishers Inc.
Wright, H.K. (1996) E-mail in African studies. *Convergence* 2 (1), 19–29.
Zeitoun, E., Yu, C-h. and Weng, C-x. (2003) The Formosan Language Archive: Development of a multimedia tool to salvage the languages and oral traditions of the indigenous tribes of Taiwan. *Oceanic Linguistics* 44 (1), 218–232.

Websites

BBC Wales Learn Welsh: *http://www.bbc.co.uk/wales/learnwelsh/index.shtml*
BBC Wales Vocab/Geirfa: *http://www.bbc.co.uk/cymru/vocab/*
Clwb Malu Cachu: *http://www.clwbmalucachu.co.uk/*
Cymdeithas yr Iaith Gymraeg: *http://cymdeithas.com/*
Cymru ar y We: *http://www.cymruarywe.org/*
Cymuned: *http://www.cymuned.org/*
Eurolang: *http://eurolang.net/*
European Charter for Regional or Minority Languages: *http://conventions.coe.int/Treaty/en/Treaties/HTML/148.htm*
euskaraz.tv: *http://www.euskaraz.tv/*
Flickr: *http://www.flickr.com/*
Formosan Language Archive: *http://formosan.sinica.edu.tw/*
gwales: *http://www.gwales.com/*
maes-e: *http://maes-e.com/*
Meddal: *http://www.meddal.com/*
Morfablog: *http://morfablog.com/*
Nawat language learning courseware: *http://www.compapp.dcu.ie/~mward/nawat.html*
Sgwarnog: *http://www.sgwarnog.com/*
Wikipedia: *http://www.wikipedia.org/*

Chapter 9

Linguistic Normalisation and Local Television in the Basque Country

EDORTA ARANA, PATXI AZPILLAGA AND BEATRIZ NARBAIZA

Local television in the Basque Country has seen major transformations in recent years. In the 1990s there was some hesitant progress, with the promotion of Euskara (the Basque language) as one of its main features. But more recently, the entry of the big Spanish communications groups into the sector, coupled with the Spanish state's attempts to establish a new regulatory framework, have significantly changed the situation. While it is true that local television represents only a very small part of the Basque media system, analysis of its development allows us to review the complex relationship between the media and the process of 'normalisation' of Euskara (for a discussion of normalisation, see the Introduction by Cormack (Chapter 1), and Chapter 10 by Maria Corominas Piulats). This is a story marked by ebbs and flows that reflect the powerful political tensions affecting the process of linguistic normalisation, as well as the changing conditions – political, technological and economic – within which the media operate.

The general situation in which Euskara finds itself has seen marked improvements over the last 25 years. Its presence in the media is today better than ever and the work undertaken by the media whose task it is to publish and broadcast in Euskara has largely contributed to bringing this about. The horizon is, however, by no means cloud-free, and the situation of local television stations today dramatically illustrates the difficult conditions Euskara still faces in the media.

Local media, due to their closeness to the general public and the centrality of their role in the community, have produced very positive experiences in the Basque Country in relation to linguistic normalisation. This is certainly the case if we look at the local press, which has experienced significant expansion in recent years, to a point where Euskara is today practically in a hegemonic position when compared to the Spanish language. When it comes to television, however, pressure from the big communications groups, and the partial and fragmented attempts at regulation by the Basque authorities, combined with the absence of clear communications guidelines in relation to linguistic normalisation policies, may in the end put severe limits on the possibilities inherent in the local context.

Overview of the Basque Country and Euskara

The Basque Country is the territory that is historically, ethnically and culturally Basque. The Spanish and French may call only a portion of the country the Basque Country (País Vasco, Pays Basque) and not the whole nation. Nevertheless, Basque people conceive of their country as embracing the area of the traditional seven provinces: Bizkaia, Gipuzkoa, Araba and Nafarroa on the Spanish side, and Lapurdi, Nafarroa Beherea and Zuberoa on the French side. These provinces are divided between three administrative structures. Two are within the Spanish state: the Basque Autonomous Community (formed by Araba, Bizkaia and Gipuzkoa) and the Autonomous Community of Navarre (Nafarroa). The three provinces within the French state are not autonomous. They form, along with Béarn, the French *département* of Pyrénées Atlantiques (capital Pau, in Béarn), which is part of the region of Aquitaine (with Bordeaux as its capital). The Basque Country is a small nation: just 20,864 sq. km and 2.9 million people. Only 834,000 (29%) of them speak Basque. Almost all of these are bilingual, most speaking Spanish (721,000), and the rest French.

Euskara is, then, a minority language not only within Spain and France but also within the Basque Country itself, where just a section of the population know and use it. It is also a *minoritised* language, that is to say, it has gradually been pushed by the Spanish and French languages, via mechanisms of domination and linguistic substitution, into the fringes and restricted in its use and its social role to increasingly smaller geographical spaces and to mainly oral and informal spheres and forms of expression (Odriozola, 2004: 62–67). Nevertheless, it has retained great symbolic value. In fact, Basque nationalism has transformed Euskara into the central referent for defining Basque identity, in place of other factors that might have proved more controversial or exclusive, such as concepts of race or ethnic group (Amezaga, 1995: 121–124).

From the 1960s onwards, linked to the political processes that were in play in the Spanish Basque Country (the repression instigated by the Franco regime that resulted in national and social resistance and rebellion), there was a significant shared awareness of the importance of recovering Basque culture and signs of identity, accompanied by a powerful social mobilisation whose demands centred around Euskara. This combination of consciousness and mobilisation, though initially championed and supported by nationalism, managed to incorporate increasingly broader sectors of society and, even more importantly, managed to transcend the purely symbolic and identity-related dimension of the language.

Today, beyond the confines of political positions, there is a significant social consensus in the Basque Country regarding the need to extend knowledge and use of Euskara throughout the population, and also a disposition, shared by the majority, to advance towards a bilingual society – even if the precise form such a bilingual society would take is not yet completely clear. For many nationalists, it would mean that *all* citizens would know and use Basque, along with Spanish or French. For a good number of non-nationalists, however, it would simply signify the right of Basque-speakers to use their language whenever they wanted to and to carry on their social life in Euskara. Thus, according to the sociolinguistic survey[1] commissioned periodically by the Government of the Basque Autonomous Community (CAPV), whose latest findings relate to 2001, 45.4% of the population over 15 years old are in favour of, or very much in favour of, the promotion of Euskara, 34.5% take no position either for or against, and only 20.1% are against the language.

Two important features emerge from this survey: first, the limited size of the Basque-speaking population, both in relative and in absolute terms; second, there are still important differences between territories, such as the 10.4% bilingual population in Navarre as compared to 29.4% in the CAPV, or, from a more localised perspective, the figure of 8.8% in the urban area of Lapurdi (the urban triangle formed by Baiona–Anglet–Miarritze) as against Gipuzkoa's 48%, Araba's 13.4% or Bizkaia's 22.4%. A more detailed analysis that also took local spaces into account would reveal even wider territorial differences, ranging from populations that are practically 100% bilingual, even in municipalities of a significant size, to population groups where the bilingual component is around 1%, located in more urban environments that border on other communities. From the point of view of linguistic policy, this means that the role of local communities is extremely important.

In recent years, progress regarding knowledge of the language has been positive in overall terms, with a 3.1% increase in the bilingual population between 1991 and 2001. However, this general statistic conceals a very sharp negative development in the French Basque Country, where the Basque-speaking population dropped by 8.4%, while there is a situation of near stagnation in Navarre with an increase of just under 0.8%. The overall positive result, therefore, reflects progress in the CAPV, where the increase in the bilingual population amounted to 5.3%.

These statistics reveal the existence of a direct relation between the legal status of Euskara, the level of institutional involvement in its promotion and development, and advances in knowledge of the language. Indeed, Euskara has held shared official status throughout the entirety of the CAPV since 1979, although this masks a situation of striking legal inequality between the two languages. In effect, the CAPV's Statute of Autonomy recognises that citizens of the region have the *right* to know Euskara and to express themselves in that language in the same way and in the same spheres as is the case with Spanish. However, the Spanish Constitution lays down that it is *compulsory* to know Spanish within the entire state territory, including, of course, the CAPV (Odriozola, 2004: 178–189). Euskara has also had official status within Navarre since 1982, though this applies to only a small part of its territory. There are three linguistic zones within Navarre: Basque-speaking (north and north-east), mixed (the capital and the central area), and non-Basque-speaking (south). Euskara is recognised as an official language alongside Spanish in the Basque-speaking area, in the same way as in the CAPV. It has a special status in the mixed zone and is not recognised in the rest of the territory. However over recent years restrictions have been introduced by the government of Navarre regarding the treatment of Euskara for reasons that are of a purely political nature. In the French Basque Country, by contrast, no kind of official recognition of Euskara exists. It is no accident that by 2006 France was the only state in the EU still not to have ratified the European Charter for Regional or Minority Languages. Furthermore, in the CAPV there is a complex legal and institutional network associated with the promotion of Euskara. In Navarre and the French Basque Country such structures are either weak or non-existent.

The principal base for the general expansion of knowledge of Euskara has been, without a doubt, the educational system. It was the first objective of the official language policies that began to be implemented in the 1980s and also of the social movements that, from the 1960s onwards, worked for the development of Euskara and Basque culture.[2] Thus, for the academic year 2003–2004, out of the total number of students in the CAPV within the non-university system, 70.66% were following bilingual programmes,[3] while the percentage rose to 84% for those in the primary education sector. Even in Navarre and the French Basque Country, despite the difficult institutional and legal conditions, there is a growing demand for bilingual education, reflected (for the school year 2001–2002) by a 21.1% figure for primary education in the French Basque Country and 25.4% in Navarre.

However Euskara is encountering major barriers to its penetration of other levels of the educational system such as vocational training and university education, and in fields such as the media, which, along with education, have constituted the prime areas for institutional and social intervention. Linguistic normalisation has been one of the main principles that has guided the implementation of these policies. Based on the recognition of the same rights for both Basque-speakers and Spanish or French-speakers, not only in their relation with institutions but as well in their personal and social life, normalisation would mean giving both languages the same official status. As we have already seen, that only happens in the CAPV and in a small part of Navarre. But if official status is the legal umbrella that better allows the implementation of protection and promotion policies for Euskara, what can the practical normalisation objectives of such policies be, given the enormous difference between Euskara on the one hand and Spanish or French on the other? Zalbide suggests a general formulation linked to Joshua Fishman's proposals for 'reversing language shift'. Zalbide proposes a vision of the normalisation of Euskara as a 'social process intending to retain and recoup for Euskara speakers social areas of use, so that Euskara will remain or become the usual language of relations inside the language community, in both formal and informal situations, and in oral and written interactions' (Zalbide, 1998: 365). This is a vision, then, that asks for a closer attention to the language community and to the primary environments in which intergenerational transmission of language happens, such as family, friends and the local community, but that cannot be understood as undermining the importance of the media and other social institutions for the survival of the language. On the contrary, it asks for new combinations and links to be made between the different levels of language use and transmission. So from this point of view local press and television, and indeed local media in general, appear as a strategic field for language normalisation.

The Media System

The media system in the Basque Country is the complex result of the juxtaposition of various structures (Zallo *et al.*, 2002: 11–12). There are the state-wide and centralised public and private media systems in both France and Spain. Secondly, there is the Basque public media structure created in the 1980s. Thirdly, there are the indigenous private communication initiatives. We will examine each of these in turn to see their role in the media system of the Basque Country.

Firstly, then, there are the state-wide media systems, both public and private, which are in a dominant position throughout the Basque Country. Since the 1980s in France and the 1990s in Spain, this sector has increasingly widened in accordance with the processes of deregulation in each of these countries. In the Spanish state, this sector consists of five terrestrial analogue television channels, four being free-to-air (TVE1, La 2, Antena 3 and Tele 5) and one a pay-channel (Canal +), and four general networked radio stations (RNE1, SER, Onda Cero and COPE), in addition to a whole host of specialised stations, mainly devoted to music. The situation is similar in France, with three public television channels (France 2, France 3 and Arte-La cinquiéme) and three private channels (TF1, M6 and Canal +). These broadcasters are strongly centralised. The specific territorial structures and programme schedules for the CAPV, Navarre and the French Basque Country are no more than outposts of the central organisations. They are concentrated at an entrepreneurial level in the hands of just a few media groups. Also belonging to this category are the digital pay-television satellite platforms, in addition to the main cable operators (as yet relatively undeveloped in both countries), as well as most of the specialised programming aimed at both platforms. This situation is in marked contrast to the press, where the strength of the state-wide structure is much less, benefiting a homegrown press that is fundamentally regional in nature.

Secondly, there is the public communications structure, created in the 1980s, that functions within the ambit of the CAPV and has a presence in both the television and radio sectors. As far as television is concerned, EITB (Euskal Irrati Telebista) has four main channels. Two of these are free-to-air analogue channels (ETB1 and ETB2, the former broadcasting in Euskara, the latter in Spanish). The EITB group also runs channels for satellite and cable. On satellite the channels are Canal Vasco, aimed in the main at the Basque diaspora in South America, and ETB Sat, targeting European countries. On cable there is the Superbat children's channel, which operates exclusively in Euskara. As far as radio is concerned, the Basque national radio system consists on five stations: Radio Euskadi and Radio Vitoria (general programming in Spanish), Euskadi Irratia (general programming in Euskara), Euskadi Gaztea (specialising in pop and rock music) and EITBradio (bilingual programming specialising in music and cultural events). These public broadcasters, particularly those using Euskara, do however reach a substantial part of the Basque Country. Agreements established with cultural bodies in Navarre and the French Basque Country have made this geographical expansion possible. This structure competes directly with the state-wide networks, in terms of both programming and audience, at least within the ambit of the CAPV. Thus ETB2 gets a television audience share of 18% comparable to those obtained by state-wide networks (between 16% and 24%), and Radio Euskadi is the second most popular radio station, just behind the SER network. The channels broadcasting in Euskara get much lower results both in television (an audience share of 6.2%) and in radio.

Thirdly, there are the indigenous, private media associated with three different initiatives. One is inherited from the pioneering days of the development of the press in the Basque Country and has links with conservative and anti-nationalist circles within the Basque elite. This has a particularly strong influence within the press in the Basque Country and in fact accounts for between 60% and 70% of the readership of daily news-papers. The second kind of initiative is that of publications linked with nationalism: daily newspapers, such as *Deia, Gara, El Diario de Noticias, Le Journal du Pays Basque* and *Berria,* and periodicals such as *Argia.* Some of these publications began to appear at the end of the 1970s thanks to popular support and financial donations (as was the case with the pioneering newspaper *Egin*) and were linked to the nationalist left, or were due to the initiative of groups of nationalist business people associ-ated with moderate nationalism, as occurred with *Deia,* in an attempt to gain ideological influence at an especially critical political moment, and to lay the foundations for a national Basque communications space. Nevertheless, their results, when compared to their competitors (the Vocento-Correo group with *El Correo* and *Diario Vasco,* the *Diario de Navarra* and *Sud-Ouest)* have never been particularly good (*Gara* gets about 8% of newspaper readership, and *Deia* about 4%). This is one of the most striking features of the Basque media system: the population is, in the main, nationalist, but the press it reads is clearly anti-nationalist. Also in this second category is *Egunkaria*[4] and its successor, *Berria,* a daily news-paper that is published exclusively in Euskara, developed after the frus-trating experiences of a bilingual approach in *Egin* and *Deia.*

Finally, there are the local media – the press, radio and television. The main driving force behind the local press comes from social movements associated with the normalisation of Euskara at local level. This category is very large: there are 70 publications (mostly weekly or fortnightly, though there are monthlies too), which publish around 160,000 copies and reach around 500,000 readers, following a model of free distribution financed by advertising and institutional funding. Within radio and television the struc-ture is more complex (as we shall see below when we consider the case of television) since, along with socially inspired projects, once again stemming principally from the pro-Euskara movement, important private initiatives have developed, operating from a purely commercial perspective, and, as a consequence, limiting the possible expansion of Euskara-based media.

What emerges from this complex situation is a media system subject to enormous state centralisation in broadcasting and, from the perspective of the Basque Country, one that is fragmented, unbalanced and unstructured, in addition to being prey to powerful tensions produced by political factors and to being out of step with social demands concerning the role that the media should play in a democratic society. Particularly during the last years of the right-wing government of the Parti Populare (PP) in the Spanish state, there were intense periods of pressure and media manipulation in relation to politics in the Basque Country. There is no doubt that this has left a profound feeling of irritation and mistrust within Basque society as far as the media are concerned, particularly the main state networks, and specifically regarding their news policies, leading to a growing preference for homegrown media services in this area. Social relations that are not filtered through the media – community and family environments – and the habit of checking out diverse sources of information (written and audiovisual media of varying ideological hues) have taken on a special importance in the way public opinion is formed (Zallo, *et al.*, 2002: 62–68).

Euskara in the Media

As we have already implied, the introduction of Euskara into this system was incomplete, irregular and came late in the day. Despite the extraordinary energy expended by the language movement, Euskara only really penetrated the mass media in the 1980s, thanks to the possibilities opened up by the institutionalisation of the new autonomous framework within the Spanish state. The government of the CAPV provided strong backing for the audiovisual side of the things and set up the public radio and television service, EITB. As far as the press is concerned, they gave financial aid to existing publications and supported timid initiatives to develop supplements in Euskara in the dailies *Egin* and *Deia*.

However, the initial single-channel formula of television in Euskara was rapidly called into question and was replaced by the current model comprising two linguistically separate channels, an experience that was repeated in radio. It soon became evident that the two stated objectives behind the creation of EITB, the one political (to provide Basque society with information and to encourage it to participate at a political level) and the other cultural (to promote and spread Basque culture, 'taking special account of the need to maintain a balance within the overall provision of radio and television broadcasts in the Basque language within the Autonomous Community', to quote the Founding Act of EITB) came into conflict with Euskara as the element that was to provide articulation for the system, precisely because of its minority nature. It appeared that political and cultural legitimation, the securing of wide political influence and the goal of achieving linguistic normalisation did not necessarily go hand in hand, something that had previously been revealed also by the nationalist dailies *Egin* and *Deia* when they were launched in Spanish. Indeed, this issue has been a constant within the Basque debate on communications since that time. The well-known Basque writer Jon Sarasua expressed this dichotomy between the political community and the linguistic community with a metaphor that possesses special weight within the symbolic world of Basque culture: the 'house of the father' (*aitaren etxea*, the political structure that might be considered to give form to the Basque-speaking community) versus the 'fire of the mother' (*amaren sua*, the preservation of the language that holds the community together) (Garzia, 1998).

In addition to this, the development of this audiovisual model and the chances it offered as a lubricator for the normalisation of Euskara were challenged by new factors. On the one hand, there was the inability of the Autonomous Communities to regulate and have an effect on the Spanish and French audiovisual systems, neither of which provide any space whatsoever for Euskara in their broadcasts. On the other hand, there is the fact that the Basque government displayed what seemed to many to be an incomprehensible lack of interest or perhaps even a political incapacity regarding the provision of more precise guidelines for radio, at least in the area that came under their jurisdiction, and failed to establish their own audiovisual legislation, for example by defining specific criteria (quotas, recommendations, etc.) concerning the use of Euskara in the media. Thus, given the absence of limits on production or on networked broadcasting, practically all the radio licences granted by the Basque government ended up within the control of Spanish networks, and broadcast only in Spanish. In addition, the Navarre government has constantly attempted not only to put spokes in the wheels of EITB but even to hamper the development of Basque-language broadcasts.

Finally, there are the processes of deregulation in the state-wide systems, within the parameters of commercial competitiveness and technological development, and which brought in their wake a pronounced increase in competition within the Spanish state and put paid, once and for all, to the original intention of achieving a balance between broadcasts in Euskara and those in Spanish and French, as well as obliging EITB to develop scheduling policies based increasingly on competitive criteria.

Today, although the Basque-language channels within the CAPV's public radio and television system constitute an undoubted point of reference on the Basque audiovisual map, it is also evident that they have been losing their place in the system taken as a whole, both for their non-

Basque-speaking and Basque-speaking audiences. For instance, in 2005 a viewer in Bilbao was able to watch eight channels in Spanish and only one in Euskara. What is more, EITB's programming policies have led to the Basque-language channel (ETB1) to specialise in children's and sports programmes, where there is higher audience potential, but this implies the imposition of substantial limits on the freedom of choice as far as Basque-speaking viewers are concerned.

In contrast, the opposite has occurred in the press. The daily newspaper *Euskaldunon Egunkaria* managed to consolidate an increasingly extensive product for an audience that, nevertheless, remained stable (approximately 15,000 copies sold for a readership of around 25,000). Strangely enough, the response to the police's closure of *Euskaldunon Egunkaria* in 2003 was not just the appearance of a new daily paper, *Berria*, but also a significant increase in sales and readers: a print run of more than 21,000 for a readership of roughly 40,000. But it was actually the Basque Country's local press that succeeded in overcoming a barrier that had previously seemed insuperable for the Basque-language media: it finally reached broad mass audiences, clocking up readership figures that had not before been seen. This occurred via various initiatives involving bodies created at the municipal level to promote the use of Euskara, amongst which Arrasate Press, in Arrasate, holds an unquestionable position of prominence. Through a fluid and swift sharing of experiences and the generation of services in common (through the Topagunea Federation, which acts to bind these bodies together), diverse organisational and business models that followed an approach of free home distribution coupled with a high degree of self-financing through advertising have been developed, with the support of public funding from institutions at a municipal, provincial and autonomous community level.

One of the keys to this success was, of course, to be found in the nature of the content, characterised by a familiarity with the audience and an awareness of its needs, backed up by easy-to-read language and a straightforward modern style of presentation. Another key lies in the exclusive character of this press as against Spanish-language newspapers in most of the places where it took root. That is to say, the local Basque press was largely built up using only the Basque language and, despite the existence of important gaps where its geographical distribution is concerned, especially in the French Basque Country, Navarre, Bizkaia and Araba, this exclusiveness has armed it with significant competitive advantages when compared with its Spanish equivalents.

Given that availability of accessible daily and weekly newspapers is one of the keystones to the normalisation and survival of a language, as well as one of the trickiest areas to penetrate (Etxegoien, 2004: 9–13), this singular success story within the press sector aroused the interest of other media in relation to local communications. This is demonstrated by the intense activity generated within Basque radio in recent years, with the setting up of new free radio stations, as well as the establishment of a network for the exchange and creation of programmes. It is the first time that there has been participation from both sides of the French–Spanish border in a collaborative framework of this kind. However, the local television stations are facing a very different situation.

Local Television

The first local television stations in the Basque Country were developed at the end of the 1980s mainly by individuals with audiovisual skills and by social groups with no profit motive in mind. The emergence of these local stations took place in the face of a legal threat, for there was no specific legislation regulating local television. Nevertheless, experience spread rapidly and the first stations were soon followed by various commercial initiatives, especially in cities such as Bilbao, Iruñea and Donostia. But after the vibrant early years, a long period of crisis and slow growth began, due not only to the enduring absence of a legal framework governing local television, but also to the high cost of equipment and programming maintenance and to the lack of interest in the media and social communication on the part of Basque municipal institutions. Without public support, local television stations became very difficult to manage both for the social groups, many of them linked to the promotion of Euskara, and even for the commercial initiatives that were in the main small companies not linked to other media groups. In contrast, other parts of the Spanish state such as Catalonia and Andalusia, saw a great proliferation of local television channels, due to wide public support in the former and to extreme commercialisation in the latter.

In 1995 the Spanish government – then in the hands of the Socialist Party – passed a law to regulate the sector, provoked by the development of local television in Catalonia, the aim being to protect the eminently local and public service dimension of this kind of television service from the most dominant commercial tendencies. But this law was never enforced. Instead, under the new right-wing PP government, local television developed after 1996 in a particularly unbridled manner, subject to pressures of an increasingly commercial nature. What is more, from the end of the 1990s a new phenomenon was to strikingly alter the shape of the sector: networks were created, both by companies already operating in local television and by the major Spanish media groups (Prisa, Vocento,

COPE etc.) who detected in this de facto deregulated sector the opportunity to create a new free-to-air state-wide television network (to add to the already existing networks). This development also affected the Basque Country, as the Basque and Navarre authorities too were partial to laissez-faire policies. Thus new stations were created while existing ones went through a major restructuring process.

As a consequence, local television in the Basque Country is today a complex world where there are nearly 50 local television stations showing a combination of highly diverse origins, situations and features: stations belonging to small municipalities, together with stations covering larger areas, television stations developed by bodies in the public sector with social objectives and those created as trading companies with profit motives, as can be observed in Table 9.1.

But this apparent diversity masks a far more homogeneous reality where, due precisely to the strategies of the networks and big media groups, a sort of dual local television system has been created. These groups have privileged the provincial capitals where, since the late 1990s, they have bought existing stations in economic difficulties or have created new ones so that in each of the Basque Country's provincial capitals there are today three, and in one case four, local television stations. Moreover, all the stations in the capitals belong now to large media groups. These groups have imposed a televisual model based on the following parameters: high investment and budgets (more than a million euros per year); an ever-widening broadcasting range, easily exceeding local or regional limits and increasingly reaching the borders of provincial range; 24-hour broadcasting; broad general programming based more on state-wide networked content and on programmes already transmitted through the

Table 9.1 Channels currently broadcasting, grouped according to province

Province	Stations	Public sector/ associations	Part of TV network	Providing complete programming	Presence of Basque language
Araba	5	1	4	3	1
Bizkaia	8	1	3	7	3
Gipuzkoa	15	3	4	11	8
Nafarroa	22	10	4	8	4
Total	50	15	15	29	16

major state-wide networks than on local content; an appreciable capacity for in-house production (3 or 4 hours a day) that in general takes the specific form of daily news bulletins, magazine programmes and local reports; and, finally, an almost total absence of Euskara, which at best only occupies fringe spaces, in the form of short reports during morning slots or the odd bit of news. In the shadow of this dominant model, outside the capital cities, small and very small television stations struggle to survive and develop. A few of them are on budgets around or over €150,000 (exceptionally, some even reaching €450,000), while the vast majority are restricted to 'survival' budgets that do not exceed €60,000.

In relation to their programming, at least four kinds of local television station can be identified. There is a small group of stations that have fallen prey to the expanding strategies of the networks. Compared to the ones located in the capitals, they have a very limited capacity for programme production, so their scheduling is almost completely dependent on the networks' supply. Secondly, there are very small commercial channels that attempt to get by through complementing the meagre news bulletins and local reports they are able to offer (from half an hour per day to just one hour per week) within the scant commercial resources they have at their disposal, with programmes supplied by the providers of services such as home shopping and clairvoyance programmes (highly popular in the Spanish state) or by connecting up to programming offered by satellite television. Most of the programming broadcast by these stations is in Spanish and only in a very few cases are programmes in Euskara. Thirdly, there is a large group of stations, located mainly in Navarre, that are in reality public access channels offered to the locality by a cable operator. Most of these stations broadcast only occasionally and are associated with local events such as fiestas, cultural events and so on. Broadcasts are almost exclusively in Spanish.

Finally, there is a small group of stations, where publicly owned stations and commercial ones coexist, that have developed regular scheduling based on programmes produced in-house and centred around daily local news bulletins, backed up, when possible, by local sports programmes, reports, magazines and such like, which are repeated on a programmed basis and supplemented by local teletext information services. A majority of the television stations in this fourth group follow bilingual models or broadcast exclusively in Euskara, the most prominent examples being those managed by precisely the same bodies that publish the local press, using a multimedia strategy of optimisation and diversification of resources.

The main example of this model is GOIENA, which operates in the Debagoiena area (Arrasate, Bergara, Eskoriatza, Aretxabaleta, Antzuola,

Oñati) and is involved in the press, radio, television and the Internet, all at a local or regional level. Promoted by local associations for the promotion of Euskara, it has succeeded in incorporating institutions and other bodies plus local agents within a cooperative local communications project in Euskara for the entire population in that area, and is achieving very interesting results through integrating the values of closeness inherent within a local communications model (based on participation, integration and social cohesion, the creation of community feeling, and cooperation with local bodies) with those of linguistic normalisation. In television, in particular, they have achieved attractive programming that spreads outwards from an information-based structure towards the cultural, sports and even entertainment spheres, while always remaining within the limits of technical and economic feasibility. To this end, programme planning has to take advantage of multi-broadcast systems (which deal with the timing of broadcast repeats in such a way as to avoid too monotonous a schedule) and automation mechanisms (software packages that automatically fill certain slots in the schedule with such material as weather forecasts, traffic information and so on).

Thus the development of the main local television stations and networks and the lack of regulation and of public support for local communication projects has ended in a process of colonisation of the local space that has prevented the existing small stations from developing in their own way. Only a small group of mostly bilingual or Euskara broadcasting stations have developed the capacity to produce an appreciable and regular amount of programming embedded in the local environment. Euskara has therefore been one of the main factors that has helped to avoid the total colonisation of the local space by the big companies. On the other hand, the current domination of the local television scene by Spanish-language broadcasting has put at risk the overall development of Euskara in television broadcasting.

In effect, the general process of deregulation has resulted in a reduction of the significance and visibility of Basque-language services. The development of thematic channels for cable and satellite is progressing very slowly and up to now their use of Euskara is restricted to a children's channel. In this situation the local dimension can provide Basque-language broadcasting, as has been the case in the press, with certain supplementary and differentiating factors such as provision of local information, participation of local actors, and quality of the language (not just the standard version but a language much closer to that which is actually used by people) that should make it more attractive, and easier to follow for Basque-speaking audiences. Nevertheless it is important not to forget that in the press there have also been other very important reasons that have made it possible to take a great leap forward at the level of language use, such as the exclusiveness of publications in Spanish even in the provincial capitals, with the exception of Bilbao and a few other localities.

The situation in local television may soon change as a result of new legislation established recently by the Spanish state. In accordance with this legislation, local television will be one of the props of digital terrestrial television: local television licences will be granted for digital transmission, though a time period will be allowed for broadcasts using both analogue and digital systems; local television demarcations will no longer be municipal but regional; a minimum of 4 hours of original programming per day and 32 hours per week will be stipulated, to be broadcast during prime time, and networked programming will be limited to a maximum of 5 hours per day and 25 hours per week. Following this legal framework, it will be up to the Autonomous Communities to advertise and allocate the licences (it is thought that there will be four for each local digital frequency), which means that they will be able to establish specific conditions that respond to the needs of each Community. The state, however, reserves for itself control over networks that cover more than one Autonomous Community.

These conditions will have a significant impact on local Basque television. Digital broadcasting will require a level of investment that only the larger television stations are equipped to cope with, given the budgetary limitations affecting small television services and the institutional passivity of Basque town councils – the production and transmission of four hours of programming per day is something that, yet again, will only be within the reach of television stations supported by considerable budgets. Consequently, institutional responsibility in the reorganisation of the system will be of key importance. The regulations they establish, including measures regarding linguistic use, and the steps they take to provide economic funding for the setting up and running of local television stations will determine whether we have televisual provision in the service of linguistic normalisation or if there will simply be a de facto legalisation of the existing situation and, therefore, an entrenchment of the linguistic status quo. Also of great importance will be the creation of forms of collaboration between the different local stations and even with ETIB in order to extend broadcasting times and content in Euskara.

Conclusion

Experience demonstrates the importance of a communications model that is itself centred within the linguistic community in order to secure effective results in terms of linguistic normalisation (Zuberogoitia, 2003). In the press, bilingual models developed taking Spanish as their starting point have generally ended up reproducing the marginalisation of Euskara in a quantitative and functional sense and contributing, even despite themselves, to a deepening of the situation of diglossia (Basterretxea, 2000). But the combination of the Basque-language press with the local environment has been demonstrated to be a sustainable and successful model attracting new audiences and creating new loyalties for exclusively Basque-language media. It is uncertain if similar results are possible in television due to its specific characteristics, but the colonisation of the local space by the major networks and the weak situation of Basque institutions, on both the regulatory and the economic sides, risks condemning not just the development of Basque-speaking local television but also, more generally, the development of Basque-language broadcasting.

Notes

1. *Euskararen Jarraipena III: 2001eko Soziolinguistika Ikerketa.* Since 1991 the Department of Culture of the Basque Government has carried out five-yearly sociolinguistic surveys concerning knowledge and use of Euskara. The statistics we have employed here are taken from the latest study, which is for the year 2001 published in 2003 (Eusko Jaurlaritza, 2003). The universe of reference comprises members of the population above 15 years old and from the different territories of the Basque Country: the Autonomous Community of the Basque Country and the Comunidad Foral de Nafarroa, in the Spanish state, and Iparralde in France. The first two territories, which are referred to as Hegoalde when taken together, possess a certain degree of political and administrative autonomy, although they constitute two regions that are politically and administratively differentiated. Iparralde, however, does not constitute a specific political or administrative entity and is included within the broader entity of Aquitaine.

2. The social dimension of the promotion of Euskara has been a constant from its first beginnings through to the present day and it is noteworthy that, despite the formal institutionalisation of linguistic policies, in the CAPV in particular, these social organisms have not disappeared from the map. On the contrary, they are still active and functioning and on occasion there have been significant clashes between both these spheres. One of the central organisms in this process was unquestionably the *ikastola* network. These were centres of primary and secondary education that made their first appearance at the end of the 1960s and start of the 1970s, founded on popular support within a cooperative framework and dedicated to the creation of an

exclusively Basque-language based educational approach. Two important organisations that must also be mentioned are the AEK (devoted to fostering adult literacy) and the UEU (Basque Summer University).

3. Four models exist: D, based on immersion in Euskara; B, a bilingual model with various gradations depending on territory and local environment; A, carried out in Spanish or French but including Euskara as a language to be learnt; and X, in which Euskara is not a subject for study. Model X constitutes an exception in non-university education in the CAPV and in the Basque-speaking and mixed areas of Navarre, while it still has a notable presence in the French Basque Country.

4. *Egunkaria* was shut down by judicial order in 2003 and a number of its executive directors were detained and tortured. One of them has spent more than a year and a half on remand. By 2005 the case had still not been heard. *Berria* emerged to step into the gap that same year, backed by popular campaigns of support and financial donations.

References

Amezaga, J. (1995) *Herri kultura: euskal kultura eta kultura popularrak*. Leioa: EHU / UPV.

Basterretxea, J.I. (2000) Hedabideak eta hizkuntza: erdararen aldeko erreprodukzio mediatikoa. In NOR ikerketa-taldea *Hedabideak eta Euskal Herria* (pp. 199–218). Bilbao: UEU.

Etxegoien, F. (2004) *Neurona eta Zeurona*. Iruñea: Pamiela.

Eusko Jaurlaritza (2003) *Euskararen Jarraipena III: 2001eko Soziolinguistika Ikerketa*. On www at: http://www.euskadi.net/euskara

Garzia, J. (1998) *Jon Sarasua bertso-ispiluan barrena*. Irun: Alberdania.

Odriozola, J.M. (2004) *Euskalgintzaren lekukoak*. Donostia: Elkar.

Zalbide, M. (1998) Normalización lingüística y escolaridad: un informe desde la sala de máquinas. *Revista Internacional de Estudios Vascos* 43 (2), 355–424.

Zallo R., Azpillaga, P. and De Miguel, J.C. (2002) *Komunikabideak hemen: egitura mediatikoa Euskal Herrian*. Irun: Alberdania.

Zuberogoitia, A. (2003) Globalizaio garaiotarako biziraupen-estrategia bat euskal hizkuntza-komunitatearentzat: komunikazio-esparru autozentratua. *Bat Soziolinguistika aldizkaria* 48, 27–38.

Chapter 10

Media Policy and Language Policy in Catalonia

MARIA COROMINAS PIULATS

Language plays a significant role in communication systems, but the place of individual languages in specific systems becomes increasingly important and controversial in contexts where there are competing languages and linguistic communities. There are often substantial inequalities in terms of the prominence of different languages in media contexts. In modern societies, where mass media are essential tools of communication, the languages chosen for use by media practitioners and the contexts in which these languages are used are of critical importance. In Catalonia, a historic nation within the Spanish state, the transition to democracy that took place after General Franco's death (1975), was accompanied by the linguistic 'normalisation' of the Catalan language, a process that relied heavily on the mass media. The policy of language normalisation implied, firstly, the creation of public Catalan-speaking audiovisual media and, secondly, the promotion of Catalan-speaking private media. The initiatives undertaken through this policy have brought about considerable enlargement of Catalan language content in all media, though with different proportions and significance. Consequently, in spite of a continuing unbalanced position in favour of Spanish-speaking media, there has been a general increase in Catalan language media consumption.[1]

The evaluation of the policy of language normalisation needs to be considered in two key stages, which roughly correspond to landmarks in the evolution of language and media policy in Europe. The first stage of policy development, which emerged during the 1980s was rooted in the profound political changes in Spain in the immediate post-Franco era. These policies focused on the process of political democratisation and its impact on the mass media. The role of the media changed profoundly during this period as the authoritarianism of Franco gave way to high levels of social participation and activism in all key cultural institutions including media organisations.

In terms of broader policy debates, this stage was linked to discussions about a New World Information and Communication Order (NWICO) at international level, which led to the publication of the MacBride Report

168

and UNESCO's subsequent crisis. In spite of emerging debates about communication rights at international level, these policies were always considered in terms of the capacities of nation-states. In Catalonia, policy-makers and politicians called for the inclusion of minority cultures and stateless nations within this policy debate arguing that the incorporation of these voices was a prerequisite for democratic communication (Gifreu, 1986; Moragas & Corominas, 1988). During this period, much media policy in Catalonia focused on language normalisation but the scope of policy development was not limited to language issues. Reform of the media was seen as essential to the creation of a true democracy.

The second stage of media and language policy development in the nineties was marked by the adaptation of the broader Spanish state to European Union (EU) policies. The EU played an increasing role in the formulation of media policy, particularly in terms of broadcasting, as well as in the development of policies for the convergent sector of telecommunications. There was considerable emphasis on the integration of economic and technological policies with broader European policy trends. A growing emphasis was placed on the liberalisation of markets, and commercial criteria gained force over cultural and social considerations. During the 1990s, language policy continued to be a very important dimension of media policy, but not the sole concern of Catalan media policy-makers.

Since 2000, increasing globalisation and digitalisation have provided the dominant frame for media and language policies in Catalonia. The linguistic situation has been re-defined as a result of the challenges raised by broader economic and cultural changes linked to globalisation. Although the Catalan language has increased in use, this use still falls behind that of Spanish. Catalan speakers now have to face new challenges from other languages, most notably English, which is achieving global dominance.[2]

In terms of minority language cultures, the Catalan language community presents an unusual profile. Firstly, Catalan speakers represent one of Europe's largest linguistic minorities with up to 10,000,000 speakers. Catalan is a romance language that has official status within the autonomous communities of Catalonia and the Balearic Islands. The Valencian autonomous community has two separate linguistic areas: one with Spanish as the sole official language and the other one with two official languages: Spanish and Catalan (which is described officially as Valencian). It is also spoken in an eastern strip of the autonomous community of Aragon, although the language is not officially recognised in this region. Outside Spain, Catalan is the official language of the micro-state of

Andorra in the Pyrenées, and is also spoken in France (in Roussillon). A small Catalan-speaking community also exists in the Italian town of L'Alguer (Alghero, Sardinia). Thus the Catalan-speaking community is a complex one that is diffused through a number of distinct political and administrative boundaries and exists within a number of regions and states where other romance languages such as Spanish, French and Italian have a majority status.

According to the 2001 linguistic census within the region of Catalonia itself, 94.5% (5.8 million people) of population aged 2 years and over understands Catalan. Some 74.5% (4.6 million) can speak the language and a similar number (74.4%) can read it. About half of the population aged 2 years and over (49.8%; 3.1 million) can write Catalan. Shifting from knowledge to use, the 2003 *Statistics of Linguistic Uses in Catalonia* (the first official survey) shows that 48.8% of residents declare that Catalan is their *own* language, whereas 44.3% say it to be Spanish; 5.2% say both languages and 1.8% of residents identify other languages as their own language.

Besides the number of Catalan speakers, Catalonia shows other particularities in relation to minority languages and cultures. Firstly, the mass media have been developed at both local and autonomous community levels. Secondly, the number of media outlets, the reach of mass media and the productive capacity of the industry are unusually high, particularly book publishing, where Catalonia as a publishing *country* could be ranked fifth in Europe and tenth in the world (Jones, 2003). Notwithstanding this progress, there is a substantial difference between the Catalan language media industry and the media capacities of national language communities with a similar number of speakers where the state fully supports the position of the national language in defining and implementing public policies.

Despite these disparities, analysis of the Catalan case can provide a model or a pathway for a minority language community in terms of language and media policy. The Catalan autonomous community has attempted to articulate policies that try to foster the knowledge and the social use of the minority language, keeping pace as far as possible with the main policy developments of every period, starting from the transformation of the state's system of political organisation (from dictatorship to democracy, and from a highly centralised model to a decentralised one). Therefore, within Catalan media policy, language policy plays a constant and considerable role but other issues such as political reform also inform policy formulation.

Media and Language Normalisation in Catalonia

Public policies and power distribution

The Spanish Constitution (1978) states that Spanish is the official language of the state (art. 3.1), and that 'the other Spanish languages are also official in respect to Autonomous Communities in accordance with their Statutes' (art. 3.2). The Catalonian Statute of Autonomy (1979) states that 'the language of Catalonia is Catalan' (art. 3.1), and that Catalan enjoys official status within the region equivalent to the status of Spanish in the rest of the state of Spain (art. 3.2). In this sense, the Catalonian Statute defines a linguistic model where Catalan (minority language) is declared official throughout the whole autonomous community, together with Spanish.[3]

The Catalan autonomous government (*Generalitat*) guarantees to oversee both the 'normal' and official use of both languages (art. 3.3). Accordingly, the Catalan Generalitat developed a language policy that was designed to promote the Catalan language in order to redress some of the damage done when the language was banned under the Franco regime.[4] Thus, the starting point of language policy was the recognition of a strongly unbalanced situation where Catalan had been disadvantaged in relation to Spanish. Catalan language policy-makers decided to promote a policy of language normalisation, meaning the recovery of public use of Catalan language in all fields. The expanded use of Catalan in the mass media was explicitly included in this policy programme.

Despite being kept in the domestic domain during the Franco period, to a certain extent, the Catalan language continued to hold a high status, in that it represented a way to democratically oppose and resist Francoism. Demands for linguistic normalisation of Catalan language, requiring its *normal* use in mass media (as well as in school, where it was required to be the teaching language) were made throughout this period by a wide range of people in different social sectors who linked language freedom to democratisation.[5] A sign of the political and social consensus that had emerged around this point became evident in 1983 when the Catalan Parliament unanimously passed the Law of Linguistic Normalisation that aimed to (art. 2):

(1)   shelter and foster the use of Catalan by all citizens;
(2)   give legitimacy to the official use of Catalan;
(3)   *normalise Catalan use as the means of social communication* [own emphasis];
(4)   assure the spreading of Catalan knowledge.

Reform of mass media organisations, as well as school and public institutions, was explicitly designated as a main pillar of this policy.

The 1978 Spanish Constitution recognises (art. 20) freedom of speech and provides for the future regulation of 'organisation and parliamentary control of state-dependent media', guaranteeing 'access to these media to social and political groups, respecting the pluralism of society and that of the different languages of Spain'. The Constitution also enshrines the state's exclusive power to oversee the 'basic norms of press, radio and television and, in general, of all means of social communication, without prejudice of developing and executing faculties corresponding to Autonomous Communities' (art. 149.1.27). In other words, it gives to the state the exclusive power to settle the legal framework for broadcasting, while autonomous communities can assume responsibility for legislative development and execution of policy.[6]

Public autonomous audiovisual media

During the period of democratic transition after the death of Franco, Spain's broadcasting system underwent a series of major changes that created a mixed model of broadcasting where public and private broadcasters could coexist and compete, in either a local, autonomous community or state-based context. The reform had a profound effect on the balance between Spanish and Catalan broadcasting. During the first stage of reform, during the 1980s, strategies were centred on public media.

On May 1983 the Catalan Parliament passed a law creating the Catalan Broadcasting Corporation[7] (Corporació Catalana de Ràdio i Televisió, CCRTV) as a public corporation. The creation of the CCRTV could be interpreted as a manifestation of the Catalan desire to follow the model developed by democratic European states with public service broadcasting corporations. However, the development of CCRTV must also be contextualised in terms of the wider process of regionalisation that was impacting on television in Europe. After the decentralisation of many state radio and television companies in the 1960s and the 1970s via the creation of second and sometimes third television channels, regionalisation became the focus of policy initiatives in the 1980s. CCRTV's television channel, TV3, was leading the way in this new trend along with Sianel Pedwar Cymru (S4C, the Welsh television channel in the United Kingdom that began broadcasting in 1982), Euskal Telebista (Basque Country, 1982) and Television de Galicia (Galicia, 1985). All of these services linked their broadcasting goals to the promotion of minority languages and cultural identities.[8] (Don Browne's Chapter 7 in this book gives the broader picture within which these developments took place.)

The promotion of Catalan language and culture is explicitly defined as one of the CCRTV's guiding programming principles (art. 14.e of the 1983 Law). However, though language concerns were central to the launch of the CCRTV, other considerations also shaped the structure and output of the service. Management focused on providing a modern television service that could compete with neighbouring television services such as TVE but which would operate in the Catalan language. This policy also resulted in the establishment of a Catalan-speaking radio channel, Catalunya Ràdio, in June 1983. The launch of these new Catalan language media services meant a significant increase in the use of Catalan in radio and a radical increase in Catalan on television, with estimates that 44% of programming would be in Catalan and 56% in Spanish by the end of 1987.[9]

The Catalan language had a small media presence prior to this period of media reform. From December 1976 Ràdio 4, a Catalan-speaking station belonging to the public state-owned radio network (*Radio Nacional de España*), was on air (with some 18 hours per week of programming, but this service did not reach all Catalonia). On television, Spanish public state-owned television (Televisión Española, TVE) also was broadcasting some 1310 hours per year in Catalan in 1984. In this context, the establishment of TV3 (and Catalunya Ràdio) implied a considerable advance for Catalan language normalisation. The increased amount of Catalan language content was received warmly by audiences. Catalunya Ràdio was, by the end of 1987, the second largest station in Catalonia. In 1987, TV3's audience share began to overtake TVE 1, Spain's premier television channel.[10]

With the introduction of private television in Spain (Law on Private Television, 1988), the context of television broadcasting changed and three licences were given to services to broadcast programming on a state-wide basis. Exploiting this development, CCRTV launched a second Catalan television channel, Canal 33 (April 1989), in an attempt to reinforce its dominant position in the market and increase Catalan programming in television.

Catalonia was the second autonomous community to create a second television channel, after ETB2 was launched in the Basque Country in 1986. However, the two autonomous communities adopted quite different approaches to the second service, which was linked to their individual social, political and linguistic situations. Catalan speaking Canal 33 was specialised in terms of content; while ETB2, broadcasts mainly in Spanish (except for children's programmes) and was designed to reach the whole population, Basque and non-Basque-speaking alike (López & Corominas, 1995: 186–187).

These initiatives emerged at the same time that three other Spanish autonomous communities launched their own (first) television services: Andalusia, Madrid and Valencia (all in 1989). The establishment of the channels for Andalusia and Madrid was driven mainly by socio-economic rather than linguistic considerations as these are Spanish-speaking communities. However, the Valencian service was driven by similar sociolinguistic concerns to those that prompted the development of the Basque, Catalan and Galician models. During the same period, the Spanish public television was engaged in a process of decentralisation through the creation of 'Territorial Centres' in all autonomous communities, in order to adapt to the Statutes of Autonomy. By the end of the 1980s, the use of Catalan in public radio and television had started to become *normal* in Catalonia, due to a combination of media and language policies that received wide public acceptance and support.[11]

Local communication

A characteristic of the Catalan communication system is the existence of a large amount of local and regional media. Catalan local communication provides a different approach to media and language policy integration. A plurality of media initiatives, which include linguistic initiatives, exist and have been developed by civil society organisations in accordance with their broader political agenda. These initiatives provide a clear example of bottom-up approaches to media reform.

The structure of local communication systems in Catalonia is a legacy from the final years of Francoism,[12] where the local and regional press played a role in the nationalist and democratic resistance to the dictatorship (Moragas & Corominas, 1988: 10–16). During the democratic transition (from 1979 onwards), municipal radio and local television stations followed the example of the press and were actively trying to defend and promote democracy and Catalan identity.

Municipal radio and local television stations spread rapidly during this period, numbering respectively 138 and 46 stations by the end of the 1980s, although there was a lack of formal legal recognition.[13] The lack of a legal basis for these services as well as the support of municipalities generated an access and community-based approach to the local broadcasting movement, which came to be represented by two organisations: the EMUC (1980), the association coordinating all municipal radio stations, and FTLC (1985), the group of a large set of local television stations.[14] In both cases, these organisations were built around the principles of democratic, social participation and Catalan linguistic normalisation. Within these local services, the Catalan language was *normally* used on radio and television and the linguistic issue was important in local services. These services were also part of a process of political and media democratisation.

Media and Language Policy in Catalonia

Once the public sector of Catalan broadcasting and the mainly local, Catalan-speaking audiovisual media were organised and consolidated, the next step undertaken was the expansion of media and language policy to private media. A new language policy[15] tried to promote Catalan language use within the media through the provision of a quota system in private radio and film dubbing. This policy represented an attempt to create equality of supply between Catalan and Spanish language material. At the same time, private sector commercial interests in the press were acting to create the same type of parity: in 1997 two Spanish-speaking dailies, *El Periódico de Catalunya* and *Segre*, introduced a double language version, in Catalan and in Spanish.

However, in reviewing overall changes in media and language policy during the period which began in the 1990s, it is possible to identify some contradictions. There seems to have been a lower degree of consensus about the need for language and media reform compared to previous periods. For example, the Law of Linguistic Policy of 1998 was passed by a majority of the Catalan Parliament, but not unanimously.[16] Secondly, Spain's entrance into the EU in 1986 resulted in the incorporation of a number of new actors into public policy debates. The increasing internationalisation and globalisation processes affecting member states led to a general consensus that cultural and communication issues could no longer be kept solely under the aegis of nation-states.

Globalisation affected Catalan media in a number of ways. Competition between advertising-funded television services greatly increased with the liberalisation of media markets and the establishment of three Spanish private terrestrial television channels as well as Spanish and non-Spanish satellite channels. Globalisation also impacted on the film sector in Catalonia, which remains dominated by global media corporations. These organisations successfully objected to the introduction of a quota system for film dubbing into the Catalan language, in spite of the fact that the Catalan government declared it was ready to pay for it.

The Law of Linguistic Policy (1998) and its application

The 1998 Law of Linguistic Policy has, among its general objectives 'normalising and promoting the use of Catalan language in administration,

education, the means of social communication, cultural industries and the
socio-economic world' (art. 1.2.c). As in the previous law, the media
continues to be identified as a central actor in language normalisation, but
now its role is integrated with cultural industries as well as the private
sector. Provisions for public (Generalitat's and municipal) audiovisual
media have been kept unchanged, in that the 'language normally used
must be Catalan', and municipal stations may take into account the nature
of their audience (art. 25.1). According to these provisions, the Catalan
language should completely dominate public radio. Catalan is the only
language used (apart from music and songs) on the four CCRTV stations:
the general Catalunya Ràdio (1983), the specialised Catalunya Música
(1987), Catalunya Informació (1992) and Catalunya Cultura (1999).[17] On
municipal radio stations, in spite of the legal provision for linguistic diversity, Catalan is also the main language used. According to Direcció General
de Politica Lingüística (DGPL, 2002: 82) out of 187 radio stations of this
kind operating in 2001, 63.1% used only Catalan (58% of the 199 existing in
1998); about one-third (30.5% in 2001 or 31% in 1998) used it between
50–99% of their output and 1% for less than half their output.

The Catalan language is also used by public service television stations.
From 2001–2002, there are seven terrestrial stations operating in Catalonia
that broadcast 24 hours a day (totalling 1176 hours per week); this year
second public channels La 2, from Spanish RTVE, and Canal 33 from
CCRTV began all-day programming (DGPL, 2001: 67; DGPL, 2002: 75). In
this context, Catalan language programming represents around one-third
of the supply of terrestrial television.

The output of the two channels of the Catalan Radio and Television
Corporation accounts for 90.4% of the Catalan language programming on
offer, while the public Spanish television channels, La Primera and La 2, tend
to have less Catalan language programmes. Data from Catalan Audiovisual
Council (CAC, 2003: 54) shows that the total amount of Catalan language on
these two channels has fallen from 1340 hours in 1998 to 951 in 2002. On
private television, Catalan is marginal.[18] One of the new features of the 1998
Law is a policy related to the new radio and television stations created under
concession by the Generalitat. The Law and subsequent norms enacting it
foresee that cable television and privately managed local television services
operating in Catalonia have to guarantee (DGPL, 2003):

(1)   at least 50% of programming produced in-house must be in Catalan;
(2)   films, television series and documentaries dubbed into a language
      different from the original must be available, if not simultaneously,
      at the very least in Catalan;

(3)   50% of the time reserved for the broadcast of European works must be devoted to the broadcast of original works in either of the official languages of Catalonia and there must be a guarantee that 50% of these works are in Catalan.[19]

In practical terms, there are not significant differences among private and public local stations in terms of language use. Almost all stations, whether public or private, claim to broadcast exclusively or mainly in Catalan. More relevant are the signs of internationalisation and economic integration. Because some local television are re-broadcasting satellite channels, English appears to be the second language in terms of broadcasting presence after Catalan, and Spanish the third. In 2001, Catalan was used during 86% of broadcast time for local stations, English in 10% and Spanish 3%, while the remaining 1% was Catalan and Spanish without distinction (Prado & Moragas, 2002: 56–57). But when limited to programming, Catalan language stands for an overwhelming 91%, Spanish represents 7%, and 2% are bilingual.

Integration and co-operation have also developed at the local level, where stations, whether public or private, have grouped around networks such as Consorci Local i Comarcal de Catalunya (some 60 stations, mainly private) or Xarxa de Televisions Locals (with more than 60 stations, public and private, from Catalonia and Balearic Islands, is the biggest distribution network in Catalonia). According to the 1998 law, radio stations under concession of the Generalitat (all stations on FM, there not having been any new AM stations since then) must guarantee a minimum of 50% of broadcast time in Catalan, although in this case the percentage can be changed by the Generalitat according to audience characteristics (art. 26.3). The decree (269/1998) developing these provisions stipulates that the use of Catalan must be spread over all time slots in equitable terms.[20]

The implementation of this Law has brought an increase of Catalan language in commercial private radio, both in terms of stations using it and in terms of slots allotted. Data from the General Directorate of Audiovisual Media[21] reveals that in 1998 there were 29 stations (39% of all stations of this kind) using Catalan in more than 50% or programmes, while in 2001 there were 67 (representing 71%). At the same time, the number of radio stations, broadcasting exclusively in Catalan, increased from 20 (27%) in 1998 to 45 (48%) in 2001. A survey of radio schedules conducted during January 2003 showed a general trend for stations belonging to Spanish networks to solely (or mainly) use Catalan while they were broadcasting in an opt-out context. This practice means that the amount Catalan language is strictly dependent of the amount of opt-out time available, which ranged from 11.45 hours per week up to 88. The same survey showed that in the commercial sector, Catalan was the language used by the six networks belonging to the so-called autochthonous groups,[22] and by the three stations not linked to networks.

Another new reform introduced by the 1998 Law is related to music. This policy is trying to ensure that Catalan is not only used as a spoken language in radio and television but also as a sung one, and requires stations to guarantee an 'appropriate presence of Catalan artists and Catalan-produced songs' and at least 25% of songs in Catalan (or 'Aranès', a linguistic variety of Occitan, spoken by some 4000 people in the Pyrenean Aran Valley, Catalonia).[23] In defining a quota system for songs, Catalan policy was inspired by the French model of policy on this issue. In 1994, France (Law of 1st February) set a quota of 40% for songs in French (in response to the encroachment of English language music) for most radio stations under concession.[24] This language policy measure has an economic-industrial dimension, in that it aims at developing the recording and video industries in Catalan, which have, by and large been dominated by global corporations, producing commercial English-speaking products (Jones, 2003). The law makes an explicit reference to the link between media and language policy, as it states that one of the criteria used by the government in the adjudication of radio concessions should be the use of Catalan in higher percentages than the minimum required.

Finally, in cinema, the 1998 Law foresees the possibility of introducing linguistic quotas in film distribution and exhibition (art. 28). This aspiration was later detailed via a decree in which dubbing requirements for all children's animation works were specified.[25] Before this decree, the Catalan government had a policy of financially supporting production, but Catalan language cinema was in a marginal position and very far from being *normalised*. Taking into account the existing film dubbing tradition (into Spanish), this policy was an attempt to normalise the presence of Catalan language in commercial cinema. However, these provisions were not accepted. Cinema companies strongly objected to the new measure. In recognition of this opposition from the distribution and exhibition industries, the decree's operation was postponed and finally repealed in May 2000 in negotiations between the Catalan government and the distribution sector.[26] An agreement was reached that the major American distributors would dub a significant number of commercial films in Catalan, especially children's films, and would progressively increase the scope of this process while the Generalitat would continue to provide financial help for dubbing.[27]

The presence of the Catalan language in cinema continues to be minimal in spite of signs of recovery in the sector in terms of audience and revenues visible at the beginning of 2000. Around one thousand films per year are exhibited in Catalonia. Between 1997 and 2003, the number of films with a Catalan version increased from 55 in 1999 to 92 in 2002 and, according to provisional data, 103 in 2003. However, in relative terms these figures represent between just 5% and 7% of films distributed in Catalonia.

Media and private sector initiatives

In Catalonia, as in other European countries, the press has been dominated mainly by private companies, who depend on market criteria, although there has been public funding available from the Generalitat for publications using Catalan. Under these conditions, the printed press and daily newspapers circulating throughout the entire region were in Spanish, except for one title (*Avui*, launched in 1976), whilst Catalan-written dailies tended to be aimed at local audiences. However, a major change took place with the launching of a double edition of the formerly Spanish-only daily, *El Periódico de Catalunya*. From 28 October 1997, the paper, which has a large circulation, was published in Catalan and in Spanish. In 1998, this newspaper on average sold 81,364 copies of its Catalan edition and 120,952 copies of its Spanish edition. Putting this figure in relative terms gives a better idea of the magnitude of this initiative: *El Periódico* consists of half (51.5% in 1998) of the circulation of Catalan-written dailies in Catalonia.

With this double edition, Catalan has become normalised as a press language. *Segre*, a Lleida-based daily, started the same double edition process in September 1997: 4947 copies of the Catalan edition and 7847 of the Spanish edition are sold daily (1998 data from Oficina de Justificación de la Difusión, OJD). Along with these new state-wide Catalan editions, there are 7 Catalan-written dailies (5 of which are mainly regional) and 10 exclusively or mainly Spanish-written.[28] This double edition process has been facilitated by technological developments in automatic language translation (with human revision) applied to news media. In general, this technological innovation offers a key opportunity to increase the numbers of minority languages in the press. This increase of Catalan in the press is also being promoted by the private sector as Catalan-speaking dailies are seen as viable and profitable projects. In spite of the increase of Catalan-written dailies, of the 550,000 copies of newspapers are sold in Catalonia, the majority have continued to be mainly in Spanish in a proportion of 1:3. This trend remained steady from 1998–2003, although the general press recession at the beginning of 2000 had a stronger effect on Catalan-written dailies than Spanish language publications.[29]

In terms of debates about economic liberalisation, it is clear that private sector media interests have developed particular initiatives in order to reinforce their market position and have used the Catalan language as part of this process. In response to a period of stagnation in circulation figures, eight private press publishers and an electronic publication firm,[30] all publishing in Catalan, formed an alliance, Comit, in 2001. The alliance has been created to coordinate different locally based, Catalan-language projects, as well as attempting to build a Catalan communication space. Representing 420,000 readers, Comit provides leadership for the Catalan-written press, not only in Catalonia but also in the Catalan-speaking world. The alliance has been involved in the promotion of *El Punt* as a *national* daily, and the joint distribution of a Sunday supplement. In January 2002 Comit also launched the first Catalan-written sports daily: *El 9 Esportiu de Catalunya*, bringing Catalan language normalisation to a market that had previous only had Spanish language publications: sports dailies.[31] Market liberalisation has had considerable impact on the press, through new free dailies, like *Barcelona y más*[32] and *Metro Directe*,[33] launched in Barcelona in 2000–2001 though the free press is largely written in Spanish.

Local media

Local communication systems in Catalonia changed significantly during the 1990s. The law regulating municipal radio stations was passed in 1991, and in the aftermath the movement that had unified radio interests within the sector was disbanded. Local television stations are still awaiting full regulation. The access approach to broadcasting became marginalised and replaced with an ethos of professionalisation as private and public interests began to lay great emphasis on quality. The growth of this professional approach has contributed to a reinforcement of the role of the private sector in local communication. Private enterprises in association with communication groups of different sizes are entering the sector and extending their commercial presence.

From a linguistic point of view, there are clear signs of Catalan use being consolidated and increased since 2000. The Comit alliance, even though its future remains uncertain, is one sign of this increase, as is the overall consumption of Catalan-written local weeklies and fortnightlies. The increased Catalan language consumption in local radio and television is also encouraging. However, there are signs of the reinforcement of the presence of Spanish. Circulation figures for the local press written mainly in Spanish are recovering, although at the moment it is not clear whether the increase is due to language or to the style of the newspapers on offer.[34] The new metropolitan free press, which has a high circulation, mainly uses Spanish. In spite of an overwhelming use of Catalan in local television, a new worrying trend also seems to be emerging. Spanish language content is being increased as some stations broadcast Spanish language drama and dubbed films.

Finally, new local media that define their identity more in terms of community interests than geography and language, have developed strongly since 2000. Newspapers of different periodicity and radio stations aimed at migrants tend to feature Spanish, but also languages such English (for example, with the free daily *Catalonia Today* launched in 2004), Russian, Chinese and Urdu. Therefore developments in local communication systems indicate that strong interdependence exists between different levels within the communication system, from multinational to local, yet despite all the pressures, the Catalan language still seems to retain its dominant position.

New Challenges

The presence of the Catalan language has increased in all media, both in terms of supply and of consumption, as a result of complex processes involving the intersection of political, private sector and civil society interests to support the language. In spite of this increase, at the beginning of the 21st century, the Catalan language occupies second place in the media. Even with the project of normalisation, the language remains secondary in state-wide media although it is dominant in local communication services. In terms of consumption, the relative percentages of consumption between Spanish and Catalan language content is: 58:42 in general radio, 68:32 in specialised stations; in television, it is 70:30; in the daily press 75:25 and in cinema 93:2 (with the remaining 5% being in other languages, see below). A closer analysis of radio and cinema, respectively the most and the least normalised media, allows us to evaluate the situation in more detail. Although not entirely homogeneous linguistically, available data for different periods illustrate the success of language normalisation within the radio sector. There has been an increase from four Catalan language stations (or five if we include one station using it for 95% of airtime) out of the 31 stations operating in 1981, to half of total radio output in 2002 (Barril, 1997; Bonet, 2000; Carreras, 1987; Gifreu, 1983: 282; Martí & Bonet, 2003).

This steady rise of Catalan radio has occurred with a parallel increase in the consumption of the medium as a whole. In 2003, the numbers of listeners to general Catalan-speaking radio had increased to 47.8%, from 35.5% in 2000, 40.2% in 2001 and 42.7% in 2002. Another indicator of the success of language normalisation in radio is the continuing dominance of Catalunya Ràdio in terms of audience. In the period 2000–2002, the total audience for specialised radio decreased from 2,026,000 listeners in 2000 to 1,894,000 in 2002. In this case, it is important to note that specialised radio is by large devoted to music where the Catalan language is marginal.

In cinema, the increase in audience for Catalan language versions of films is clearly visible: from 435,986 viewers in 1998 to 1,073,898. However, this doubling in numbers must be viewed in light of the overall increase in cinema-going in Spain. When this general increase is considered, there is just a slight variation in audiences for Catalan films of about 2–3%. This marginal position of Catalan cinema is also reflected in the distribution of different language versions of films. An overwhelming 93% of people view Spanish versions of films; with around 5% of audiences opting for films with 'other languages' while 2–3% opt for films in Catalan (DGPL, 2001: 103).

New media systems are creating key challenges as the digital divide potentially created by the Internet could threaten minority languages. In fact, in terms of language issues, the Internet must be examined using different criteria. Within conventional media such as press, radio, television or cinema, analysis focuses on proportions between different languages. However when examining the Internet, one must simply focus on the question in terms of presence or absence. In terms of the Catalan language, the data available show conflicting tendencies. The Open Directory Project (www.dmoz.org), which monitors web-use and content, ranked Catalan in twelfth place in terms of language on the Internet in March 2002, with 7981 websites, behind English, German, Spanish, French, Polish, Italian, Swedish, Dutch, Japanese, Danish and Korean – all of which are backed by nation-states.

According to 2001 official data provided by Catalan Government,[35] scarcely half the Internet users in Catalonia visited websites in Catalan (48.9%) while 82.7% go to websites in Spanish. English language websites are in third place (44.5%). Therefore the Internet has generated a new type of linguistic competition for Catalan where the language is no longer in competition with Spanish, but also with English.[36] The same data-set shows that plurilingualism on the Internet tends to decrease, as the proportion of users that visit only websites in Catalan and/or in Spanish increases.

The Internet also provides a contemporary example of social activism. In 1997, a group of citizens organised on a voluntary basis under the name

Softcatalà (www.softcatala.org), in order to translate software into Catalan and make it available without charge. However, this activism cannot, by itself, counteract the absence of Catalan in the more market-driven areas of the Internet.

In terms of media and language policy, Catalonia constitutes an example of a state that still has relatively limited power in managing communication networks, both at *national* and local levels. Until recently, this powerlessness has been at least in part counteracted by social dynamics at the local level, where, as in the case of local television, the long-term situation of alegality has been actively and positively used by a majority of the sector in order to support the language. This lack of regulation is being exploited in a similar manner in activity underway to support the language on the Internet.

Media and communication systems always depend on language, and policy-makers today face very special challenges monitoring the rapid pace of change in new telecommunications networks and in the transformation of audiovisual systems. In the context of the profound changes in radio, television and the Internet, even national languages with state support and majority status feel threatened. Expanding liberalisation as well as technological innovations are making visible the strong links between different levels of communication systems. The profound changes in media and cultural industries suggest that neither public policies nor social initiatives alone will be enough to ensure a specific Catalan language media space and new kinds of co-operative strategies need to be created in order to ensure the future of the language.

Notes

1. This chapter has been prepared under the framework of the research project *Catalan Language in the Media in Catalonia (Press, Radio, Television, Internet, Cultural Industries, 2001–2003)* of the research programme of Institut d'Estudis Catalans.
2. Another element of change comes from the internal level. From 1980 to 2003, the political coalition ruling in Catalonia was the same (nationalist Convergència i Unió). The general election of November 2003 brought in a new ruling coalition between three political forces (socialists, green-socialists and republicans).
3. In Spain, the autonomous communities of Balearic Islands (Catalan), Basque Country (Basque) and Galicia (Galician) share this model, while Valencian Community (Catalan, called *Valencian*) and Navarra (Basque) territorially distinguish two zones, only one of which has two official languages.
4. Departament de Cultura (1983).
5. See Gifreu (1983) Parés *et al.* (1981) Costa, P.O. *et al.* (1981) *Autonomia i mitjans de comunicació.* Barcelona: Institut de Ciències Socials. Diputació de Barcelona.

6. Catalan Statute of Autonomy provides for Generalitat power in these areas in article 16.
7. The Spanish Third Channel Law (1983) had not yet been passed, and that was a source of conflict between the Spanish central and the Catalan governments. See López and Corominas (1995: 177).
8. Concerning regionalisation of television in the (then) 12 member states of the European Union, see Moragas and Garitaonandia (1995).
9. Data from CCRTV in Corominas (1989).
10. It has to be borne in mind that a vast and increasing majority of the population understood Catalan. In 1981, 81% of people aged 2 years and over, 90.3% in 1986, and 93.8% in 1991.
11. An economic indicator of Catalan autonomous television consolidation is that, although it is the autonomous television with the highest budget, in 1991 it was 83% self-financing (through advertising). In 1993, the figure had dropped to 74% (López & Corominas, 1995: 188).
12. Local and regional press in Catalonia was born in 19th century, but after the Spanish Civil War (1936–1939) almost all publications disappeared and the few remaining ones had to be published in Spanish.
13. See Moragas and Corominas (1992).
14. EMUC and FTLC illustrate this model, which indicated at the same time that there was a rather negative connotation associated with television business initiatives which were linked to privatisation and profit-making. Note the difference between *municipal* (public, linked to the municipality) radio and *local* (public or private) television.
15. Instead of the linguistic normalisation law of 1983, this one was of linguistic *policy* (Llei 1/1998, de Política Lingüística. *Diari Oficial de la Generalitat de Catalunya, DOGC* 2553, 09.01).
16. In contrast to the vote of the 1983 Law, the nationalist ruling coalition (Convergència i Unió), Partit dels Socialistes de Catalunya, Iniciativa per Catalunya and Partit per la Independència were for; Partido Popular and Esquerra Republicana de Catalunya were against, although for different reasons. Partit dels Comunistes de Catalunya abstained.
17. Catalan is also used in Ràdio 4 (from Radio Nacional de España) and in COMRàdio, a public radio initiative promoted by Consorci de Comunicació Local with more than one hundred municipal stations.
18. Notwithstanding, in public consumption the Catalan-speaking TV3 has tended to be the leader – with a share of 21% by itself and an accumulative one of 28% with Canal 33 – while in second position was the private company Telecinco (19–20%) in 2000–2002.
19. The EU's Television Without Frontiers Directive (1989, renewed 1997) setting a majority quota of European works to be broadcast, was incorporated into Spanish legal system in 1994.
20. As radio in Spain has been for long highly concentrated in networks, the decree allowed stations belonging to statewide radio channels when the regulation came into effect to be excluded from the obligation to broadcast in Catalan for up to a maximum of six consecutive hours, which would not count when setting the basis for quota calculation (DGPL, 2003: 77).
21. Direcció General de Mitjans Audiovisuals. Generalitat de Catalunya. On www at: http://www6.gencat.net/dgma/catala/ccatala.htm. Data included in Corominas, M. (2003).

22. Networks or groups of stations resulting, specially, from the licensing process conducted by the Generalitat from 1998 onwards.
23. Decree 269/1998 excludes music stations which specialised in classic or folk music (art. 6.g).
24. There are other models for promoting songs in languages different from English based on voluntarism as in Denmark, where the Information Centre of Danish Music (Ministry of Culture) and the Authors Society (KODA) promoted *Play Danish Day* on 31 October 2002. See Ferro (2002).
25. Decree 237/1998 established the dubbing into Catalan of all works distributed in dubbed versions in Catalonia and longer than 60 minutes if there were more than 16 copies or if they were animated films for children. At least 25% of annual dubbed copies distributed in Catalonia should be in Catalan (art. 3.2). In exhibition, at least one day of Catalan-dubbed films for every three dubbed into Spanish or other languages.
26. See Jones (1999) and DGPL (2001).
27. Generalitat's film dubbing funding raised from €300 million in 1998 to €2104 in 2002 (DGPL, 2003: 13).
28. Including the Catalonian editions of three state-wide dailies.
29. Between 1999 and 2003 Catalan-written issues sold in Catalonia have decreased by 5.96% while Spanish-written have decreased by 3.89%.
30. Editing *El Punt, Segre, Regió 7, El 9 Nou* (in Catalonia), *Diari d'Andorra* (in Andorra), *Diari de Balears* (Balearic Islands), *El 3 de Vuit* and *L'Hora del Garraf* (also in Catalonia); and the electronic publication VilaWeb.
31. In Catalonia (and in Spain) sports dailies are important in terms of circulation: 171,088 copies in Catalonia in 2001 (combined circulation of *Sport* and *Mundo deportivo* from Barcelona; plus *Marca* and *As* initially from Madrid).
32. Launched in November 2000 by Multiprensa y más, which in July 2002 was taken over by the Swiss company 20 Min Holding AG (from the Norwegian multimedia group Schibsted) and the newspaper was renamed *20 minutos de Barcelona y más*.
33. Launched in March 2001 by Metro International, a division of the Swedish company Modern Times Group, Publisher of some 20 free dailies mainly in large cities in 15 countries in Europe, Latin America and North America.
34. See the contribution of J. Vicenç Rabadán (2003).
35. Secretaria per a la Societat de la Informació (2002).
36. The trend was confirmed in a survey conducted in June 2002 and May 2003 concerning the websites of the 50 biggest companies in Catalonia, where the Catalan language is in third place, behind Spanish and English.

References

Barril, J. (1997) Ponència: Llengua i comunicació radiofònica. In *Actes del 1r congrés de la ràdio a Catalunya. Barcelona, 4 i 5 d'octubre de 1996* (pp. 201–208). Barcelona: Societat Catalana de Comunicació.

Bonet, M. (2000) La ràdio local. In M. Corominas and M. de Moragas (eds) *Informe de la comunicació a Catalunya 2000* (pp. 222–227). Bellaterra (Barcelona): Institut de la Comunicació.

Carreras, Ll. de (1987) *La ràdio i la televisió, avui*. Barcelona: Edicions 62.

CAC (Consell de l'Audiovisual de Catalunya) (2003) *Informe de l'audiovisual a Catalunya 2002* (Quaderns del CAC. Número extraordinari). Barcelona: Consell de l'Audiovisual de Catalunya.

Corominas, M. (1989) Política lingüística i política de mitjans a Europa (Radio y televisió). Doctoral thesis, Universitat Autónoma de Barcelona, Facultat de Ciències de la Informació.

Corominas, M. (2003) La llengua. In M. Corominas and M. de Moragas (eds) *Informe de la comunicació a Catalunya 2001–2002* (pp. 247–264). Bellaterra (Barcelona): Universitat Autònoma de Barcelona.

Costa, P.O. *et al.* (1981) *Autonomia i mitjans de Comunicació*. Barcelona: Institut de Ciències Socialis. Diputació de Barcelona.

Department de Cultura (1983) *Llibre blanc de la Dirreció General de Política Lingüística*. Barcelona: Department de Cultura. Generalitat de Catalunya.

DGPL (Direcció General de Política Lingüística) (2001) *Informe sobre política lingüística 2000*. Barcelona: Direcció General de Política Lingüística. Departament de Cultura. Generalitat de Catalunya.

DGPL (Direcció General de Política Lingüística) (2002) *Informe sobre política lingüística 2001*. Barcelona: Direcció General de Política Lingüística. Departament de Cultura. Generalitat de Catalunya.

DGPL (Direcció General de Política Lingüística) (2003) *Informe sobre política lingüística 2002*. Barcelona: Direcció General de Política Lingüística. Departament de Cultura. Generalitat de Catalunya.

Ferro, Ch. (2002) Play's the thing for Danish music scene. *Billboard* 114 (48), 52.

Gifreu, J. (1983) *Sistema i polítiques de comunicació a Catalunya. Premsa, ràdio, televisió i cinema (1970–1980)*. Barcelona: L'Avenç.

Gifreu, J. (1986) *El debate internacional de la comunicación*. Barcelona: Ariel.

Jones, D. (1999) Catalunya davant la prepotència de Hollywood. Mercats globals í cultures minoritaries. *Trípodos* 7, 47–59.

Jones, D. (2003) Indústries culturals d'edició discontínua: editorial, fonogràfica, videogràfica, multimedia. In M. Corominas and M. de Moragas (eds) *Informe de la comunicació a Catalunya 2001–2002* (pp. 139–170). Bellaterra (Barcelona): Universitat Autònoma de Barcelona.

López, B. and Corominas, M. (1995) Spain: The contradictions of the autonomous model. In M. de Moragas and C. Garitaonandía (eds) *Decentralization in the Global Era: Television in the Regions, Nationalities and Small Countries of the European Union* (pp. 175–199). London: John Libbey.

Martí, J.M. and Bonet, M. (2003) La ràdio. In M. Corominas and M. de Moragas (eds) *Informe de la comunicació a Catalunya 2001–2002* (pp.45–60). Bellaterra (Barcelona): Universitat Autònoma de Barcelona.

Moragas, M. de and Corominas, M. (1988) *Local Communication in Catalonia (1975–1988). Media Spaces and Democratic Participation*. Barcelona: Barcelona City Council.

Moragas, M. de and Corominas, M. (1992) Spain, Catalonia: Media and democratic participation in local communication. In N. Jankowski, O. Prehn and J. Stappers (eds) *The People's Voice. Local Radio and Television in Europe* (pp. 186–197). London/Paris/Rome: John Libbey.

Moragas, M. de and Garitanondia, C. (eds) (1995) *Decentralization in the Global Era. Television in the Regions, Nationalities and Small Countries of the European Union*. London: John Libbey, updated in Moragas, M. *et al.* (eds) (1999). *Television on your Doorstep. Decentralization Experiences in the European Union*. Luton: University of Luton.

Parés, M. *et al.* (1981) *La televisió a la Catalunya autónoma*. Barcelona: Edicions 62.

Prado, E. and Moragas, M. de (2002) *La televisió local a Catalunya. De les experiències comunitàries a les estratègies de proximitat* (Quaderns del CAC. Número extraordinari). Barcelona: Consell de l'Audiovisual de Catalunya.

Secretaria per la Societat de la Informació (2002) *Estadístiques de la Societat de la Informació Catalunya 2001*. Barcelona: Generalitat de Catalunya.

Vicenç Rabadan, J. (2003) La comunicació local (in the Observatori de la comunicació local). In M. Corominas and M. de Moragas (eds) *Informe de la Comunicació a Catalunya 2001–2002* (pp. 214–218). Bellaterra (Barcelona): Universitat Autònoma de Barcelona.

Websites including English version

Consell de l'Audiovisual de Catalunya (Audiovisual Catalan Council): http://www.audiovisualcat.net

Generalitat de Catalunya. Catalan Language Web: http://www6.gencat.net/llengcat/index.htm

Generalitat de Catalunya. General Directorate for Audiovisual Media: http://www6.gencat.net/dgma/scripts/catala/index.asp

Generalitat de Catalunya. Institut d'Estadística de Catalunya (2003) *Cens linguistic de 2001. Principals resultats*. Barcelona: Generalitat de Catalunya. Institut d'Estadística de Catalunya. On www at: http://www6.gencat.net/llengcat/socio/docs/censling2001.pdf

Generalitat de Catalunya. Institut d'Estadística de Catalunya (2004) *Estadística d'usos linguistics a Catalunya. Document de presentació*. Barcelona: Generalitat de Catalunya. Institut d'Estadística de Catalunya. On www at: http://www6.gencat.net/llengcat/socio/docs/usos2003.ppt

Chapter 11

The Territory of Television: S4C and the Representation of the 'Whole of Wales'

ELIN HAF GRUFFYDD JONES

The quest for media in one's own language has been and continues to be an ambition shared by many minority language communities worldwide. While some language communities have succeeded in establishing a plethora of media institutions operating in their own languages, others are still striving for very basic levels of provision in this field. It is certainly notable that despite the pronounced scepticism expressed by minority languages guru Joshua Fishman (Cormack, 2003; Fishman, 2001) when he referred to the 'mass-media fetish of some language activists', minority language pressure groups and institutions – Wales being a case in point – remain either unaware of his observation or at least undeterred by it as they continue their efforts to seek media in their own language.

In fact, as each new medium appears – the emergence of the web, for instance – many minority language activists feel that it is imperative that they embrace the inherent challenges posed by all new technological developments in media and communication so that their language is not 'left behind'. Having access to communication media in one's own language can simultaneously be symbolic of the very essence of the struggle to ensure the future survival of the language in the modern world and provide a practical tool to enhance communication opportunities through the medium of that language and hence add to its use and usefulness. In the Welsh context, initiatives to establish a presence for the language in the media, from the early years of radio broadcasting in the 1920s right through to the present day, have largely been instigated by language campaigners rather than provided as routine developments on the part of the media institutions themselves. There are a few notable exceptions to this. The Welsh language digital television platform, S4C Digidol, was established by the Broadcasting Act of 1996 as a result of forward thinking by the broadcaster rather than overt, public and political lobbying by pressure groups. The BBC's online service in Welsh, BBC Cymru'r Byd was launched in 2000 and according to its executive producer Grahame Davies (2004: 28), 'no *external* protesting or lobbying was needed in order for it to be created' (my italic, my translation); 'ni fu angen protestio na lobïo allanol i'w greu ychwaith.' These are exceptions nonetheless and language supporters' efforts have led to significant developments in Welsh language press and broadcasting media over the years. Naturally, the campaigns and initiatives have taken various guises; from the legendary political lobbying and direct action that led to the creation of S4C, to the long standing labour of love provided by thousands of volunteers involved in producing and distributing the 55 community newspapers (*papurau bro*) published monthly all over Wales for the past 20 years (Huws, 1996). It can currently (2006) be seen in the entrepreneurial project to establish a daily newspaper *Y Byd* (The World) in the language for the very first time. As Grahame Davies (2004: 27) notes 'the language has – or more correctly, the language's supporters have – an amazing vitality' (my translation); 'y mae i'r iaith – neu yn fwy cywir, ei charedigion – hyfywedd hynod'.

The political campaigns undertaken by language-focused pressure groups and political parties have played a crucial role not only in arguing the case for media in minority languages and in particular television but have also ensured that the arguments in favour remain live issues for debate in the public arena for prolonged periods of time and often by means of heavy investment in human campaigning resources. The campaign to establish S4C in Wales led by Cymdeithas yr Iaith Gymraeg (the Welsh Language Society) and Plaid Cymru lasted over a decade and involved many thousands of campaigners, participating in non-violent direct action and mass civil disobedience campaigns (Hourigan, 2001; Phillips, 1998). The declaration in May 1980 by Gwynfor Evans that he would begin a fast unto death from 6 October of the same year (if the Conservative government did not reverse its decision and continue with its manifesto promise to establish a Welsh language television channel) was undeniably the single definitive act that transformed the political climate and led to the establishment of S4C and indeed it could not have been realised by any other individual, yet it took place, one must remember, against a backdrop of sustained collective action.

Indeed, it can be argued that campaigns in favour of television in minority languages represent the best known and most effective of all public campaigns to democratise the media, both in terms of broadcasting structures and television content, certainly in this part of Europe. In comparison, and despite a certain level of public debate and concern by other non-dominant sections of society such as those represented by Trade Union movement and other groups within the political Left about matters such as editorial control and the effect of private monopolies, the absence of particularly sustained or high profile non-language related campaigns is quite noticeable.

Fears arising from the uncertain future for a minority language, coupled with the explicit link between language and the very nature of communication media, have provided clear and unambiguous *raisons d'être* upon which dedicated campaigns can be based and concrete, tangible goals can be set as a source of continuing inspiration for campaigners. Indeed, with the language as a focus, campaigns have been portrayed as a matter of the language itself needing media in order to survive into the modern world as seen in one of the popular slogans used by Cymdeithas yr Iaith Gymraeg during a decade of protesting for Welsh language television provision, 'Bywyd i'r Iaith' (Life for the Language).

The Functions of Television in a Minority Language Community

Language, as observed by postcolonial writer Ngũgĩ wa Thiong'o (1986: 13), has a 'dual character…both as a means of communication and a carrier of culture'. Communication and culture are of course at the heart of television, but the television industry also has a role in the economics and status of a language community as well as a contribution to make to the language's linguistic repertoires. These five primary functions of television – communicative, cultural, economic, status and linguistic – form the basis of the arguments why this medium is essential for the well-being of any (minority) language community. They also point to the limitations that a language community might experience if it does not have its own television service.

It is commonly recognised that television enables a language community to speak to itself and that it can build and strengthen that community's sense of collective identity. Outside the particular field of minority language media, the idea that 'the media are both a product and reflection of the history of their own society and have played a part in it' (McQuail, 1994: 121) are commonplace. In the context of Wales, it has been argued that 'to a greater extent than perhaps any other country in Europe, broadcasting has played a central role, both positive and negative, in the development of the concept of a national community' (Davies, 1994). Creating 'communicative spaces' or 'espais de comunicació' (Moragas Spà, 1988) for minority language communities, echoing the Habermasian notion of communication in the public sphere, are indeed perceived by commentators as just as necessary for minority language groups as they are for other social groups. In reviewing the first decade of S4C it was observed that 'a language is a group of people speaking to each other, and...in modern conditions much of that communication occurs through the media, so that a language denied access to media is discriminated against, accorded inferior status, and is unlikely to survive' (Thomas, 1997).

Television, it is said, creates a mediated representation of society, not a mere reflection, and in the case of a minority language, like Welsh, the linguistic experience that it projects is quite clearly not identical to that encountered in 'real life'. Welsh language television creates a world in which the language is used for all kinds of communication in its factual and fiction programmes. However in the 'real world', or in the public sphere outside television, public institutions in the Welsh context, as indeed in many others where they exist, seldom use their language to conduct their business to the same extent as corresponding institutions operating in majority language communities use theirs. Despite the existence of the Welsh Language Act of 1993 which states that 'in the conduct of public business and the administration of justice in Wales the English and Welsh languages should be treated on a basis of equality', very few public bodies actually use the Welsh language to anywhere near the same degree as they use English. In this context, television performs an important communicative function in Welsh society as an arena for public debate in the Welsh language between institutions. Jeremy Isaacs, the founding chief executive of Channel Four UK noted in his memoirs:

> What is clear is that S4C has demonstrated, as have television in Catalonia and the Basque country, and radio in the Gaeltacht, that broadcasting has a vital role in the cultural life of a people, and particularly of a people whose nationhood is not evinced in a self-governing autonomous state. (Isaacs, 1989: 96)

The expectations of what television can achieve are multiple and the notion that it can and must in some way compensate for other missing elements in a nation's life is highlighted time and again in the Welsh case. As early as 1941 in a pamphlet produced by Plaid Cymru, Gwynfor Evans, the party's leader at the time stated that:

> Mae'r teledu yn gymaint mwy na chyfrwng adloniant, ac hyd yn oed o addysg i Gymru...Gallai wneud mwy nag unrhyw un sefydliad arall i gynnal a hybu'r iaith ac egni deallusol y Cymry, ac i sicrhau na chaiff etifeddiaeth y canrifoedd ei herydu.

> Television is so much more than a medium of entertainment and even of education for Wales... It could do more than any other institution to sustain and promote the language and the intellectual energy of the

Welsh people and to ensure that the heritage of the centuries is not eroded. [my translation]

Similarly, producing one's own cultural output rather then being 'the *objects* of others' study and gaze' (as noted by Thomas, 1995) is an essential role for all communities with access to television. The level of home production is one of the defining criteria against which 'good', 'quality' or 'public service' television is repeatedly judged. Television performs a distinct function in the formulation of the collective memory of a community with regard to the creation and dissemination of its cultural canons. It is not without significance that the BBC, for instance, has produced a television adaptation of Jane Austen's 1813 novel *Pride and Prejudice* at least every 15 years since it started broadcasting television.

In addition to communicating within the group, Welsh language campaigner Ffred Ffransis of Cymdeithas yr Iaith Gymraeg (1985: 107–108) expresses the aspiration that television will enable Welsh people to view the world through their own eyes:

> To all intents and purposes, English is the language of television and radio in Wales and the programme material is Anglo-American. Hence our people are conditioned to forget the Welsh language and the values of our civilization; we are conditioned to think like the English and to see the world through the eyes of the English. [my translation]

> I bob pwrpas, Saesneg yw iaith y teledu a'r radio yng Nghymru ac Eingl-Americanaidd yw deunydd y rhaglenni. Fel hyn, cyflyrir ein pobl i anghofio'r iaith Gymraeg a gwerthoedd ein gwareiddiad; cyflyrir ni i feddwl fel Saeson ac i edrych ar y byd trwy lygaid Seisnig.

The analogy of seeing the world through one's own eyes recurs in the current Welsh context in the campaign to set up a daily newspaper in Welsh. The novelist Emyr Humphreys, who writes mainly in English, states: 'Hawl cenedl aeddfed a chyfrifol yw gweld y byd yn ddyddiol drwy sbectol ei phriod iaith arbennig hi ei hun a neb arall.' ('It is the right of a mature and responsible nation to view the world daily through the spectacles of that nation's own particular language and no other.' – my translation).

If, in the early years, the case for a separate television channel for Wales which would broadcast in the Welsh language, was seen as 'a purely cultural one' (Isaacs, 1989), it has subsequently become evident that the television industry in Wales has made a significant contribution to the country's economy. Studies undertaken from perspectives of cost effectiveness (Grin & Vaillancourt, 1999) and local economic impact (Fuller-Love & Jones, 1999; Zendoia Sainz, 1997) emphasise the economic wealth and job creation that would not have been possible were it not for the cultural specificity of the media product. The television industry provides attractive job opportunities where the language is central, the production companies and channels are vibrant economic entities, and this – in addition to the mere fact of seeing the language being used on television – accords status to the language. As expressed in the context of web based media, Catalan journalist and director of VilaWeb, Vicent Partal (n.d.) who has been operating online media in Catalan since 1995, states:

> Si l'idioma de la comunicació al nostre país és l'espanyol o el francés els beneficis aniran a parar a Los Angeles, París o Miami. No està en joc només la supervivència d'una cultura. Estan en joc milers de llocs de treball que es crearan gràcies al català o que no es crearan en el nostre país.

> If the language of communication in our country [Catalonia] is Spanish or French, the profits will end up in Los Angeles, Paris or Miami. The survival of a culture is not the only issue at stake. It's the thousands of jobs which will be created because of the Catalan language, or the jobs that won't be created at all in our country. [my translation]

'Home-grown' media, and language specific cultural products cannot be easily sourced from elsewhere (or 'imported'), and thus the jobs involved in their production are not easily exportable to countries where labour costs are cheaper. Welsh language television production companies, like small businesses in other sectors, also spend proportionately more of their turnover locally than larger businesses (Fuller-Love *et al*, 1997) therefore a television industry that has a large proportion of small, indigenous businesses can contribute greatly to the economic well-being of the language in the area.

The linguistic function of television within a minority language community such as Wales is particularly influential due to the fact that other major institutions seldom perform all their social and communicative functions in the minority language. The absence of the language in the private retail sector means that the vocabulary for goods and services are not coined and disseminated in these fields proper but only in mediated communication. Similarly, not all academic and vocational subjects are taught through the medium of Welsh and as such mediated debate contributes greatly to the overall public debate of that subject in the language. Television programmes alongside print and electronic media often perform the role of a hothouse for coining new vocabulary (see Awbery, 1995; Jones, 2003) and occasionally have to do so instantaneously as news stories break. The language policies and linguistic practices of a television channel can have a far-reaching effect within a minority language community. The fundamental televisual convention of juxtaposing the audio and the visual within the mise-en-scène lends itself to the practice of using lesser-known or new forms of speech in a context that is reinforced by paralinguistic elements and the use of images. This can extend the dissemination and comprehension of new or unfamiliar linguistic elements within the language community that in turn may well lead to further dissemination and use by third parties. Similarly, it can promote mutual understanding of different dialects, if it chooses to allow or encourage its presenters and scriptwriters to use dialect forms of speech in addition to (or instead of) contributing to the development of a 'standard oral language'. In debating a wide compass of subject areas in all manners of speech from international politics to home improvements, it can provide a public context for new modes of expression and thus contribute to the expansion of linguistic registers of the language. 'The difference between developed and underdeveloped languages is fundamentally one of register range' (Ferguson, 1968 in Williams, 1992).

Towards a Typology of Television Provision in Minority Languages

S4C in Wales can be categorised alongside other minority language television channels as a dedicated television channel operating under public ownership. Other channels that form part of this first model of television in minority languages (Jones, 2002) include TV3 and C33 in Catalonia (1984 and 1988), TVG in Galicia (1985), TVV in Valencia (1989), Omrop Fryslân in Friesland (1994) and TG4 in Ireland (1996). The channels (and broadcasting authorities) were established either by autonomous parliaments or as a result of state legislation (usually preceded by protest and lobbying). Some of these channels have a clear and specific linguistic brief (though they may at the same time serve a particular region or country) while others were created under a geographical remit, but use the language – or languages – of the territory in question. The Basque Language Normalization Act of 1982 refers to the government's responsibility to 'increase the presence of the Basque language within the media'. In the UK, the Broadcasting Acts of 1980/1981 established the Welsh

Fourth Channel Authority with the function to 'provide television programmes of high quality for broadcasting' and 'to secure that the programmes broadcast on the Fourth Channel in Wales [S4C] between the hours of 6.30 pm and 10.00 pm consist mainly of programmes in Welsh'. The specific aim of these broadcasters was to improve the language's presence in the media and many have since set up new channels, especially in the light of digital technology.

The second model of television in minority languages is that of private television channels that broadcast wholly or partly in the minority language and sometimes exist in communities where the public sector has failed to provide or on occasion alongside public provision. Long-term advances in status and use of minority languages usually involve commitment from the public sector, and for the private sector to provide where the public sector has failed is unusual. As such, fewer examples of this type have existed, the main ones being TV Breizh in Brittany and Tele Südtirol.

The third model is that of the specific slots or individual programmes that some minority language communities have on majority language channels. This is very often the situation in places where there is limited recognition for the language, as is the case in France, where there has been little development in the provision of television since the 1960s. However, in the case of Scottish Gaelic, a significant increase in investment was made in the 1990s as well as changes in the scheduling of Gaelic television programmes on English language channels in Scotland so that they were no longer confined to off peak hours. Recent language legislation requires the Italian broadcaster RAI to substantially increase its provision for up to 12 minority languages. However, the existence of minority language programmes on majority language channels is not always an indication that one has no channel of one's own. For instance, the Spanish state network TVE produces opt-outs for Catalonia in Catalan.

Finally, a fourth model has appeared in recent years, that of local television channels that emerged during the 1990s in particular within the language communities of the Spanish state, some of which are not surprisingly in local community ownership (Arana et al., 2003; see also their Chapter 9 in this book). Representing the whole country: 'Sianel Gymraeg, ie, ond ar gyfer Cymru gyfan' – a Welsh language channel, yes, but one for the whole of Wales. The dedicated television channel or corporation has by far the best resources to fulfil the appetite for television in minority languages. In their schedules they include a variety of programmes typical of those found on similar channels in the majority language of the state – news, sport, current affairs, documentaries, light entertainment, fiction, children's programmes and other genres as they emerge. Their creation often marks a new age in television in that particular area. Minority language television channels seldom have exact counterparts operating side by side in the majority languages of the area. Indeed, more often than not, majority language television does not serve the same territory as minority language television. Moreover, the territory of linguistic minorities rarely corresponds in its entirety to that of an official administrative area. With the exception of the Basques and the Irish, no other minority language community has established a fully fledged TV channel to broadcast in its own territory using the majority or dominant language. The Basque language channel, ETB-1 is accompanied by a Spanish language TV channel for the area, ETB-2. However, Spanish language ETB-2's programme content differs significantly from that of Basque language ETB-1, one major difference being that ETB-2 aims exclusively at an adult audience and shows no children's programmes, these being broadcast in Basque on ETB-1. (For a critique on the lack of synergised strategy between ETB-1 and ETB-2, see Amezaga & Arana, 2005). The situation of the Irish language as a minority language where it is also the first official language of its own state is somewhat of an anomaly in many aspects of comparative analysis between minority languages and their social contexts, and the media context is no exception. The Irish public service broadcaster, RTÉ has always broadcast predominantly in English. Occasional calls have been made for such a television service to be set up, in the context of Wales at least, but with little political support, no sustained campaigns and possibly still some confusion as to its cultural *raison d'être*. Welsh, like most other minority languages, does not operate in a culture of 'twinned unilingualism' where both languages are used by two distinct and mainly unilingual communities, it is spoken in all parts of the country to varying degrees. Hence, the dedicated minority language television channel is more often than not the only television channel that serves the territory of the language community.

The Geography of On-screen Wales

It is significant that almost all of the channel's Welsh language programme output is produced in Wales (98.6% in 2000 against a target of 95%). The practice of dubbing imported programmes is generally limited to the genre of children's animation. The option of dubbing English language fiction (film, drama, soap and comedy) produced either in the UK or in other anglophone television contexts was never really considered suitable for Welsh language television. It is not simply the case that the Welsh audience may have already seen the original versions in English on one of the British channels as suggested by some observers (Thomas, 1995) because successful Welsh language versions of the *Teletubbies*, *Denis a Dannedd (Dennis the Menace)* and other children's programmes contradict this. There is also the perceived reluctance to view any subtitled programmes or material than is known to be dubbed as this is also the case in the context of imported programmes originally broadcast in languages other than English. *Ros na Rún* – the Irish language soap opera broadcast on TG4 – was broadcast in Irish with Welsh subtitles during the infancy of S4C Digidol (S4C Digital, set up in 1998) as were other drama series from other European countries. However, as the number of households in Wales with access to the digital channel increased, this practice faded away and perhaps it is no coincidence that in S4C's Annual Report of 2000 chief executive Huw Jones stated that '...our own audience's resistance to dubbed material (like that of viewers in other parts of the UK) works in favour of the creation of high quality original material, notwithstanding the challenge that this represents'.

The need to create indigenous programmes right from the onset of S4C sets Welsh language television somewhat apart from its counterparts of the first 'wave' of minority language dedicated channels set up in the 1980s. The schedule of ETB-1 for example contained programmes such as *Cagney eta Lacey* and *St Elsewhere Ospitalea* for many years and the first, long standing Basque soap opera *Goenkale* did not appear until 1994, some 12 years after the channel first started broadcasting. *Pobol y Cwm* (BBC), also the first British soap opera to go daily on weekdays, precedes the establishment of S4C and celebrated its thirtieth anniversary in 2004.

Indigenous production carries the expectation of counteracting the images of Wales and the Welsh produced by outsiders and these are generally considered from the inside to be extremely stereotypical. Gwenno Ffrancon (2003: 9) in her volume on the films of 1935–1951, a period that included several Hollywood 'blockbusters' set in Wales such as *How Green Was My Valley* (John Ford, 1941), observes:

> Yn sgil y cynnyrch hwn [ffilm], er da ac er drwg, daeth darluniau o'r fam Gymreig, y chwarelwr, y glöwr a'r Cymro duwiol a cherddorol â'i fryd ar hunanwellhad yn rhan o ymwybod miloedd o bobl.

As a result of this product [film], for better and for worse, the images of the Welsh 'mam', the quarry man, the collier and the godly and musical Welshman with his aspiration to better himself became part of the consciousness of thousands of people.

Contemporary Welsh television fiction still uses the old quarrying land-scapes and the former coal mining areas to provide the backdrop for its stories. Religion and music too have their place within S4C's broadcasting schedule. The problematic nature of stereotyping lies in the awareness of an image being too limited in its depiction of those whom it claims to portray rather than it being inherently negative or having no truth in it at all and also in the complexities of the relationship between the producer of the image and the audience in terms of 'insiders' and 'outsiders'. Huw Jones, chief executive of S4C at the time claimed:

> Mae cyfresi fel Y *Palmant Aur* a'r *Wisg Sidan* yn dangos fod ein hanes ni yr un mor ddiddorol a'r un mor ddilys fel ffynhonnell drama ag unrhyw gyfres focs siocled sy'n clodfori moesau aristocrataidd Seisnig. Y gwahaniaeth pwysig yw mai ein hanes ni, ein moesau ni sy'n cael eu darlunio yn y cyfresi hyn.

> Y *Palmant Aur* and Y *Wisg Sidan* demonstrate that our history is as interesting and as valid a source of television drama as any other chocolate box series which pays tribute to the values of the English aristocracy. The important difference is that it is our history and our values that are depicted in these series. [my translation]

What kind of Wales is represented on screen through the television programmes of S4C and has the channel developed its own particular way of broadcasting? This question can of course be approached from a number of perspectives. The annual reports of S4C reiterate the channel's aim of 'ensuring that the programme service reflected the whole of Wales'. From the mid-1990s onwards, this notion has been interpreted as having a geographical meaning and specific reference has been placed, at least in the intention if not always in outcome, to 'see programme ideas coming forward set in areas not hitherto represented, including North East Wales and the valleys of South East Wales'. To what degree therefore does the output of S4C reflect 'the whole of Wales' in a geographical sense?

Analysis of Locations in Welsh Language Television

A frequent observation made by viewers in public meetings hosted by S4C around Wales was that they wanted to see more programmes from their own areas on television. Strong local allegiances and identities are prevalent in Wales as in many other minority language communities and this may be in part due to the lack of a democratic, all-Wales tier of polit-ical institutions for most part of the 19th and 20th centuries, until the establishment of the National Assembly under the Government of Wales

Act 1998. Cardiff became the official capital of the country as late as 1955. However, it is true to note that during these two centuries, some all-Wales bodies were formed mainly in cultural and religious contexts and more often than not closely linked to the language.

The importance of the local in Welsh culture is also evident in the fact that the most popular printed media in Welsh by far are the local community newspapers. These sell a total of 55,000 copies between them each month, which is 12 times more per issue than any of the weekly national publications (Huws, 1996). In addition, local dialects are recognised throughout the country and it is difficult to speak Welsh without revealing some trace of regional accent.

Research conducted by the Monitoring and Research Unit into Broadcasting Compliance, at the Department of Theatre, Film and Television Studies at the University of Wales Aberystwyth investigated regional representation on Welsh language programmes on S4C in two separate studies. The first study involved an analysis of the works of fiction broadcast on the channel between 1996 and 2000. The second focused on a content analysis of the whole schedule during three non-consecutive weeks of broadcasting between October 2002 and October 2003. The results of both studies revealed specific patterns that can be said to characterise Welsh language television broadcasting.

Television Fiction and the Regions of Wales

The first study, an overview of television fiction broadcast over a five-year period from 1996 to 2000, produced a data set of over a hundred television programmes comprising film, drama series, single plays, situation comedy and children's drama. It was decided not to include *Pobol y Cwm* (BBC) in the data, because as the channel's soap opera with five episodes a week (260 per year) each screened three times and running throughout the year, it dominates the schedule unlike any other fiction programme. In addition, it is not subject to the same commissioning process as other works of fiction because it is principally provided as part of the BBC's contribution to S4C as laid out in the establishing Act. Also, although fictionally located in a valley in Carmarthenshire, it is widely known that the purpose-built set is in Cardiff.

The data were analysed and the main locations identified for each piece of fiction. The main pointers used to identify the (perceived) location were programme information from S4C marketing, accents of the 'local' characters, references to real places in the dialogue and scene-setting location shots. The vast majority of productions were set in what could be defined as one main area (though some had minor locations too). The data were organised according to area. No weighting was given to the total length of the production or to the number of times it was broadcast, though these were quite varied. Sequel or multiple series broadcast during this five-year period were counted as separate commissions and thus included in the data as such.

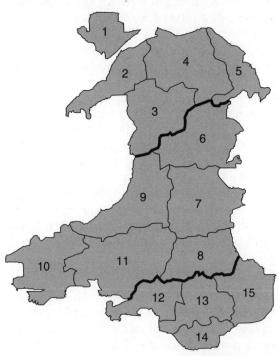

The North
1. Môn / Anglesey
2. Arfon and Dwyfor (Caernarfon area and Llŷn peninsula)
3. Meirionnydd
4. Conwy and Denbigh
5. Flint and Wrexham

Mid-Wales and The West
6. Montgomery
7. Radnor
8. Brecknock
9. Ceredigion (including Aberystwyth)
10. Pembrokeshire
11. Carmarthenshire (including Llanelli)

The South
12. Swansea and Neath–Port Talbot
13. The Valleys (including Pontypridd)
14. Cardiff and Vale of Glamorgan
15. Gwent (including Newport)

Figure 11.1 Wales, divided into 15 areas

Table 11.1 Analysis of television fiction by location 1996–2000 (excluding daily soap opera, *Pobol y Cwm*)

Main location used in the programme	Number of productions (figures in brackets refer to number of 'period' pieces)	Productions as percentage of total
North West – Gwynedd, Môn and Conwy (areas 1, 2, 3 and Western part of 4 on Figure 11.1)	36 (5)	48
North East – Flint, Denbigh and Wrexham (areas 5 and Eastern part of 4)	2 (1*)	3
Mid-Wales – Ceredigion and Powys (areas 6, 7, 8 and 9)	7** (5)	9
South West – Pembrokeshire, Carmarthenshire and Swansea (areas 10, 11, 12)	13 (2) *Pobol y Cwm* (BBC) not included	17
South East – the Rhondda Valleys, Cardiff and Gwent (areas 13, 14, 15)	17	23
Total	75 (13)	100
No real location, not identifiable or locations outside Wales	32	
Total	107	

Notes: * period film shot mainly outside Wales (in Poland); ** Aberystwyth in its function as a minor location (usually to represent university life) not included.

The figures in Table 11.1 represent the number of productions commissioned over the five-year period and do not represent actual proportions of on-screen time for each region in televisual works of fiction. Table 11.1 shows that the North West dominates televisual fiction, followed by the South East and the South West, though it must not be overlooked that *Pobol y Cwm* is not included in the data. The North East only appears twice (both single productions, not series) during these five years of fiction on television.

Table 11.2 compares the data in Table 11.1 with the percentages of the Welsh speaking population of Wales and that of the total population of the country living in each area. By taking these factors into account, the North West is overrepresented and North East underrepresented, both in

Table 11.2 Distribution of Welsh speakers and population in Wales, according to the census of 2001 and percentage of fiction commissions 1996–2000

Region	Percentage of total number of Welsh speakers in Wales	Percentage of population	Percentage of commissions (as in Table 11.1)
North West – Gwynedd, Môn and Conwy (areas 1, 2, 3 and Western part of 4 on Figure 11.1)	25	10	48
North East – Flint, Denbigh and Wrexham (areas 5 and Eastern part of 4)	11	13	3
Mid-Wales – Ceredigion and Powys (areas 6, 7, 8 and 9)	11	7	9
South West – Pembrokeshire, Carmarthenshire and Swansea (areas 10, 11, 12)	28	23	17 (excluding *Pobol y Cwm*)
South East – the Rhondda Valleys, Cardiff and Gwent (areas 13, 14, 15)	25	47	23
Total	100	100	100

terms of population and Welsh speakers. The percentage of works of fiction located in other areas roughly corresponds to that of the country's Welsh speakers or population living there. The representation of Mid-Wales in fiction during this period mainly in the various series of *Y Palmant Aur* (Opus), which chronicles the lives of families associated with the milk route from Ceredigion to London in the interwar years. Fiction located in the South East included several contemporary series set in the valleys, a film in and around the city of Newport as well as productions in Cardiff.

However, the counties of Gwynedd and Ynys Môn (Anglesey) have the highest concentration of Welsh speakers in all of Wales (69% and 60% respectively, according to the census of 2001). This is important when considering the penchant within contemporary television drama series towards the social realist tradition. Dramatic portrayals of the lives of ordinary or working-class Welsh people in towns and villages in the North West are some of the most prevailing images of television fiction in Welsh. Also this area has the largest concentration of television production companies outside Cardiff and creating a television industry in this Welsh heartland was a decision made in the early 1980s in order to bring the economic advantages of the industry to a strong Welsh-speaking area. Many of the production companies located in this area have produced drama series and other works of fiction for S4C including *Rownd a Rownd* (Nant), a children's drama series broadcast since 1996. Prominent scriptwriters are based here or have strong links with the area, and one successful commission often leads to the next. Also, short travelling distances for crews and cast from base to outside locations reduce production costs.

The main geographical area of Wales underrepresented in televisual fiction during this period is the North East. This would come as no surprise to television viewers in Wales, and is probably typical of the output of Welsh language television in any given year. Some 14% of the populations of the border counties of Flintshire and Wrexham speak Welsh. While this percentage is admittedly lower than the national average (21%) and indeed lower than anywhere outside the industrial South, in terms of actual numbers of people (around 38,000 in total) it is equal to the number of speakers in either Ceredigion or Anglesey. To expand further on the suggested correlation between the locations used in works of fiction and the actual location of television production companies, it is worth noting that not one television company is located in the North East of Wales. The first ever contemporary television drama series located in this area *Mostyn Fflint n'aye!* (Teledu Elidir, 2004) was broadcast in the autumn of 2004, was produced by a Cardiff-based company, and did not make a second series. On the other hand, *Treflan* (Alfresco), an imaginative adaptation of a sequence of novels written and set in 19th-century North East Wales by Daniel Owen (the 'Welsh Charles Dickens') is regarded by S4C as one of its most ambitious projects and has run to several series since it was first broadcast in 2002. However, *Treflan*, being a period piece and filmed entirely on a purpose built set in a warehouse in the South of the country, did not seek to portray the present-day reality of living in the North East of Wales. Indeed, the absence of modern fiction set in this area means that a whole repertoire of linguistic dialects are hardly ever heard in contemporary television drama, the images of the North of Wales are almost exclusively those of the Western part and the reality of life in the industrialised towns in the North East or in the rich farmland of its inland vales including the experience of living on the border with England are rarely examined. Television fiction therefore cannot claim to reflect the whole of Wales, though it does reflect substantial parts of it.

The 'Whole of Wales' in All Programmes

The second study was based on a quantitative content analysis of all programmes broadcast on the channel during three non-consecutive weeks of broadcasting (7–13 October 2002, 17–23 February 2003 and 29 September–5 October 2003). The methodology of three full but non-consecutive weeks was used instead of Monday Week 1, Tuesday Week 2, Wednesday Week 3 and so on in order to see whether during the space of one full week of broadcasting S4C had shown something from 'every part of Wales'. In collecting the data, each location shown (those referred to in speech only were not included) was recorded exactly as it was presented within the programme, more often than not using very local units of individual villages, towns, suburbs of cities rather than in larger units of counties etc. This in itself was indication that presenters expected a relatively high level of familiarity with the geography of the country on the part of viewers. Studio-based discussions referring to particular places were not included, unless accompanied by footage reporting. In the case of fiction, the location was taken to be the perceived location, as in the previous study.

Taking the whole week of broadcasting into the sample meant including repeats and multiple broadcasts. This quantitative approach is based on a large sample of data; a total of 252 hours of broadcasting. No weighting was given to the length of the programme, the length of the appearance of the location, the time of broadcast, whether it was a repeat or whether it was broadcast on both analogue and digital platforms or only on digital.

Table 11.3 uses almost exactly the same regional divisions as those used in Tables 11.1 and 11.2. These data show that there is a better balance between the regions of Wales when all programmes – not just fiction alone – are considered. Mid-Wales, though rural and sparsely populated for the most part, features often in factual and lifestyle programmes. Also, news coverage is closer to the percentage of the population – not just the Welsh speaking population – living in each area. From this analysis it can be said that S4C did in fact represent all parts of Wales during each of these three randomly selected weeks of broadcasting.

However, for those viewers in public meetings and other participants and observers of Welsh life these regions could be considered too vast.

Table 11.3 Analysis of locations used in Welsh language programmes during three non-consecutive weeks 2002–2003 (data presented in five regions)

Region	Percentage of total number of Welsh speakers in Wales	Percentage of population	All prog-rammes	News prog-rammes	Other prog-rammes (except news and drama)
North West – Gwynedd, Môn and Conwy (areas 1, 2, 3 and Western part of 4 on Figure 11.1)	20	6	26	22	28
North East – Flint, Denbigh and Wrexham (areas 5 and Eastern part of 4)	16	16	8	10	8
Mid-Wales – Ceredigion and Powys (areas 6, 7, 8 and 9)	11	7	17	7	24
South West – Pembrokeshire, Carmarthenshire and Swansea (areas 10, 11, 12)	28	23	26	29	22
South East – the Rhondda Valleys, Cardiff and Gwent (areas 13, 14, 15)	25	47	22	32	19
Total (figures do not total 100 due to rounding)	100	99	99	100	101

Indeed the cultural meaning of 'place' is an important organising concept in the field of minority languages. In colloquial terms, the country is often regarded as North and South, though there is no agreement or consistency for that matter on where large areas of Mid- and West Wales belong in that divide. None of the official divisions of the country – such as the 40 political constituencies, the 22 local authorities, the 4 police force zones etc. – lend themselves as a suitable model for this study. They lack a recognisable cultural identity, divide cities, their boundaries are unclear and in the case of the 22 local authorities do not have any real consistency in numbers of populations (Cardiff the largest with 300,000 and Merthyr Tydfil the smallest with 55,000). On the other hand, non-official bodies, or grassroots organisations with an all-Wales dimension, such as the Young Farmers' Association and The Urdd (national youth organisation) operate using some 15 regions, which are much more meaningful and identifiable in cultural terms.

The data were redrawn using 15 regions, as shown in Figure 11.1. Some areas coincide exactly with single local authority areas (Anglesey, Ceredigion, Pembrokeshire and Carmarthenshire). Two local authorities were subdivided further using previous district councils, Gwynedd into two areas ('Arfon and Dwyfor' and 'Meirionnydd') and Powys into three (Montgomery, Radnor and Brecknock). The other areas are clusters of neighbouring local authorities. Presented this way, the data can be also interpreted using other social realities, such as 'North/South', 'Welsh speaking heartland/Anglicised areas', 'East/West', 'rural/industrial' etc. S4C's own audience and viewing figures refer to three regions, the North, the West (including Mid-Wales) and the South, so this was also incorporated into the presentation of data. The number of Welsh speakers living in each of these three regions is similar, but the population as a whole is more concentrated in the South.

Even though the total number of locations used over the three weeks varied from 180 in Week 2 to 280 in Week 3, the division between the three regions was fairly constant during each of these weeks. The percentage of locations used in any one region was not higher than 42% or lower than 27% in any individual week. In the case of news programmes only (all of which are produced by the BBC for S4C), the regional profile reflected the population density to a greater degree than other programmes.

In the case of works of fiction shown during these three weeks, the sample was very small (54) and only comprised of a handful of productions and the daily soap, *Pobol y Cwm* (BBC). Yet interestingly it produced results that largely coincided with those of the earlier study (Tables 11.1 and 11.2) as the North West, Carmarthenshire, Cardiff and the Valleys were the only areas represented. However, it is remarkable that each of the 15 areas appeared at least once during each of the three weeks with only one exception, that of Radnorshire (home to 1% of the population) in Week 3. Some areas, namely Carmarthenshire, Arfon and Dwyfor, Cardiff and Ceredigion dominated in all genres (though Ceredigion did not in news programmes), but no one single area featured in more than 19% of the total of any week or any genre.

Table 11.4 Analysis of locations used in Welsh language programmes during three non-consecutive weeks 2002–2003 (data presented in 15 areas and 3 regions)

	Percentage of total number of Welsh speakers of Wales	Percentage of the population of Wales	All programmes		News		Other programmes (except news and drama)	
1. Môn (Anglesey)	7%	2%	56	8%	9	4%	43	9%
2. Arfon Dwyfor	13%	4%	113	15%	31	15%	71	15%
3. Meirionnydd			27	4%	4	2%	23	5%
4. Conwy Denbigh	9%	7%	32	4%	7	3%	25	5%
5. Flint Wrexham	7%	9%	27	4%	14	7%	13	3%
The North	**36%**	**23%**	**255**	**34%**	**65**	**32%**	**175**	**36%**
6. Montgomery			18	2%	4	2%	14	3%
7. Radnor	4%	4%	15	2%	0	0%	15	3%
8. Brecknock			9	1%	2	1%	7	1%
9. Ceredigion	7%	3%	88	12%	9	4%	79	16%
10. Pembrokeshire	4%	4%	22	3%	6	3%	16	3%
11. Carmarthenshire	15%	6%	121	16%	31	15%	58	12%
Mid-Wales and The West	**30%**	**17%**	**273**	**37%**	**52**	**26%**	**189**	**39%**
12. Swansea, Neath–Port Talbot	9%	13%	54	7%	21	10%	32	7%
13. The Valleys	11%	20%	38	5%	19	9%	18	4%
14. Cardiff and Vale of Glamorgan	8%	14%	103	14%	33	16%	65	13%
15. Gwent	6%	13%	22	3%	13	6%	9	2%
The South	**34%**	**60%**	**217**	**29%**	**86**	**42%**	**124**	**25%**
Total	100%	100%	745	100%	203	100%	488	100%

Note: Numbers have been rounded to nearest integer

Some particular programmes made a significant contribution to the number of individual locations used and covered vast areas of the territory of Wales. These were mainly news and current affairs, factual and light documentary programmes with a rural brief and a children's magazine programme. The channel's weeknightly general magazine programme now known as *Wedi 7* (Tinopolis) featured the highest number of locations used and across the three selected weeks had items from all parts of Wales with the exception of two rural areas, Brecknock and Radnorshire. This programme was established in 2002 with a specific mission to reflect all parts of Wales whereas its predecessor *Heno* (Agenda) (controversially known for its remit to use English language items and casual or 'slack' registers of Welsh) had a specific geographical focus on industrial Carmarthenshire, Swansea and its valleys, an area of large numbers of Welsh speakers but where language transmission rates and literacy levels and other vitality indicators are reportedly lower than the average. This policy decision indicates a shift in focus in order to reflect more of the whole country.

Conclusion

These data strongly suggest that S4C's policy of reflecting the whole of Wales in a geographic sense is being implemented across its programmes' service. Certain areas are indeed better represented than others in terms of the frequency of appearances on screen and the range of programme genres in which they feature; namely the capital and Western areas with high percentages or high numbers of Welsh speakers. However no area can claim to be totally disregarded by Welsh language television. A comparative analysis of English language television programmes produced in Wales would yield interesting results as would studies other countries, states and regions.

The presence of so many identifiable locations used during each of these individual weeks implies that the televisual Wales, or perhaps more correctly the televisual Cymru, is constructed as a 'community of communities' and does not follow in the same capital-centric or centralist tradition of television that is associated so often with British and other state broadcasters. In that sense, it could be argued that Welsh language television replicates structures found in other Welsh language institutions – such as the National Eisteddfod and others previously mentioned in this chapter – which have a decentralist approach or are made up of strong local components. The study reveals that Welsh language programmes regularly visit communities all over Wales as part and parcel of the business of making television. This suggests that the relationship between watching Welsh language television and participating in the programmes is one of cultural proximity.

Further studies are needed to analyse the way in which linguistic minorities with access to their own media produce images of themselves, especially given the societal context in which many of these television channels were created. The conditions under which these media entities operate – levels of funding, structure of the industry, commissioning processes etc. – are crucial elements in the construction of the image of the community on screen. It is the subject of current debate what these conditions might be in the UK at least where television programming is increasingly market-led and the date for the impending analogue switch-off becomes imminent as digital television is now available in a majority of homes. At this turning point in the broadcasting environment, it is legitimate for S4C as the only broadcaster of Welsh language television to function under conditions conducive to fulfilling the needs of a full television service in Welsh. One of the slogans used by Cymdeithas yr Iaith Gymraeg in the last stages of the television campaign was 'Amodau teg i'r sianel' (Fair conditions for the channel). A quarter of a century since it started broadcasting, it seems as relevant as ever.

Bibliography

Amezaga, J. and Arana, E. (2005) Two television channels in the Basque Country: Ignoring each other or working in the same direction. Paper given at the 4th Mercator International Symposium on Minority Languages. On www at: www.aber.ac.uk/mercator/cymraeg/events/ MercSym2005papurau.html

Arana, E., Amezaga, J., Basterretxea, J.I. et al. (1999) A. La oferta de ETB-1. On www at: www.euskonews.com/0026zbk/gaia2606es.html

Arana, E., Azpillaga, P. and Narbaiza, B. (2003) Local television stations, Basque and minority language normalization. Mercator Media Forum 7, 86–98.

Awbery, G. (1995) The Welsh used on television. Mercator Media Forum 1, 77–87.

Broadcasting Act 1981, Part II Section 47 (1) (a) and (3). London: HMSO.

Broadcasting Act 1996, Part I, Section 29. (1) (b). London: HMSO.

Census 2001. On www at: www.statistics.gov.uk

Cormack, M. (2003) Developing minority language media studies. Mercator Media Forum 7, 3–12.

Cymdeithas yr Iaith Gymraeg (1985) S4C: Pwy dalodd amdani? Aberystwyth: Cymdeithas yr Iaith Gymraeg.

Davies, G. (2004) Dechreuadau: Y Gymraeg a'r Cyfryngau Newydd. Cyfrwng 1, 26–41.

Davies, J. (1994) Broadcasting and the BBC in Wales. Cardiff: University of Wales Press.

Edwards, J. (1994) Multilingualism. London: Penguin.

Ellis, G. (forthcoming) Twin Town, ffilmiau'r nawdegau a'r etifeddiaeth ffilm Gymreig. In E.H.G. Jones (ed.) *Astudiaethau Prifysgol: Ffilm, Teledu a'r Cyfryngau*. Cardiff: University of Wales Press.

Ffrancon, G. (2003) *Cyfaredd y Cysgodion: Delweddu Cymru a'i Phobl ar Ffilm, 1935–1951*. Cardiff: University of Wales Press.

Fishman, J.A. (ed.) (2001) *Can Threatened Languages Be Saved?* Clevedon: Multilingual Matters.

Fuller-Love, N. and Jones, A.G. (1999) Small businesses in the media industry in Wales. *Contemporary Wales* 12, 173–192.

Fuller-Love, N., Jones, A.G. and Dennis, C. (1997) *The Impact of S4C on Small Businesses in Wales*. Aberystwyth: University of Wales Aberystwyth. Study funded by the Economic and Social Science Research Council ESRC Ref No. R000221667.

Grin, F. and Vaillancourt, F. (1999) *The Cost-effectiveness Evaluation of Minority Language Policies: Case Studies on Wales, Ireland and the Basque Country*. Flensburg: European Centre for Minority Issues.

Habermas, J. (1989) *The Structural Transformation of the Public Sphere*. Cambridge: Polity Press.

Hourigan, N. (2001) New social movement theory and minority language television campaigns. *European Journal of Communication* 16 (1), 77–100.

Huws, G. (1996) The success of the local. *Mercator Media Forum* 2, 84–93.

Isaacs, J. (1989) *Storm Over 4: A Personal Account*. London: Weidenfeld and Nicholson.

Jones, E.H.G. (1997) The future of languages in world-wide networks. *Mercator Media Forum* 3, 45–51.

Jones, E.H.G. (2002) La televisión en lenguas minorizadas: hacia una tipología de modelos para crear espacios de comunicación. Paper given at Escuela de Serronda, Asturias, 8 December 2002.

Jones, E.H.G (2003) Cyweiriau Iaith Teledu [the language registers of television]. Paper given at 12th International Congress of Celtic Studies.

Ley de normalización del uso del euskera 1982. Vitoria/Gasteiz: Gobierno Vasco/Euskojaurlaritza.

McQuail, D. (1994) *Mass Communication Theory*. London: Sage.

Moragas Spà, M. de (1988) *Espais de Comunicació: Experiències i Perspectives a Catalunya*. Barcelona: Edicions 62.

Ngũgĩ wa Thiong'o (1986) *Decolonising the Mind: The Politics of Language in African Literature*. London: Currey.

Partal, V. (n.d.) La Nació Digital: les tecnologies de la informació i el futur del nostre país'at. On www at: http://vilaweb.com/AREES/placa/congres/nacio.html

Phillips, D. (1998) *Trwy Ddulliau Chwyldro: Hanes Cymdeithas yr Iaith Gymraeg*. Llandysul: Gomer.

S4C Annual Report 1995. Cardiff: S4C Authority.

S4C Annual Report 1996. Cardiff: S4C Authority.

S4C Annual Report 2000. Cardiff: S4C Authority.

Thomas, N. (1995) Linguistic minorities and the media. In P. Lee (ed.) *The Democratization of Communication*. Cardiff: University of Wales Press.

Thomas, N. (1997) Sianel Pedwar Cymru: The first years of television in Welsh. Paper presented at the International Symposium on Contact and Conflict, European Centre for Multilingualism, Brussels.

Ure, J. (1982) Approaches to the study of register change. *International Journal of the Sociology of Language* 35.
The Welsh Language Act 1993. London: HMSO.
Williams, G. (1992) *Sociolinguistics: A Sociological Critique.* London: Routledge.
Y Byd. On www at: www.ybyd.com
Zendoia Sainz, J.M. (1997) The Basque language media: An assessment of their economic importance. *Mercator Media Forum* 3, 75–86.

Chapter 12

Translation and Minority Language Media: Potential and Problems: An Irish Perspective

EITHNE O'CONNELL

As pointed out in the Introduction to this collection of essays (Chapter 1), the emergence of minority language media studies is a fairly recent development and the discipline is still in the process of determining its own breadth and scope. In this context, it seems important to make an early claim for input from linguists, translators and intercultural experts if the full significance of the *language and translation* element in minority language media is to be usefully explored and understood. Too often, especially in the largely monoglot, English speaking world, the particular nature and perspective of individual languages is overlooked or the particular is taken to be general. Even the acclaimed linguist, Noam Chomsky, speaks of language but cites only examples from English. And yet much of modern linguistic research has pointed again and again to the differences, not just in structure but also in perspective, to be found even in languages from the same historical linguistic family. Attention has been drawn by Whorf and Sapir, and Jakobson, among others, to the deeply complex links between culture and language. Tymoczko writes of 'the recognition that there is no Platonic reality represented in various ways by various languages, but that reality is constructed by language itself' (1999: 24).

Language, but very significantly language that is not representative of a dominant culture, is at the heart of minority language media. The language of minority language media gives a voice to the 'other', offering hitherto not widely heard perspectives. Thus it is no coincidence that when the state Irish language television station, TnaG, later renamed TG4, was founded in the Republic of Ireland in 1996, it chose '*Súil eile*' (i.e. another eye/another way of seeing) as its slogan. This foregrounding of what linguistic minorities have to offer, namely different perspectives inextricably linked to their particular mode of self-expression, is central to the minority language media studies project. Moreover, even the most superficial examination of minority language communities will show that where a minority language survives in close proximity to one or more other languages, translation is likely to be a significant linguistic activity and sometimes even a vital survival strategy for the minority language culture. Any investigation of the language element of minority language media, therefore, also needs to address the question of the role of translated language in the minority language culture, in general, and in the media, in particular.

Importance of Minority Language Media

One powerful tool that linguistic communities can exploit for language planning purposes is the media, especially the audiovisual media. Yet, for more than a decade now, a note of caution has been sounded in some quarters in relation to claims about the power and influence of minority language media in the context of language revival and maintenance. This is due in no small part to Fishman's (1991: 395) assertion that the domain of the media is far less important than home, community, education or work. He followed up this claim a decade later with a rather sceptical reference to the enthusiasm of some minority language activists for mass media as a 'fetish' (Fishman, 2001: 473). As a result, there has been an understandable reluctance to make grand claims for the role of minority language media in the revival and / or maintenance of minority languages. Nevertheless, as Cormack (2004: 4) points out, while it is difficult to determine exactly the full potential of the media in a minority language context (and it would be foolish to exaggerate its likely role), we should not be blind to the obvious contributions they can or could clearly make.

Four important benefits of minority language media are summarised by Cormack (2004):

(1)   their symbolic role for language communities;
(2)   the attendant economic boost to minority language communities, e.g. by providing some attractive careers prospects;
(3)   their role in creating a public sphere within the minority language community; and
(4)   their representational role both for the smaller minority language and wider external community.

Further positive claims for minority language media are made by Riggins who states that

> ...ethnic minority media are making a substantial contribution to the continued survival of minority languages. The skills of imperfect speakers are improving, languages are being modernised by the addition of new technical vocabulary related to contemporary life...Ethnic

minority media give the young an opportunity to relate to role models speaking their native language. The public validation of minority languages by their use in the media is important for their survival especially in the eyes of the young who would be most tempted to speak exclusively the majority language. (1992: 283)

An interesting point which Riggins includes in his list of advantages of minority language media is the way in which they can help in relation to corpus planning matters by improving aural/oral skills and disseminating new technical vocabulary. A similar point is made by O'Connell (2003: 60) in a study looking at the dubbing of a television animation series for children from German into Irish, referred to below. She recommends the exploitation 'in this age of mass communication, … [of] Irish-language broadcasting…for the initial transmission and repeated reinforcement of new terminology, especially for the benefit of young viewers…' (2003: 60). Yet if minority language television carries major language subtitles as is the case with TG4's English language subtitles on Irish programmes, new Irish technical and other terms are less likely to be picked up by viewers because they will be focused on the English language technical vocabulary in the subtitles.

These references from Riggins and O'Connell are cited here because although the topic under discussion is minority *language* media, paradoxically, relatively little has been written about the specifically *linguistic* aspect of minority languages. It is true that Cormack (2000: 6–9) provides a good overview of research conducted to date on the topic of language in the mass media. Most interestingly, he points out that the traditional assumptions about the use of high register and formal, standardised language in the media, especially print media, are not borne out by recent research. Rather both print and broadcast media 'present different solutions to a similar problem, namely that of finding an appropriate non-formal register for use in a mass, public medium' (2000: 8). Though different, these solutions have in common their attempt to identify a linguistic form 'which is not (in the main) either strongly regional, nor too obviously received pronunciation, neither strongly working class, nor too much upper middle class, neither too formal nor too informal' (2000: 9). However, it is crucially important to note that Cormack's literature review is based largely, if not entirely, on analyses of language used by *major language* media.

Language in Minority Language Media

But what of the *language* aspect of minority language media? It could surely be argued that the language of minority language media is likely to have a greater potential influence on the linguistic ability of its audiences than the language of major language media is likely to have on its audiences, at least in situations of *diglossia* such as pertain in Ireland. For our purposes, a diglossic situation can be said to exist when a minority language is restricted in use to a limited number of domains, such as home and school, while the major language is used in other more numerous and often more prestigious domains, such as workplace, hospital, local government. Where clear functional separation exists in the diglossic use of the major and minority languages, we can speak of stable social compartmentalisation. If it does not, intra- or inter-generational language shift from the minority to the major language is likely to occur, placing the minority language in danger of terminal decline. In this context, it should be noted that in Ireland as elsewhere, the media, especially the audiovisual media, is a high prestige domain – one of very few such domains in which Irish is used. On the other hand, English is used in a much wider range of domains and therefore its relative influence in the particular domain of the media is not as great.

In Ireland, there is little evidence of stable social compartmentalisation and therefore, language shift at both intra- and inter-generational level is a grave cause for concern. Indeed, bilingualism and minority language decline are so far advanced that there are no longer any monolingual speakers of Irish. Native speakers amount to approximately 100,000 out of a total population of over 3,500,000 in the Republic of Ireland, while almost 1,500,000 (over 40%) citizens claimed in recent census returns to speak Irish. In Northern Ireland, approximately 142,000 people (10% of the population) made the same claim. A realistic estimate of actual competency is made by Walsh, who states for the Republic that 'about 5 per cent have a high active competence in Irish, a further 10 per cent have a good competence, while a further 20–30 per cent have a lower passive ability in the language' (2003: 545–546). Rather like Scotland, many native and very active speakers are concentrated in rural Irish-speaking areas, known as the Gaeltacht(aí), mainly along the western seaboard, but significant numbers also live in Dublin and other urban centres. Yet while the language declines in the former rural strongholds, increasing numbers of all-Irish schools spring up due to popular demand throughout the rest of the country.

Thus, there is no longer any semblance of a homogeneous community of Irish speakers to be served by the media: poorer farming communities in the Gaeltacht and prosperous urban dwellers may be equally interested in TG4. The language that was long associated with remote terrain and cultural backwardness now garners support from parents in working class and middle class areas, many of whom want something for their children that they themselves do not have, namely fluency in Irish. Irish speakers have become a fragmented, dispersed, heterogeneous community, many of whom live virtually surrounded and inundated by English. Moreover, as explained above, many speakers of Irish, even native speakers in the Gaeltacht regions, find themselves able to use Irish only in a very restricted number of domains while they often have no choice but to use English in all others, including most if not all high prestige domains.

One of the most striking and significant differences between major and endangered minority languages and their respective media is the extent to which the minority languages may have to rely on substantial amounts of *translated* material rather than *original* minority language material. A major or world language may engage in inward translation as an attractive add-on or luxury, a kind of cultural self-indulgence or diversion, although with minoritisation this is changing too. But for minority languages translation may be an absolute necessity, a matter of linguistic life or death. Hoffmann has pointed out that the stigma of technical, cultural and linguistic backwardness so often associated with minority languages, mainly as a result of various geographical and economic factors, has provided minority language planners with one of their greatest challenges. She states:

> It is generally accepted that in order to secure the survival of a minority language as a living entity, it is necessary not only to gain legal recognition for it, but also to prove that it has at its disposal all the linguistic resources needed for successful communication in a modern, industrially advanced world. (1994: 240)

Since endangered minority languages, by definition, do not have all these necessary domestic linguistic resources immediately at their disposal, one shortcut or temporary solution may be found in translation, which offers an important alternative means of enriching the minority language with both new ideas as well as words and phrases to describe them. Notwithstanding the obvious benefits of translation for minority languages, the necessary partial reliance on translation can also be potentially problematic. For example, Cronin (1995) describes possible implications for Irish of over-reliance on translation from English as follows:

> If [translators] translate allowing the full otherness of the dominant language to emerge in the translation, inviting rather than eliminating anglicisms from their Irish translations, then the language into which

they translate will become less and less recognisable as a separate linguistic entity capable of future development and become instead a pallid imitation of the source text. (Cronin, 1995: 90)

That this danger does not exist for major languages when engaged in inward translating is explained by Danan in a study of dubbing for the cinema. She explains that major languages are '...more capable...of resisting external intrusions and relegating translation to a secondary position, so that translated texts will not affect the main cultural norms of the target system' (1994: 14). Minority languages, on the other hand, she describes as 'weaker, open systems' (1994: 14) and as such, they are not in a position to resist or limit source language influence in the same way as major languages have been able to.

Translation and Power

One strand of investigation within translation studies, strongly influenced by postcolonial theory, has made a significant contribution in recent years to the study of the power relations that exist between languages and are often expressed by translation activity. Venuti (1992) introducing a series of essays intended to demonstrate the powerful, though frequently invisible and therefore rarely examined role of the translator in the establishment of literary canons and cultural identities, makes the following observation:

Translation continues to be an invisible practice, everywhere around us, inescapably present, but rarely acknowledged, almost never figured into discussions of the translations we all inevitably read. This eclipse of the translator's labour, of the very act of translation and its decisive mediation of foreign writing, is the site of multiple determinations and effects – linguistic, cultural, institutional, political. (Venuti, 1992: 1)

Venuti's observation is perhaps even more true of audiovisual translation than it is in the case of literary translation where the translator may at least be named. Indeed, it has been claimed that when a programme has been well dubbed, it is quite possible that the audience will never suspect that it has in fact undergone translation. Niranjana (1992: 1) has identified an inequality of relations between major and minority languages or languages of different status, as she refers to them and, in particular, shows how this is expressed through translation in terms of the relative volume of material that is translated between different language pairs and the main direction of translation activity. Looking at the phenomenon from a global perspective, Jacquemond (1992) presents the inequality in translation relationships as mirroring the economic power relations that persist between the former imperial powers and their erstwhile colonies stating 'the global translation flux is predominantly North-North, while South-South translation is almost non-existent and North-South translation is unequal: cultural hegemony confirms, to a great extent, economic hegemony' (Jacquemond, 1992: 139).

Venuti (1995) sees the USA and UK, aided by foreign publishing houses, engaging primarily in outward translation of English language texts, much to their globalising cultural and financial benefit, because the extent of the imbalance is enormous and the traffic is almost all one way:

> By routinely translating large numbers of the most varied English-language books, foreign publishers have exploited the global drift toward America's political and economic hegemony in the post-war period, actively supporting the international expansion of Anglo-American culture. (Venuti, 1995: 14)

This global tendency to translate predominantly from major languages into minority ones can lead to a chicken and egg situation whereby the relative dearth of translated material *from* minority languages seems to support the widespread view within dominant language cultures that minority languages, e.g. through their literary and audiovisual production, have little of interest to say. Such perceptions fuel the drive towards monolingualism, the globalisation of English and the suppression or, at least, benign neglect of minority languages. Indeed, even amongst those major language speakers who adopt a more 'live and let live' approach to minority languages, one can often detect a somewhat uncritical tendency to believe translators can be relied on to bring the linguistic riches of the wider world *intact* into major language cultures. Such passive approaches to translation from minority languages may be based on the common, but erroneous, assumption that once two languages have been mastered by a competent translator, there is little involved in the process of translation other than routine transfer or mapping of information from the source language onto the target language. This can result in a casual, unquestioning acceptance that any well-translated text, such as a subtitled or dubbed television programme, conveys exactly the same as the original. But such an attitude fails to take into account the hermeneutic realities of the act of translation – the idea that every competent translation is still but one possible version: any translation is simply the result of one possible reading of the source text and one possible rendering in the target language. Moreover, no translation can be viewed as neutral since it is undertaken as a result of a complex series of decisions taken by people ranging from the publisher or broadcaster who commissioned the translation in the first place, to the translation company or agency and ultimately to the individual translator or translation team.

Translated language

But there is a further problem with over-reliance on translated material. Interestingly, recent research suggests that translated language, regardless of the source and target language pair, may constitute a very distinctive kind of language that is untypical of what is generated by writers of original texts. Researchers have identified certain linguistic features that appear with regularity in translated texts and their existence has given rise to the notion of translation as a distinctive form of language or *third code*. The term was coined by Frawley (1984: 168), who claims that translation is 'essentially a third code which arises out of the bilateral consideration of the matrix and target codes: it is, in a sense, a sub-code of each of the codes involved'. Øverås (1998) has compiled a list of the distinctive features that have been identified as occurring to a greater or lesser extent in translations. These include: '*a high level of cohesive explicitness* combined with a *specific type of distribution of exotic features* (Baker 1993), a *low degree of lexical repetition* (ibid.), a *relative absence of colloquialism* (Gellerstam 1986) as well as *occasional metaphor* (Koller 1988)' (Øverås, 1998: 586). Although each of these features also appears in original texts, Øverås argues that when their distribution is studied in both original and translated texts, they may constitute 'parameters within which to identify a text as a translation' (1998: 586).

If the assertion that translations are marked texts is correct, it follows that cultures that rely heavily on translated texts are exposing speakers to an atypical form of language. Yet there seems to be little awareness of this possibility and, in particular, of the implications of this for language maintenance in minority language environments. The percentage of translated material broadcast by minority language broadcasters needs to be established and the implications studied.

As pointed out above, the assumptions underlying uncritical minority language attitudes in relation to heavy reliance on translated material mirror a common major language view that there is no value per se in learning or supporting a minority language, however interesting its output, since what is said in it can be rendered without loss through translation. It is precisely this kind of powerful, invidious logic that minority language awareness projects need to tackle head on. Indeed, at the very core of all justifications for the protection of minority languages is an appreciation of the ability of each and every language, whether major or minor, to express human experience in a unique fashion. The crucial fact that translation can only struggle to, but never completely succeed in, rendering this uniqueness is well put by the Irish language poet, Biddy Jenkinson, who does not encourage the translation of her own poetry into dominant language of her own bilingual country:

> The writing is a matter of love...a sustaining through my veins and verbs of something infinitely precious, a stretching back along the long road we have come...I prefer not to be translated into English in Ireland. It is a small rude gesture to those who think that everything can be harvested and stored in an English-speaking Ireland. (Jenkinson, 1991: 34)

Here Jenkinson is simply making a very pertinent point about the power relations between major and minority languages (i.e. unequal), the role of the translation (in the case of poetry translation perhaps, to appropriate ideas without engaging directly with the minority culture), the location (in Ireland, i.e. a bilingual society) and direction of translation (from the minority language, Irish, into the major one of the same territory, namely English). It is interesting to note that she is perfectly happy to have her work translated, for example, into French in Canada, where the relevant political, linguistic and cultural factors and relative power dynamics are quite different.

Translation and Minority Language Media

While some individual minority language writers, like Jenkinson, may feel at liberty to eschew the chance to have their work translated into certain languages under certain circumstances, such options are unlikely to be so freely available to those working with minority language media. Minority language television is always struggling to strike a balance between its ambitious goal of helping to forge and/or maintain a virtual linguistic community by means of high quality output, on one hand, and remaining commercially viable, on the other. Pressures on minority language media finances are aggravated by the wish to achieve sufficient variety to satisfy the interests of the intended audience. The audience, while identified for the purposes of minority language broadcasting by virtue of its minority language skills, is in fact anything but homogeneous. It is rather made up of many different people, all of whom have multiple identities and interests, which need to taken into account and reflected in the programming. As Cormack puts it, 'the content of minority language media sometimes gives the impression that the linguistic identity is the only one that matters, but other identities – political, sub-regional, religious – can cut across linguistic lines' (2000: 11).

Even if the necessary creative talent and skill is available in the minority language to produce sophisticated programmes ranging from, say, animation and drama to wildlife documentary, the cost is often simply prohibitive. Rather than settle for a small number of shoestring home productions, any minority channel with good business sense and a wish to maintain good average production values has to face up to the possibilities offered by the translation of foreign language productions. Many of these productions may have been made to the highest standards with generous budgets and have already paid their way in their home territory. When offered on the international market, any additional monies the original programme makers earn may well constitute unexpected additional profit. From the minority language broadcasters' point of view, the only challenge to be faced is that of language transfer from the original major language into the minority one.

The two main language transfer techniques for the screen are re-voicing (which includes dubbing, voice-over, narration and free commentary) and subtitling. Much of the early literature on audiovisual translation suggests that preferences for one or other type of transfer can be explained in terms of national traditions, with large countries such as France, Germany and Spain being identified as traditionally dubbing countries and smaller ones like Belgium, Denmark and Sweden cited as examples of subtitling ones. These distinctions are based on a historical view of translation for the cinema and are hopelessly simplistic in this age of multimedia where translation for cinema, television, video and DVD audiences cannot be casually lumped together. Neither the decision to dub, rather than subtitle, nor the reverse, can be explained away simply. A complex interplay of factors of an economic, political and cultural nature all have a part in the selection of appropriate translation strategies, as do programme genre, audience profile, cost, time and, of course, the relationship between the source and target language (e.g. major/minority language) (O'Connell, 1996: 152).

The Case of Irish

If we take the examples of English and Irish language television broadcasting in the Republic of Ireland, we can see that that English language broadcasters, whether working for the state channels, RTÉ One and Two, or the independent TV3, are in no way dependent on translated audiovisual texts and could easily decide to transmit only material that originated in the English language. Even if these channels had a strong intercultural agenda and wished to engage actively with other societies and cultures as well as perhaps saving money by buying material produced abroad (rather than relying exclusively on more expensive – because of economies of scale – home productions), there would still be plenty of scope to source English language material from other Anglophone countries such as the UK, Canada, the USA, New Zealand, Australia etc. It is relatively rare for Irish broadcasters to purchase foreign language material for translation and rebroadcast. Thus translated language is not typically found in major language media in Ireland.

On the other hand, minority language broadcasters in Ireland, like the rest of their counterparts in Europe, have to purchase and translate foreign language material. Thus audiovisual translation features promi-nently in Irish language audiovisual post-production activity, particularly on the Irish language television station, TG4. Indeed, such activity can be viewed as a matter of commercial survival and translations typically account for a significant proportion of minority language audiovisual texts.

The methods of translation most frequently used to adapt audiovisual material are dubbing and subtitling. To date, there has been an unfortunate tendency within the international post-production industry to view this dubbing or subtitling primarily as a technical task, which can be admirably completed given state-of-the-art post-production studio facilities, rather than viewing it as also a considerable linguistic or translation challenge. However, there is now a small but growing awareness, not least as a result of research in the field of translation and intercultural studies, that transla-tion is a complex activity and there is much more to translation than simple linguistic transfer or routine mapping of source language onto target language (O'Connell, 2004a: 31–33). Indeed, various linguistic, social, polit-ical and financial choices and constraints may impact on the translation process and have marked effects on the translation outcome (O'Connell, 1998). Since translation so often underpins minority language media production, minority language translation practice needs to be investigated critically, in the first instance, with a view to understanding better its current effect on minority language maintenance and development. Critical analysis of translation is also required in order to formulate recommenda-tions for the most appropriate use of different translation approaches and strategies when translating into and from the minority language.

An example of what is meant here is provided in some detail in O'Connell (1994: 367–373) where it is pointed out that it would be possible to adopt two different translation approaches in order to provide the same Irish programme with alternative sets of subtitles in English depending on the broadcaster's priorities. For example, if the purpose of the subtitles is to win as large an audience as possible, the translation approach will be much the same as adopted when providing English subtitles on foreign films. But if the broadcaster sees the role of minority media as dove-tailing with language maintenance and development initiatives, then different, possibly more literal, subtitles that help the minority language learner to understand the audio track might be used.

A quick look at some practical examples of shifts in translation policy and practice within TnaG/TG4 since its foundation in 1996 may help to suggest some of the kinds of issues worthy of investigation that may arise in minority language audiovisual media where there is heavy dependency on translated material. When the station started broadcasting in 1996, there was an awareness amongst senior management that subtitling could have an important role and there was an interest in the linguistic impact of subtitles of various kinds on viewers. On this basis, the station expressed its intention to broadcast many programmes in Irish only, in the first instance. English language subtitles and, subject to cost considerations, Irish language subtitles, would be used also but only on re-broadcasts. The logic was clear – at least from a language planning and maintenance point of view: the first broadcast would be aimed at native speakers and those with good Irish. Re-broadcasts carrying English subtitles would facilitate those with weaker or no Irish, as well as those with hearing problems, thus opening up Irish language programming to those directly excluded because they did not have sufficient mastery of the minority language. In addition to assisting Irish speakers with hearing difficulties, the use of Irish language subtitles, on the other hand, would also facilitate the viewing of those native speakers unfamiliar with Irish language dialects other than the one they speak themselves. An indirect benefit of providing subtitled text in Irish would be to improve the reading skills of the very many native speakers who do not regularly read Irish language material. With this in mind, it was decided that Irish language subtitles should be written in the official standard form of the language.

Over the years, the practice within the station in relation to the use of subtitles has changed significantly (Mac Dubhghaill, 2005). The primary motivation for the changes that occurred was the wish to increase the audience base. However, the *linguistic* implications for the minority language, which are quite serious, have largely been ignored. Nowadays, most Irish language programmes already carry English language subtitles on the first broadcast and these are what are known as 'open' subtitles, i.e.

they cannot be switched off. This practice has won a larger audience for TG4, which is doubtless extremely important in terms of the continued survival of the station. In commercial and political terms, it has probably been a wise move. But in terms of minority language maintenance and development, the changes are anything but positive. In effect, the station now broadcasts most of its programmes in a bilingual, rather than minority language, format. It should be noted that the fact that an audio track is in Irish and the subtitles are in English does not even mean that the linguistic split is really 50/50. On the contrary, as shall be explained in more detailed later, written text has a greater impact than the spoken word so ostensibly Irish language programmes on the minority language channel have now become predominantly English language programmes with merely a minority language veneer.

Translation from Irish

The negative linguistic consequences of this kind of practice for the speakers of the endangered minority language have been discussed elsewhere in some detail (O'Connell, 1996, 2001). Nevertheless, TG4 has tried with some success to legitimise this bilingual trend citing data from surveys of viewers' attitudes conducted between 1997 and 2005 (Mac Dubhghaill, 2005). The surveys reveal that the majority of native speakers questioned are not critical of this exposure to English subtitles on Irish language programmes and these findings are used to justify the continuation of the station's current policy. However, it is one thing to be a minority language television viewer and quite another to be an expert in issues relating to language maintenance and development. Looking to viewers for opinions concerning broadcasting policy decisions is appropriate if the main goal of the station is entertainment. If, however, the potential importance of minority language audiovisual media as a high prestige domain was recognised and harnessed to also serve as a component in a broader minority language planning project, television channels would also need to seek and take seriously the views of researchers in relevant areas.

Approaching the question of the use of English subtitles on Irish language programmes from a language learning perspective, it is possible to evaluate the linguistic implications of TG4's subtitling policy in a new light. There is considerable evidence, based on research conducted in several countries over the last two decades and beyond, as to the positive, reinforcing effects of subtitles on foreign language learning (O'Connell, 2004b). The current expert view is that an English-speaking intermediate level student of German, for example, can make substantial progress, especially in relation to vocabulary acquisition by watching what are called *reverse subtitles*, i.e. English films with German subtitles. This approach has been found to be more effective than watching German films with English subtitles. The reason for this is thought to be that the information received through the aural channel is much weaker than the visual information in the subtitles, which requires considerable cognitive processing. This has implications for minority language media's use of translated materials. Clearly, most Irish speaking viewers are simply not aware of the subliminal effects of their bi-modal viewing on their linguistic ability, i.e. it is likely that it is their *English language skills* that are being reinforced and developed as they watch programmes with Irish audio tracks and English subtitles, for the reasons outlined above, rather than vice versa.

Translation into Irish

Inward translation, as explained above, occurs where non-Irish language programmes are acquired elsewhere and need to be translated for broadcast on Irish language television. Depending on such factors as programme genre, target audience, age group, source language and available time and budget, the material may be dubbed or subtitled into Irish, but most are in fact dubbed. For example, programmes for children are nearly always dubbed, even though this is the more expensive option, because children are unlikely to have the reading skills to be well served by subtitles. Thus, given the high cost of home-produced material, most of the animation viewed by children on TG4 features Irish language that is based on *translated* dubbing scripts. As we have seen, this means that these texts in Irish bear *third code* hallmarks that distinguish them from texts that originate in Irish.

A study conducted in recent years (O'Connell, 2003) looked at a sample of episodes of *Janoschs Traumstunde*, a German animation series that was dubbed into Irish. Even with just a small corpus of six videos in German and their Irish translated/dubbed versions, there were many different aspects of the translations that could have been fruitfully investigated. But since terminology creation, standardisation and dissemination have traditionally been problematic language planning issues for minority languages, it was decided to focus on the ways in which specialised German terms were rendered in the Irish language translations. A consistent pattern of lexical simplification was found in the passages investigated. In other words, technical terms were translated in less specific ways and the general level of lexical complexity of the original was not matched in the translations. The simplification identified resulted from the fairly consistent use of a number of translation strategies including:

- the use of superordinates, e.g. *Hecht* (a type of freshwater fish called *pike* in English) was translated as *iasc* (fish);
- the use of general words instead technical terms, e.g. *Revolver* was translated simply as *gunna* (gun);
- the use of conventional forms instead of creative ones, e.g. *Bananenmilch mit Mandelkernen* (literally *Banana milk(shake) with almonds*) was translated as *cáca mór milis* (a big sweet cake);
- the use of paraphrase, e.g. *der Erfinder* (*the inventor*) was translated as *an té a rinne* (*the person/one who made*).

There is some justification for thinking that this marked tendency towards lexical simplification in the translations could be explained primarily by the German/Irish language pair. In other words, some lexical simplification that occurs in translations into Irish might be due to the fact that a minority language such as Irish might not yet have coined all of the technical terms that occur in the German or if the words do exist in Irish, they might only be available in specialised glossaries. When checked however, it was found that more than 90% of the terminology investigated could be found in Irish general dictionaries – it was not even necessary to go to specialised lexicographical sources to find them. However, it may be the case that the status of Irish as a minority language was still a significant factor in the translator's decision to simplify vocabulary. As we have seen, Irish speakers live with their use of the language limited to certain domains, while the dominant language is used in the more numerous and prestigious public domains such as those of commerce, science and technology. On this basis, the translator may have decided that the linguistic level of native speaker children and/or children attending Irish language primary schools would not generally be as high or developed as that of their German speaking counterparts and on that basis, simplification of vocabulary may have seemed appropriate. Or for that matter, the translator may have aimed the text at the lowest common denominator, namely children who are only in the process of learning Irish as a normal school subject.

In any case, the Irish versions of *Janosch* were professionally produced to a high standard and the quality of translation and dubbing was high. There is no wish whatsoever to suggest otherwise here. What is interesting and worthwhile here, in the context of translation and minority language audiovisual media, is rather to identify simply that particular translation choices were made systematically. These, like all other linguistic choices that find expression in translated audiovisual media material, have cumulative implications for minority language usage that should be studied. Interestingly, where subtitling is used, two languages are presented simultaneously thereby providing the possibility of critical comparison by those who know both. But in the case of dubbing, comparative scrutiny of source and target texts by researchers is particularly important because viewers do not have access to the original material for the purposes of comparison.

As we have seen, every translator has to adopt a specific approach and make particular choices: go down one particular linguistic road, leaving another or several other roads untaken. Providing the translation is of a professional standard, this is not in itself problematic. It is simply the case that translation policy and practice need to be identified as important and monitored so that the effects of minority language broadcasters' reliance on translated material can be both fully understood and potentially exploited to the benefit of the minority language community.

Conclusion

No serious effort to develop minority language media studies as a discipline in its own right, complementing media studies on the one hand and minority language studies on the other, can make significant headway unless it takes a long, detailed look at the specifically linguistic elements of minority language media studies. In this context, the language of the media per se is a useful starting point just as the language of particular types of media in specific cultures is also of relevance. Moreover, when sharpening the focus on the language of minority language media, in particular, the question of the extent, direction, techniques and effects of translation as a powerful act of intercultural communication should not be ignored.

References

Cormack, M. (2000) Minority language media in a global age. *Mercator Media Forum* 4, 3–15.
Cormack, M. (2004) Developing minority language media studies. *Mercator Media Forum* 7, 3–12.
Cronin, M. (1995) Altered states: Translation and minority languages. *TTR* 8 (1), 85–103.
Danan, M. (1996) *From Nationalism to Globalization: France's Challenges to Hollywood's Hegemony.* Ann Arbor, MI: UMI.
Fishman, J.A. (1991) *Reversing Language Shift.* Clevedon: Multilingual Matters.

Fishman, J.A. (ed.) (2001) *Can Threatened Languages be Saved?* Clevedon: Multilingual Matters.

Frawley, W. (1984) Prolegomenon to a theory of translation. In W. Frawley (ed.) *Translation: Literary, Linguistic and Philosophical Perspectives* (pp. 159–175). London and Toronto: Associated University Presses.

Hoffmann, C. (1994) *An Introduction to Bilingualism.* Harlow: Longman.

Jacquemond, R. (1992) Translation and cultural hegemony: The case of French-Arabic translation. In L. Venuti (ed.) *Rethinking Translation* (pp. 139–158). London: Routledge.

Jenkinson, B. (1991) A letter to an editor. *Irish University Review* 21 (1), 27–34.

Mac Dubhghaill, U. (2005) *Harry Potter and the Wizards of Baile na hAbhann: Translation, Subtitling and Dubbing Policies in Ireland's TG4, from the Start of Broadcasting in 1996 to the Present Day.* Paper delivered at the Mercator Media Conference, Aberystwyth, Wales.

Niranjana, T. (1992) *Siting Translation: History, Post-structuralism and The Colonial Concept.* Berkeley, CA: University of California Press.

O'Connell, E. (1994) Media translation and lesser-used languages: Implications of subtitles for Irish-language broadcasting. In F. Eguíluz, R. Merino, V. Olsen, E. Pajares and J.-M. Santamaria (eds) *Transvases Culturales: Literatura, Cine, Traducción* (pp. 367–373). Vitoria: Facultad de Filologia.

O'Connell, E. (1996) Media translation and translation studies. In T. Hickey and J. Williams (eds) *Language, Education and Society in a Changing World* (pp. 151–156). Clevedon: Multilingual Matters.

O'Connell, E. (1998) Choices and constraints in screen translation. In L. Bowker, M. Cronin, D. Kenny and J. Pearson (eds) *Unity in Diversity? Current Trends in Translation Studies* (pp. 65–71). Manchester: St Jerome Publishing.

O'Connell, E. (2001) The role of screen translation: A response. In H. Kelly-Holmes (ed.) *Minority Language Broadcasting: Breton and Irish* (pp. 83–88). Clevedon: Multilingual Matters.

O'Connell, E. (2003) *Minority Language Dubbing for Children.* Bern: Peter Lang.

O'Connell, E. (2004a) Serving our purposes: Audiovisual media, language planning and minority languages. *Mercator Media Forum* 7, 29–41.

O'Connell, E. (2004b) Subtitles and language learning. In M. Smith (ed.) *Readings in the Teaching of Culture: Culture: Mine, Yours, Whose?* (pp. 75–77). Dublin: ITE.

Øverås, L. (1998) In search of the third code: An investigation of norms in literary translation. *META* 43 (4), 571–588.

Riggins, S.H. (1992) The promise and limits of ethnic minority media. In S.H. Riggins (ed.) *Ethnic Minority Media* (pp. 276–288). Newbury Park, CA: Sage Publishers.

Tymoczko, M. (1999) *Translation in a Postcolonial Context.* Manchester: St Jerome Publishing.

Venuti, L. (ed.) (1992) *Rethinking Translation.* London: Routledge.

Venuti, L. (1995) *The Translator's Invisibility: A History of Translation.* London: Routledge.

Walsh, J. (2003) Irish Language. In B. Lalor (ed.) *Encyclopaedia of Ireland* (pp. 543–546). Dublin: Gill and Macmillan.

Chapter 13
Signs of Change: Sign Language and Televisual Media in the UK

PADDY LADD

The re-emergence of sign language-using communities – Deaf peoples – is one of the most recent developments in minority language studies. These communities are starting to impact on disciplines as diverse as geography, sociolinguistics, education, politics, psychology, literature, cultural studies and anthropology, and beginning to contribute to or challenge traditional theories concerning ethnicity, bilingualism and post-colonialism. This chapter, the first Deaf formal narrative of sign language television and its relationships with majority society media is thus the first entry into the field of minority language media studies.

These positive developments are the latest manifestation of the Deaf Resurgence (Ladd, 2003), which began in the late 1970s, a belated response to the liberation movements of the 1960s. This belatedness is indicative of the extent to which sign language communities were forced into isolation by the hegemonic discourses responsible for their suppression for over a century, and which still continue to dominate majority society media's representations of Deaf peoples.

These discourses, which construct sign language peoples essentially as biologically deficient beings (Lane, 1993), continue to retard access by liberal or radical 'lay' persons to the knowledge and resources of sign language communities. Thus some participants in minority language policy discourses cannot grasp the appropriateness of sign languages becoming part of their domains. It is hoped that this chapter will enlighten and empower such readers to become allies in removing the barriers and ceilings that still exist.

Thus it is necessary for this chapter to introduce readers to Deaf communities themselves and the history of suppression of their languages.[1] The absence of any previous academic discourse on their relationship to minority language media means that wider theoretical issues cannot be discussed here in depth. Instead this narrative is intended to enable readers to make comparisons with other language minority groups. Similarly, those working within Deaf/sign language television in other countries may examine this narrative to locate patterns of oppression and strategies for cultural revivification, which can later be drawn into theoretical frameworks. Feedback from any of the above is greatly welcomed.

Sign Language Peoples – a Brief History

The virtual absence of census data means that estimating the numbers of sign users and/or native 'speakers' is a contentious matter. This chapter uses an estimate based on statistics of one in 1000 born profoundly Deaf and one in 1000 born 'hearing impaired'. If all such persons in the UK were permitted access to their native, British Sign Language (BSL), the BSL community would number 120,000. Hearing children of Deaf marriages (thus BSL users) may number as many as 60,000, whilst 100,000 'hearing' people have learned BSL over the last 20 years. The relative status and social cohesion of each group, their BSL skills and their degrees of bilingualism cannot be discussed here, but the figures above may prove helpful for defining sign languages in respect of minority language type (cf. Edwards, 1995).

Although sign communities have existed throughout recorded history, modern Deaf communities began once Deaf schools were founded from the 18th century onwards. Their graduates grouped together in the newly emerging towns and cities of the 19th century in 'Deaf clubs', gradually developing regional, national and international organisations by the 1890s. As the 19th century gathered pace, a convergence of three significant cultural developments and discourses negatively impacted on sign language communities (Ladd, 2003). These were the emergence of scientism (that is, a growing reification of science as embodied in the trope of 'progress'), medicalism (a similar reification of the medical profession) (cf. Foucault, 1979), and colonialism. Although the latter is generally understood as applying to physical territories being invaded and economically controlled by Western nations, more recent definitions (cf. Merry, 1991) have emphasised that suppression of languages and cultures are primary characteristics of some colonialist interventions.

These three developments manifested themselves within Deaf domains from the 1880s onwards as a worldwide movement of non-Deaf people espousing a doctrine known as Oralism, whose objectives included the removal of sign languages, Deaf teachers, and thus Deaf cultures, from Deaf education. They then enforced the sole use of lipreading and speech in the national majority languages through a range of physically and psychologically abusive strategies. The equation of sign with the 'languages of savages' (documented by Lane, 1984) thus facilitated what became a colonialist approach towards Deaf communities (Ladd, 2003).

Although Deaf communities resisted for several decades they were unable to overturn the formidable discourses ranged against them, and for the next century were forced into effective invisibility. Nevertheless they refused to give up using their languages, surreptitiously maintaining them at school and later openly using them within their daily lives and their local and national communities.

It is interesting to note that the first known use of sign language on film occurred as early as 1913, and was developed specifically as a tool for language survival. The US Deaf communities watched with alarm as Oralism began to spread outwards from Europe and their National Association of the Deaf decided to make several films to record their language for posterity. As they put it 'there is but one known means of passing on the language; through the use of moving picture film'. These films were indeed preserved, and have recently been re-released. In one, the words of one of their leaders, George Veditz, give some idea of the elevated tone of their discourses in respect of Oralism:

> They have tried to banish sign from the schoolroom, from the churches and from the earth...so our sign language is deteriorating... 'A new race of pharoahs that knew not Joseph' are taking over the land...As long as we have Deaf people on earth, we will have signs...It is my hope that we all will love and guard our beautiful sign language as the noblest gift God has given to Deaf people. (Quoted in Padden & Humphries, 1988: 36)

Although the languages survived (not entirely undamaged) it was not without immense cost to the users. The first independent national study of Oralism, one hundred years after its inception, found that Deaf school leavers had an average reading age of eight and three-quarters had largely unintelligible speech, and lipreading skills no better than an untrained hearing person (Conrad, 1979). Subsequent studies have highlighted rates of acquired mental illness among Deaf people as double that of the majority society (Hindley & Kitson, 2000), unsurprising when one considers that many Deaf children, never seeing a Deaf adult, thought they would either die or become hearing when they were sixteen (Ladd, 2003). Many other forms of personal, social and cultural damage have also been identified (Ladd, 2003).

In the 1970s, a Deaf Resurgence took place across Western Europe and the USA. Ladd (2003) identifies eight features, including:

- the recognition of sign languages as bona fide languages by linguists;
- the return of these languages and Deaf teachers to Deaf education;

- the growth of sign language television;
- recognition of the concepts of Deaf history and Deaf culture;
- the founding of Deaf Studies.

The Resurgence can be thus seen as a *decolonisation process*, that is, a sustained attempt to restore sign language communities and culture not only to Deaf education, but also to their rightful place within the wider public lives of majority societies. It can be argued that this chapter contributes to a ninth feature – Deaf scholars engaging with the wider academic world and other minority language domains in order to speed up this process.

Along with other minorities, sign language communities have suffered a neo-colonialist backlash during the 1990s, with the spread of mainstreaming ideologies (placing Deaf children in isolation within non-Deaf schools) and the consequent closure of many cherished Deaf schools, several of which were over 150 years old. These changes have been exacerbated by a worldwide resurgent, intensified manifestation of medicalism and neo-Oralism via the advent of cochlear implant experimentation and genetic engineering. The intensity of this backlash makes it even more important that sign languages be recognised as minority languages, since not only is this domain the one that most closely represents their experiential reality, but also it is the only one where any degree of legal protection exists.

The particular patterns of this form of colonialism must be taken into account when considering similarities and differences between Deaf and other minority languages. The reader is directed towards the three types of linguistic and cultural oppression identified in Ladd *et al.* (2003: 22) for further consideration.

The Emergence of Sign Language Legislation

The concept of language rights and legal protection was first developed in the UK by the National Union of the Deaf (NUD). In 1982 their *Charter of Rights of the Deaf Child* identified Article 27 of the UN's International Covenant on Political and Civil Rights as the most appropriate basis for such protection, and described precisely how it was infringed by Oralism. They then proceeded to interpret Article 2 of the UN Convention on the Prevention and Punishment of the Crime of Genocide as applying to sign language communities, illustrated four sets of Oralist actions as infringing the Article, and petitioned the UN to therefore outlaw Oralism (NUD, 1982).

This remarkable campaign was unsuccessful because it was too far ahead of its time, since the UN and its agencies then (and now) could only conceive of sign communities through medicalism, i.e. as disabled people. However the campaign elevated the level of Deaf discourse to the point where official recognition of sign languages by governments was finally acknowledged as a crucial first step in the decolonisation process. Over the next 15 years, marches for recognition took place in Italy and Spain, among other countries, without much overt success outside of Scandinavia, where sign languages were recognised with minimal campaigning being required – an interesting fact, which itself deserves much closer study.

In the UK the British Deaf Association (BDA) began its campaign with the publication of *BSL: Britain's Fourth Language* in 1987 without notable success, but their intervention in the affairs of the World Federation of the Deaf (WFD) proved to be crucial. The WFD, although founded by a Italian Deaf person, was taken over by hearing persons by the 1960s, and operated subsequently from Rome through a mainly welfare colonialist discourse. By the IXth Congress in Palermo, 1983, Scandinavian countries being well advanced in the recognition of sign languages in education, were frustrated with the WFD's refusal to campaign for official recognition. Together with the BDA, they began the process of wresting the organisation away from Rome and into Deaf Scandinavian hands by setting up the concept of continental regions, and then taking control of the new regional body, the European Union of the Deaf (EUD). This achieved, the WFD then moved under Scandinavian control, and dialogue with the UN and its attendant bodies, such as UNESCO began and continues to the present day.

In Europe itself, minimal funding for the EUD was obtained from the EU, and the organisation could begin a campaign for EU-wide linguistic recognition. In 1988, the EU passed the motion submitted to them by the EUD, section 3 of which 'calls on the Commission to….grant official recognition for the Sign Languages used by deaf people in those States' (BDA, 1987). This was not binding on member states, so campaigns had to return to those individual countries to attempt recognition there. Due to political inexperience, very little progress was made in the next decade so that subsequent EU minority language legislation did not include sign languages.

The realisation that their elected leaders had let them down led to the formation of a latter-day NUD – the Federation of Deaf People – who campaigned for official recognition through the first ever UK Deaf marches in 1999, both national and local. Attracting up to 9000 people (proportionately equivalent to a march of 2 million hearing people), they succeeded in obtaining recognition by the UK government on 18 March 2003, which included a token allocation of £1,000,000 towards BSL projects.

The four year campaign re-energised the EUD, a more sustained attempt being made to dialogue with EU policy-makers, resulting in Deaf attention becoming focused on the European Bureau of Lesser-Used Languages (EBLUL) as a crucial site for membership. At the time of writing the EBLUL is resisting these requests. Another route explored resulted in the Parliamentary Assembly of the Council of Europe Recommendation 1598 (2003) on the protection of sign languages in the member states, but it is as yet unclear what this means in practice.

Indeed, space does not permit an in-depth analysis of the practical meaning of language recognition itself, nor of the discourses that currently take place around the subject. But it appears that no-one has considered the connection between recognition and guaranteed access to televisual and film media. The progress that has taken place within those domains can be said to manifest *implicit recognition* at best, and re-emphasises the need for sign communities to seek out alliances among other minority language media.

Sign Communities and Visual Media

With this background established it is now possible to turn to the subject of the relationship between majority society, televisual media and sign communities. These can be divided into two main categories – the practices of those majority society media towards the communities and the sign communities' own media. Space constraints rule out examination of how Deaf communities and sign language have been represented by other media. But certain salient points regarding sign languages are pertinent. They do not have a written form, nor can they be represented on radio. Thus unlike most European minority languages, they cannot be transmitted over distance other than through film and television. Moreover the minimal majority language literacy levels under Oralism also ruled out access to ideas transmitted through print. Given that sign languages are of course highly suited to a visual medium[2], the (expensive) media of film and television are therefore even more crucial for sign communities' development than for other minority languages. It appears that although the communities made use of film during the Oralist decades, they rarely filmed actual sign discourses, and it was not until the 1980s, when video recording became widely available, that they began to harness the form to create their own media.

Sign Language Televisual Media: A History

There is little written evidence in English-speaking countries of the use of sign languages on television prior to the 1950s. Although we do not have access to the literature of other countries, at this point in time we may posit that this may hold true across the world. The following analytical history of BSL and UK television can be used as a framework for other countries to refine, though reference is made to what is known about North American and European programming.

In the 1950s the BBC ran several series of a programme called *For Deaf Children*. Little is known of its origins, unfortunately, given that despite Oralist hegemony, sign language was the medium chosen. In what was to become a familiar pattern, organised complaints of Oralists resulted in signs being removed except for a few token lines near the end. As a consequence the programme's content mutated and Deaf-related items disappeared. Renamed *Vision On*, the programme was designed for majority society children, and to this day there has been no regular BSL programming for Deaf children.

In the 1960s, the BBC began *News Review*, a sign language programme for the adult Deaf community consisting of a 30-minute summary of the week's world news, usually including one Deaf news item on a subject decided to be of interest to them. The Oralist lobby soon succeeded in having signs removed and replaced by subtitles, the Deaf news item likewise later disappearing. Similar lobbies are known to have taken place in Holland and doubtless elsewhere. Such actions are particularly interesting since Oralism has been focused on proscribing sign language in children up to the age of 18. Its proponents realised they had no grounds, legal or quasi-legal, for trying to force adults not to sign (although they often tried to prevent Deaf intermarriage, or encourage sterilisation of Deaf couples in order to remove signers from existence). The example thus represents the first known attempts by Oralism to actively pursue these policies in televisual media, and clearly acknowledges how crucial televised sign language is for the wider decolonisation struggle. Oralists' rapid entry into the domains of adult sign communities as soon as they risked becoming publicly visible for the first time in a century tells its own tale.

Response to these events by sign communities has not yet been located. It was only when the NUD was formed in 1976, immediately focusing their priorities on gaining a TV programme in sign language, that dramatic change occurred. It is instructive to look at the terms in which this new discourse expressed itself. The NUD's first publication, *NUD 1976*, stated:

> We need to be seen. We must reach television [*sic*] (Nationwide, Open Door etc.) and put deaf people in places they have never been seen before. We need posters, badges, T shirts, pamphlets on every aspect

of deafness. Any way of showing where we stand to the public. (NUD, 1976: 14)

The intention therefore is language visibility in order to achieve better outcomes for BSL users. In *Blueprint for the Future* (1977) these intentions were refined and the 1978 Annual Report notes 13 areas of action taken by its media sub-committee, including:

> Proposals submitted to Open Door for a trial Deaf TV programme... Approached BBC to request interpreter on News Review. Reasons given for refusal highly contentious, but includes the 'fact' that hard of hearing people stopped watching the programme when sign language was used. (NUD, 1978: 11)

Open Door was a product of 1960s radicalism, the BBC's Community Programme Unit (CPU), which invited groups of viewers to make their own television programme. Selected after a two-year wait, the NUD developed *Signs of Life*, a prototype of the kind of magazine programme needed by the Deaf community. Its content was radical in its direct attack on Oralism and other areas of 'discrimination', in the prominence given to Deaf arts (sign language poetry) and the assertion that hearing people could benefit from signing.

Their vision of Deaf TV can be characterised as a *decolonising agenda*, comprising of the following programming principles, among others:

- produced, directed and presented in BSL by native users;
- forums for weekly national community dialogue (cf. Cormack's (1998) reference to the 'public sphere' in minority language media);
- agendas led and shaped by those having a vision of the range of reforms necessary for community regeneration, tailoring content and style of the programmes to carefully planned stages for each reform;
- in so doing, the power of the media to be used to actively challenge those with authority over BSL communities;
- informing majority language users about the oppression of BSL users to enable active alliances;
- portraying Deaf arts, culture and achievements, raising Deaf confidence and hearing consciousness, stimulating growth in the former;
- principles to operate in a consciously 'sequential' manner, each domain of Deaf affairs being advanced by reference to previous programmes, signposting the route to the next.

These principles are strikingly similar to the seven purposes of indigneous media described by Browne (1996).

There was controversy during the making of the programme. Despite the CPU's policy of not interfering with programme makers' intentions, they would not allow all six presenters to be Deaf, BSL-using people. Only two were permitted, the other four having to be people who could speak English and add some signs whilst doing so, reducing the sign language content to visual nonsense, so that Deaf people unable to read the English subtitles were cut off from their 'own' programme. This caused furious internal NUD debate, but it was felt there was no option but to agree.

The *NUD Newsletter 12* (1979a) following the broadcast makes useful reading for students of minority language media, presenting numerous letters sent to the NUD and the BBC by hearing viewers. The campaign continued with a seminar, *Television, Sign Language and Deaf People* (NUD, 1979b), which invited speakers and respondents from the BBC and the IBA. The report is very revealing for the numerous reasons given by broadcasters as to why sign programmes were 'not viable'.

The NUD and BDA then formed the Deaf Broadcasting Campaign (DBC), whose remit was wider than sign language television (including a demand for English subtitling, chiefly to benefit the hard of hearing, increasing the size of the lobby, but leading to later complications that cannot be discussed here for reasons of space). The DBC lobbied meetings intended to establish the new Channel 4 (whose charter specifically required them to give appropriate airtime to UK minorities) and their actions rendered Deaf people and BSL visible to many broadcasters and politicians for the first time. Engaging in a range of tactics, including being the first Deaf body to use direct action (Woolley, 1991), by September 1981 they achieved a House of Commons motion signed by 55 MPs.[3]

Thus one notable effect of the campaign was the involvement in Deaf affairs for virtually the first time of majority society viewers. Programme makers had been reluctant to disturb the 'visual integrity' of their screen with BSL signing, but in several regions of ITV (the commercially funded British television network), notably (and probably significantly) HTV, the ITV company broadcasting to Wales, once this had been tried as an experiment and then dropped, it was the positive response of hearing viewers that compelled their re-introduction (Woolley, 1991: 94).

The BBC and *See Hear*

Possibly influenced by 1981's designation as Year of the Disabled, the BBC conceded the production of a weekly programme in sign language – *See Hear*, duly broadcast as a joint CPU/Education Department production. The first series was very different from that envisaged by the NUD.

Both presenters (one deaf and one hearing) were compelled to speak and add signs where they were able to, the 25-programme series contained very few BSL-using Deaf people, and adhered to almost none of the principles noted above. Deaf protests saw the second series increase the number of Deaf subjects whilst retaining the English presentation style. It was not until the third series that one presenter was permitted to use BSL, and 1987 before the whole programme was BSL-presented.

Achievement of the Deaf agenda was therefore already compromised, and indeed could not even begin to be achieved without Deaf majority membership and editorial control of the 14-strong production team. Until the mid-1990s membership was limited to one researcher and one film director. Thus although the 'Deaf' content of the programmes increased, there were significant weaknesses, not least a tendency towards infantilisation which saw the programme derisively labelled 'Blue Peter' (a popular children's magazine programme) by numerous Deaf people (Ladd, 2003). The liberating quality of the programmes varied widely according to the relative degree of influence of the Deaf staff or the support of more radical hearing staff, among whom there was in any case a huge turnover, most simply passing through for a year as part of their training.[4]

Given the impossibility of a single programme satisfying an all-age, multiple-class, national community with its own ethnic and minority group memberships, it is interesting to note the minimal campaigning for extension of BSL coverage. One weekly programme, broadcast for 20 to 25 weeks, was felt to be sufficient or all that could be achieved, and even sustained campaigning for youth and children's programming was not seriously considered.

Nevertheless even this limited visibility had remarkable effects on the confidence of the BSL community, upon their ability to achieve political leverage, and on the numbers of hearing people wishing to learn BSL (augmented by a popular *See Hear* spin-off series, cf. Miles, 1988). There were also unexpected effects. Isolated hard of hearing and elderly deafened people, whose self-image had become understandably negative, were inspired by the on-screen achievements of those who had been Deaf all their lives. Importantly Deaf children and their parents still trapped in the Oralist system were able to access a different world-view, to aspire to a 'larger' identity, because the *cultural capital* of television far outweighed any previous prestige of an Oralist education (cf. Riggins, 1992: 284). This larger identity included aspirations towards careers not previously considered, including actually working in Deaf television and film.

Nevertheless, the NUD summarised the effect of sign language television thus:

...Deaf Pride, employment opportunities, political leverage and respect from society as a whole have resulted from [sign language on television]. But perhaps the most crucial area, that of using television programmes to nurture, control and carefully shape the growth of a national Deaf community, has not really occurred. (Ladd, 1991: 172)

During the following years one of *See Hear's* main objectives was simply to survive the various policy changes within BBC management, including attempts to cut the programme or move it to less favourable slots. That survival was achieved is to the credit of those involved, especially given that other minority programming virtually disappeared from the UK during the 1990s. It was not until around 2000 that the numbers of Deaf staff increased to any degree. Although by 2002 the programme finally had a Deaf editor, and the programme content finally became more 'Deaf-centred', the virtual absence of Deaf producers and directors meant that the decolonising agenda could not be seriously considered, and there was still a lack of investigative journalism (which Cormack (1998: 43) identifies as one of the necessary conditions of a public sphere).[5]

It is probable that growing BBC conservatism would not in any case permit such an agenda, so that overt campaigning against Oralism, main-streaming, cochlear implants and the closure of Deaf schools has become less possible. Likewise the first Deaf editor of a BBC series must, like any other minority, tread carefully the colonialist backlash, as happened in the late 1990s to other Deaf leaders who managed to gain control of a domain within their power structure (cf. Alker, 2000).[6]

Sign Language and Commercial Broadcasting

Minority language media scholars will not be surprised to learn that Deaf/sign broadcasting on commercial stations has, with one exception, been virtually non-existent. The rare examples that existed were able to do so because they operated outside the TV mainstream. One route, Adult Education departments, were also one of the few domains in which small regional ITV companies like Tyne-Tees (in the north-east of England) had a guaranteed network slot. This was used by Tyne-Tees producer Lisle Willis to produce sign teaching programmes like *Talking Hands* (1972) and *No Need to Shout* (1981). The second route, Schools' Programming, produced Yorkshire TV's (1984) *Insight*, fronted by two hearing presenters[7] but there has been only a small amount of schools programming in BSL since then. The third route, local news, has seen some token weekday use of BSL (a farcical 30 seconds in most cases) in a few regions, and a weekly half-hour programme 'interpreted' by Deaf presenters in others.

That is in effect the full picture of 50 years' 'conventional' commercial broadcasting – there have been no Deaf TV programmes on these channels, and the same holds true for non-terrestrial broadcasting. The exception to this is Channel 4, precisely because it was established in 1982 with a strong community oriented remit (Blanchard & Morley, 1982), and because in the first few years it did not have to seek its own funding, and was not therefore at the mercy of advertising.

There was therefore a window of opportunity to achieve adult BSL programming, which began in 1984 with *Listening Eye*, followed by *Sign On*. Two single-series children's programmes began soon after, *Hand-in Hand* and *D'Art*, but throughout the next 20 years even such minimal programming effectively disappeared. Two strong documentaries with a radical, bilingual educational approach followed, *A Language for Ben* and *Pictures in the Mind*, but such programming has also consequently disappeared.

The children's programmes suffered from minimal involvement of native signers, reflecting the compromises enforced by what we have earlier noted as a 'trespassing' on Oralist-controlled territory (cf. Fell, 1984). Significantly (as with the BBC), the channel's Deaf/BSL programming was situated within the Education Department, continuing the diminished, infantilised perception of BSL users within a *pedagogical conditional* (Ladd, 2003) – that is, as lesser humans who need to be 'educated' by the majority society, rather than as language users in their own right.

Despite this command structure, adult programming moved into another dimension with the Tyne-Tees-produced *Listening Eye* and then *Sign On*. These series developed a strong Deaf cultural focus, using native BSL users from the start, and most programmes focused on a specific aspect of the Deaf liberatory agenda (cf. Llewellyn-Jones, 1994). The hearing producer, Bob Duncan, aimed to recruit Deaf staff, but with the numbers of able Deaf people having been decimated by a century of Oralism, training became a priority. A proposal to train a full Deaf production team in-house at Tyne-Tees was rejected because of 'insufficient resources' – an indication that such work was not considered a priority by the industry.[8] However, they persuaded Channel 4 to co-sponsor a course, at the North-East Media Training Centre (NEMTC), and over four years, with additional funding from the EU, 17 Deaf people trained in television production.

These developments highlighted an important difference between Deaf and other minority language users. The Deaf graduates of these courses could not find work within majority language television because they could not use that language without BSL interpreters to mediate. Not only were the latter still few in number, but it was felt that the cost of employing them was prohibitive, and this, combined with an attitude that television media was a 'rapid-response workplace', gave and continues to give television companies excuses to exclude sign language users from regular television employment outside of Deaf programming. This in turn impacted on the training programmes. Being confined to the tiny Deaf broadcasting allocation suggested that it made no economic sense to invest further because of the paucity of vacancies (and *See Hear*'s unwillingness to hire such graduates), thus completing a vicious circle. However, a few graduates were able to join the *Sign On* team, so that where *Listening Eye* broadcast six to eight programmes per year from 1984–1991, *Sign On* began in 1992 with 29 programmes and in spite of tight budgets, maintained 19 half-hour programmes per year till 1996.

Sign Language Video

Once it became clear that the decolonising agenda could not be achieved through *See Hear*, there was a turn towards establishing Deaf video companies, the first being the BDA's London Deaf Video Project (LDVP) in 1985, arguably the first Deaf-run professional organisation of the entire century (and funded by the Greater London Council). Among the LDVP's achievements was the opportunity it gave to Deaf people to learn film production skills and develop Deaf and BSL production values, and many of its graduates are employed within Deaf/BSL television to this day. In the mid-1990s other Deaf video companies began to emerge and sell their work to mainstream television, notably Chase. This time period coincided with the first wave of BSL-educated Deaf children who were thus able to take up university places. Numbers of these graduated in media studies, and from these ranks such companies as Remark have emerged to make programme items for television.

The Neo-colonialist Backlash and the Closure of *Sign On*

By 1997 the relationship between *Sign On* and Channel 4 was under strain. Now that the channel had to find its own revenue, it had to make concessions for advertising revenue and market shares. This was marketed as a desire for more 'dynamic' (read 'hip') production values, which as has been widely noted, led to the channel's consequent 'dumbing down'. It was surprising that Deaf television held out for so long, when the channel's policy towards Black and Disabled programming moved away from hosting their own series into the spurious 'integrationist' approach, whereby minorities' issues were said to be covered by increased participation in mainstream broadcasts. The consequence for such groups has been virtual invisibility, the lack of a centre around which to build up their own pool of broadcasting talent, and the consequent loss of any consistent liberatory agenda. One reason for the extended life of Deaf programming was the medium's perfect suitability for sign and the obvious inaccessibility of radio, arguments that Deaf activists continued to press whenever *Sign On* was threatened.

The new ideologies and production values thus came into conflict with the Deaf/BSL production values that had been painstakingly assembled. It has also been suggested that *Sign On*'s (muted) criticism of Channel 4 in one programme over the lack of posts for NEMTC graduates added fuel to the fire. In 1998, despite widespread Deaf protests, it was axed and replaced by a programme for Deaf children *The Vibe* (and later, a youth programme *Vee TV*). The decision sent a disturbing message – rather than asserting that it was the responsibility of the Children's Department to make such programmes, the company signalled that there was but a single slot for Deaf/BSL programming, and it was they who would decide which section of the Deaf community would gain favour at any one time.

In an almost unprecedented response to community pressure, Channel 4 did bring back *Sign On* for two short series in 1998 and 1999. The 1998 series moved explicitly towards the decolonisation agenda, using the emerging concept of the 'Deaf Nation' as its focus, and began to illustrate how a radical agenda might transform the Deaf/BSL television landscape. However new levels of 'executive production' (neo-colonialist monitoring and control) were already being introduced, and by 1999 the last sad series was unrecognisable as the Deaf programme it had once been. Not only have all the subsequent youth programmes been hearing-run with token Deaf involvement, but also in closing *Sign On*, 15 years of Deaf and sign language broadcasting expertise, still badly needed by the community in the period of a growing Oralist backlash, had been single-handedly dismantled.

Two further incidents increased anger towards Channel 4. The commissioning of the first ever three-part series on Deaf history was an idea first submitted by *Sign On*, but the contract was awarded (without any tendering process) to a company whose director was involved in the decision to close *Sign On* as Channel 4's commissioning editor! Since control of how one's own history is researched, formalised and presented is crucial for any minority group, Channel 4's erasure of its founding values was complete.

During the channel's history, there was growing anger that the post of deaf advisor continued to be held by one hearing person, whilst available

Deaf expertise accumulated. Once the advisor left, it was expected that this expertise would be employed. However, all the major candidates (who could of course be expected to challenge the changes at the channel) were rejected, and a 21-year-old television-inexperienced Deaf person was appointed instead. As a result of these events, Deaf television professionals who had formed the Deaf Media Group (DMG) began to campaign for a radical change in attitude from the independent broadcasting sector, but have been unable to make any headway.

This stop-start process is familiar to minority language groups – the issue is not just their limited physical, financial and political resources, but the need to distribute them across an entire community's range of battlefields. Thus, Deaf television professionals are already engaged in fighting issues such as Deaf school closure, mainstreaming, cochlear implants and genetic engineering, as well as finding time to develop Deaf-centred training programmes for other Deaf people, interpreters, education and social welfare professionals and much, much more. These competing demands on the few who survived Oralism explains why Deaf decolonisation attempts are comparatively sporadic. In order to succeed in any one domain, persistence is a key issue, since defence of power is predicated upon outlasting the energies of its challengers. Thus the need for Deaf activists to switch from domain to domain allows neo-colonialist backlashes to succeed.

BSL and the 1996 Broadcasting Act

The DBC's continuing campaigns achieved some success with the insertion of clauses in the UK's 1996 Broadcasting Act, stipulating that by 2008, 80% of digital terrestrial television programmes must be subtitled (since voluntarily increased to a target of 100% by the BBC), and that by the same year 5% of the total output of those channels had to be broadcast in BSL. The latter was a radical step forward, but did not result in more Deaf programming. The broadcasters' response was to create a 'Sign Zone' in the early hours to repeat mainstream programmes with signers, reflecting Cormack's (1999) strictures concerning the confusion of language and culture issues within minority language media. Traditionally, on-screen interpretation was assigned to hearing interpreters, but it has become clear that with technology such as the autocue, the work could be done by Deaf translator-presenters, creating more jobs for Deaf people and (in theory) freeing up interpreters to meet the huge demands for them out in the community, thus relieving the severe shortage.

Recent Developments: Sign Language Artforms

Space does not permit a general accounting of Deaf arts and drama, except to note that these forms were severely damaged by Oralism. Although these were sporadically featured on Deaf programming, it was not (ironically) until the advent of Channel 4's *Vee TV* series with its regular youth soap strand, *Rush*, that Deaf television drama began. This was closely followed by *See Hear* with *Switch*, and the audience response revealed a deep hunger for the form.

These are scripted by hard of hearing and hearing persons, respectively, and Deaf-youth-oriented, serving to augment the already dramatic increase in young Deaf cultural activity. However, the traditional Deaf community is barely represented, and there is little sense of wider Deaf history. It is also noticeable that the 'quality' of BSL displayed by the young Deaf characters leaves much to be desired. In one sense this can be said to mirror actuality. In another it reinforces the sense that 'deep' or 'strong' BSL (and its exponents, who are closer to the heart of the community) continue to be feared or devalued by those in power. This is especially regrettable in view of the growing number of international Deaf performers who are working from within that heart to create new dimensions in Deaf performance art (Rob Roy Farmer, Rathskeller, etc.) and it remains to be seen whether this resurgence will gain Deaf television (which now of course means only *See Hear*) airtime.

Future Developments: Deaf/BSL Channels and the Internet

This long history and the recent developments mean that many Deaf/BSL users believe the only way to ensure a proper range of Deaf television programming (which mirrors the six categories put forward by Cormack (1999) plus others – programmes for Deaf ethnic and minority groups etc.) – is to set up a Deaf channel. In 2004 the BDA and the DBC together began a campaign for a Sign Language channel (in addition to the 5% BSL access already enshrined in law).[9] The BDA rented time on the Open Access Channel for two sign language television days, which met with an enthusiastic response.

The logistics are daunting, but such an approach offers an opportunity to adopt the decolonisation agenda, and help shape the communities' redevelopment. Although few majority society people may watch the channel, thus limiting the numbers who may be inspired to become allies, a significant and influential minority may still do so – not just professionals, or those who have Deaf families, friends or colleagues, but the growing numbers of hearing people learning BSL. Likewise, those students who develop an interest through essays such as this would be able to enjoy or study a consistently high standard of Deaf/BSL TV. Moreover, both *See Hear* and *Sign On* have demonstrated that the Deaf UK audience has a greater appetite for sign language programming from other (non-English-speaking) countries than the notoriously parochial mainstream hearing UK audience. The highest audience recorded for a *Sign On* programme was a Swedish Deaf drama (where investment in Deaf programming, in common with most Scandinavian countries has been proportionately greater than the UK).

These patterns suggest the potential for international sign channels is worthy of further investigation, not least because the strong grammatical similarities between sign languages allows for the development of international sign variants as a lingua franca. If accomplished, such channels would certainly stand as a monument to the extent to which the Deafhood identity is a globally felt experience. Such internationalism has been part of Deaf cultural thinking since the early 1800s, but has been rendered invisible by Oralism. Its public restoration, together with its implicit or explicit modelling of the 'world citizenship' concept, could inspire hearing people and would certainly be a benchmark for minority language TV.

Another medium with increasing visual potential is the Internet. Limited webcam broadcasting in real time has just become a possibility, and in the last few years, technology has evolved to the point where sign languages can be compressed and uploaded onto servers and websites. Thus the medium is arriving at a point where it can begin to fulfil Deaf social, artistic and educational needs. It may soon be possible to conceive of an alternative to television broadcasting, with extended programming being available on a worldwide basis for viewing or downloading. Again, the potential of international sign to reach a global audience and to model world citizenship for hearing people could become a benchmark to inspire other minority languages.

Acknowledgement

My thanks to Bob Duncan for valuable assistance with this chapter.

Notes

1. Due to lack of space, it is not possible to systematically examine communities outside the UK, or the representation of sign language users by majority society television. Likewise, English subtitling and issues of sign language interpretation ('dubbing'), the implications of sign language dialects,

programming categories (cf. Cormack, 1999), and assessments of what constitutes successful sign language broadcasting (Cormack, 1999) cannot be described here.

2. One fascinating but as yet unexplored angle is suggested by Cormack's reference to McLuhan's description of television as a 'cool medium' – that is, 'one which does not demand the same level of involvement as the "hot media" of radio and print, with their concentration on a single sense' (Cormack's Chapter 4 in this volume). Of course, for Deaf communities, that 'single sense' is exactly how sign television is received, which may also give some indication of the power of the medium for them, and the passion with which programmes can be viewed for appropriate cultural output.

3. For a valuable series of insights into Deaf beliefs and cultural perspectives in respect of television, the reader is urged to seek out the _DBC News_ from 1985–1990.

4. It has also been pointed out to me that the BBC may have seen _See Hear_ as a kind of 'departure lounge', since all five editors have retired from the BBC after their stint with the programme.

5. This chapter does not presume that Deaf people, least of all erstwhile community leaders, espouse the decolonisation agenda, or have emerged unscathed from mental colonisation.

6. For a valuable insight into the cultural perspectives of _See Hear_'s Deaf audience, see Woll and Allsop (1992).

7. That the hearing presenter was able to portray – without qualms – a character called 'Supersign', complete with cape and 'S' on chest, says much about colonialist attitudes even amongst apparent liberals!

8. It appears that the BBC have still not instituted a Deaf training programme to this day.

9. This variation in nomenclature also confirms Cormack (1999)'s concerns about confusing language with culture.

References

Alker, D. (2000) _Really Not Interested in the Deaf?_ Darwen: Darwen Press.
BDA (British Deaf Association) (1987) _BSL: Britain's Fourth Language._ Carlisle: BDA.
Blanchard, S. and Morley, D. (eds) (1982) _What's This Channel Fo(u)r?_ London: Comedia.
Browne, D. (1996) _Electronic Media and Indigenous Peoples: A Voice of our Own?_ Ames, IA: Iowa State University Press.
Conrad, R. (1979) _The Deaf School Child, Language and Cognitive Function._ London: Harper and Row.
Cormack, M. (1998) Minority language media in Western Europe: Preliminary considerations. _European Journal of Communication_ 13 (1), 33–52.
Cormack, M. (1999) Minority languages and television programming policy. _International Journal of Cultural Policy_ 5 (2), 293–313.
Edwards, J. (1995) _Multilingualism._ London: Penguin Books.
Fell, I. (1984) _Insight Year Book 1983/84._ Leeds: Yorkshire Television.
Foucault, M. (1979) _Discipline and Punish._ New York: Vintage Books.
Hindley, P. and Kitson, N. (2000) _Mental Health and Deafness._ London: Whurr.

Ladd, P. (1991) Ten years burning down the road. In R. Lee (ed.) *Deaf Liberation.* Feltham: NUD.

Ladd, P. (2003) *Understanding Deaf Culture.* Clevedon: Multilingual Matters.

Ladd, P., Gulliver, M. and Batterbury, S. (2003) Reassessing minority language empowerment from a deaf perspective. *Deaf Worlds: International Journal of Deaf Studies* 19 (2).

Lane, H. (1984) *When the Mind Hears.* New York: Random House.

Lane, H. (1993) *The Mask of Benevolence: Disabling the Deaf Community.* New York: Random House.

Llewellyn-Jones, P. (1994) *Listening Eye: A Guide to the Issues Facing Deaf People in Britain Today.* London: Tyne-Tees TV / Channel 4.

Merry, S. (1991) Law and colonialism. *Law and Society Review* 25, 889–922.

Miles, D. (1988) *British Sign Language: A Beginner's Guide.* London: BBC Publications.

NUD(1976) *NUD 1976.* London: NUD.

NUD (1978) *Report to the First Convention.* London: NUD.

NUD (1979a) *NUD Newsletter 12* (July). London: NUD.

NUD (1979b) *Television, Sign Language and Deaf People.* London: NUD.

Padden, C. and Humphries, T. (1988) *Deaf in America: Voices for a Culture.* Cambridge, MA: Harvard University Press.

Woll, B. and Allsop, L. (1992) *Summary of Findings: See Hear Research Project Prepared for the BBC.* Bristol: Centre for Deaf Studies.

Woolley, M. (1991) Deaf broadcasting campaign. In R. Lee (ed.) *Deaf Liberation.* Feltham: NUD.

Chapter 14

Minority Language Media Studies: Key Themes for Future Scholarship

NIAMH HOURIGAN

This concluding chapter attempts to assess how the preceding discussions contribute to our claim for the legitimacy of minority language media studies as a field of scholarly research. The diversity of contributions in terms of theoretical orientation, geographical focus and empirical detail illustrate the enormous range and depth of work within the field. This diversity provides one of the strongest reasons for producing a book of this nature. However, as the European Union (EU) slogan 'unity in diversity' attests, there is also grave danger of lack of coherence emerging in a field of scholarship that encompasses such a broad range of interests. For this reason, readers may have noted that there are some restrictions in terms of the orientation of this book. As noted in the Introduction (Chapter 1), the geographical scope of the research has tended to centre on the European case. Even within this limited geographical sweep, it is Western European linguistic minorities rather than Eastern European groups that have received most attention. Secondly, contributors to this text have focused on indigenous linguistic minorities rather than the new minorities languages spoken by immigrant communities within Europe. The orientation of the contributions to this collection reflects closely the current 'state of the art' within minority language media studies in Europe and provides a clear indication of the quality and range of research that has already been completed within the field. In this concluding chapter, we identify two major fields for future scholarship within minority language media studies: comparative work on new and indigenous European minority languages and research on how the various cultural, political, technological and linguistic dimensions of globalisation impacts on minority language media. Thus, we are seeking to identify a number of points of commonality where minority language media studies can intersect with current critical analysis in the related fields of socio-linguistics, geography, sociology and media studies.

Minority Language Media and New Minority Languages in Europe

Scholars of indigenous minority language media have paid relatively little attention to the experiences of immigrants to the EU, the speakers of the so-called 'new minority languages'. The increasingly complex web of definitions concerning 'minority', 'regional' and 'lesser-used' languages within the policy documentation of the EU indicates a striving to create terms that facilitate the protection and fostering of indigenous minority languages while excluding immigrant languages. The European situation differs considerably from the North American context described by Browne (Chapter 7) where immigrant minority language media have traditionally been more successful, albeit through commercial rather than statutory initiatives, than indigenous language services. In Europe, despite the participation of immigrant communities in community radio broadcasting initiatives in the UK, France and Germany, immigrants groups have relied primarily on satellite broadcasts of television services from their country of origin. Jacques Guyot (Chapter 3) notes that this model of broadcasting has created a paradoxical situation where national governments have become increasingly suspicious of these satellite services while being generally reluctant to support local services broadcasting in immigrant languages.

As the contributions from Hourigan, Corominas Piulats and Jones (Chapters 5, 10 and 11) suggest, indigenous linguistic minorities have enjoyed a relatively privileged position within the media and language policies of the EU.[1] In creating a 'Europe of the Regions', EU institutions have explicitly sought to support indigenous regional and minority identities. The 1992 European Charter for Regional or Minority Languages, which came into force in 1998, aims at the protection and promotion of 'the historical regional or minority languages of Europe'. However, while borders and boundaries within the EU are dissolving, the borders of the Union itself are solidifying, creating a new 'Fortress Europe'. EU legislation is explicit in discouraging large numbers of immigrants from Asia, Africa and the Middle East from entering the Union. As a result, policies on immigrant languages exhibit little of rhetoric of tolerance and inclusion that characterises EU legislation on indigenous minority languages. Speakers of languages such as Turkish, Arabic and Hindi have received little financial support from EU institutions and references to immigrant languages in EU legislation stress assimilation rather than cultural preservation. Extra and Yagmur note:

> In promoting linguistic pluralism, the EU has signed many documents where the language rights of minorities are protected. In theory, minori-

ties have numerous rights in relation to language. The focus of these documents however, is on regional minority groups; immigrant groups are commonly excluded with respect to such rights. (2002: 13–17)

Article 22 of the European Charter of Fundamental Rights guarantees that 'the union shall respect cultural, religious and linguistic diversity'. However, in practice while the institutions of the EU have taken a strong role in protecting and promoting indigenous linguistic diversity, their role in protecting immigrant language rights has operated in a dramatically different manner. For instance, a statement issued after a meeting of the Council of the European Union in November 2004 asserted that the primary role of the EU in relation to immigration policy was to 'assist the Member State in formulating integration policies by offering them a simple non-binding but thoughtful guide of basic principles against which they can judge and assess their own efforts'.[2] In outlining the principles of integration policy, the statement continued 'basic knowledge of the host society's language, history and institutions is indispensable to integration; enabling immigrants to acquire this basic knowledge is essential to successful immigration'.[3]

In practice, the Council and other EU institutions take little active role in assessing the linguistic implications of different integration policies adopted by the nation-states within the EU. Some EU member states advise immigrants to take classes in the national language as part of application for residency procedures, other states such as Italy provide classes through non-governmental organisations etc. In July 2005, the Dutch immigration minister, Rita Verdonk, introduced a controversial new compulsory integration policy for immigrants to the Netherlands, requiring all applicants to take a pre-entry test on the Dutch language and Dutch culture. The EU currently takes no active role in assessing how this type of policy impinges on the language rights of newly arrived immigrants or existing immigrant communities that operate through new minority languages within the EU.

Article 1a of the European Charter for Regional or Minority Languages of the Charter states that the concept of 'regional or minority languages' refers to languages that are

(1)   traditionally used within a given territory of a state by nationals of that state who form a group numerically smaller than the rest of the state's population; and
(2)   different from the official languages of that state;
(3)   not including either dialects of the official languages of the state or the languages of migrants.

However, as second, third and fourth generations of immigrants are born within European states, the capacity to make such blatant distinctions between indigenous and non-indigenous languages would appear to be diminishing.

Unlike EU policy, United Nations (UN) charters of language rights contain very few distinctions between indigenous and immigrant minority languages. The UN Declaration of the Rights of Persons Belonging to National or Ethnic, Religious and Linguistic Minorities adopted by the General Assembly in December 1992, directs nation-states

> to take measures to create favourable conditions to enable persons belonging to minorities to express their characteristics and to develop their culture, to provide them with adequate opportunities to learn their mother tongue or to have instruction in their mother tongue and to enable them to participate fully in the economic progress and development in their country. (Article 4)

Within the Universal Declaration on Linguistic Rights signed in Barcelona in 1996, there is an implied criticism of language rights charters that make a distinction between indigenous and immigrant languages. It states:

> This declaration is based on the principle that the rights of all language communities are equal and independent of their legal status as official, regional or minority languages. Terms such as regional or minority languages are not used in this Declaration because, though in certain cases the recognition of regional and minority languages can facilitate the exercise of certain rights, these and other modifiers are frequently used to restrict the rights of language communities. (Article 5)

Given the vast numbers of policy documents on language produced by EU organisations, the absence of any considerable body of work on immigrant language policy is surprising.[4] The absence of legislation on the rights of new minority language speakers is mirrored in the lack of specific policies on immigrant language education and media, a gap that contrasts sharply with the wealth of material on indigenous language communities in these contexts. In terms of educational policy, Extra and Yagmur comment that

> regional minority languages like Catalan, Basque or Frisian enjoy legal and educational support in mainstream schools but similar support is not available for immigrant languages. Although immigrant languages are conceived and transmitted as core values of culture by

immigrant language groups, they are much less protected than regional minority languages by affirmative action and legal measures e.g. education. (2002: 13)

The invisibility of new minority languages is also evident in current research within minority language education and minority language media studies. The 1985 report of the British Linguistic Minorities Project noted a research gap that remains, observing:

> The Project has been struck by how little contact there still is between researchers and practitioners working in bilingual areas and school systems, even between England and Wales. Many of the newer minorities in England could benefit from the Welsh experience and expertise. (LMP, 1985: 12)

Within conventional media studies, there have been a number of studies of the media consumption of immigrant communities in Europe (DeBruin, 2000; Frachon & Vargaftig, 1985; Ogan, 2001; Sahraoui, 1998). Almost none of this research has resulted in comparative frameworks linked to indigenous minority language media studies.[5] It is possible that the substantial differences between the two communities in terms of socio-cultural structures and patterns of media consumption have contributed to this research lacuna. For instance, within indigenous minority language communities, the desire for own-language media is often linked to a need to create a site where a specific culture and language can be cherished. However, immigrant communities establish media services with much more basic needs in mind. Radio, television and the Internet are used to provide lines of contact within the community, news from countries of origin and information about rights and entitlements in immigrant languages. Secondly, the ideological construction of indigenous minority and new minority language cultures can be quite different. While immigrant minority language groups have linguistic differences with the host community, it is often religious and cultural differences rather than language, that provoke the most profound conflict with national governments. As a result, immigrant media are often concerned with reflecting a religious or cultural world-view as well as language maintenance.

Despite the difficulties in creating comparative frameworks, it is clear that scholars of indigenous minority language media have much to learn from our colleagues engaged in research on new minority languages. Christine Ogan (2001) in her study of media consumption among Turkish communities in the Netherlands found that the broadcasting needs of first and second-generation speakers of new minority languages in European states are very often different. In contrast, studies of indigenous minority language media in Europe have tended to ignore intergenerational differences in reception. Indeed, reception studies in general have been a relatively neglected area within the field.

The emergence of the new minority languages in Europe is a phenomenon that analysts of indigenous minority language media need to consider carefully. The competition for language rights amongst French and Inuit language groups in Canada provides ample evidence that linguistic minorities with differing institutional bases do not always support each other and that conflict between competing groups can ultimately be damaging to the entire concept of language rights. It would be unfortunate if indigenous minority language broadcasters and activists who have fought so hard to gain language rights within the EU, were to allow a denial of the same rights to speakers of new minority languages.

Even if immigrant languages remain excluded from debates about minority language media in Europe, it is clear that the number of indigenous minority languages groups seeking to create a media presence within the EU is about to increase rapidly. The accession of ten new countries to the Union in 2005 means that a much greater range of *new indigenous* minority language communities will be eligible to apply for the protection and assistance of EU-funded organisations such as European Bureau of Lesser Used Languages and Mercator Media. It is unclear how many minority language groups exist in the accession countries but current estimates range from 33 to 60 (Slowinski, 1998). The consequences of this dramatic increase may be profound for existing minority language media organisations that have relied extensively on the fiscal support of EU institutions. Many language communities in Eastern European countries have no media infrastructure whatsoever and it may be difficult for West European minority language groups with considerable resources to continue their claim to funding in the context of the greater deprivation of Eastern minority language speakers. For students of minority language media, the new claims to minority status emerging from Eastern Europe and immigrant communities presents one of the most compelling routes for new research.

Minority Language Media and Globalisation

The social, political, cultural and technological processes of change that are encapsulated under the term 'globalisation' have had a particularly profound impact on questions of language and identity. Catalan geographer, Manuel Castells (1997) has characterised the growing importance of identity and identity movements as an oppositional response to globalisation, while cultural theorist John Tomlinson (1999) argues that the cultural and economic changes central to globalisation have simply forced us to re-evaluate the importance of identity within our lives. In terms of the contributions to this book, the tension between the media as a vehicle for the imperialism of national and global communications cultures and media as a site where minority language identities can be re-discovered, celebrated and supported in opposition to this process, has been a central and unifying thread of discussion. It informs not only the evaluation of language ecology, identity, history and campaigns in the early sections but also such examples as changes in work practices (Williams, Chapter 6), translation practices (O'Connell, Chapter 12) and individual conflicts between global media and minority language groups (such as the failed attempt by the Catalan government to introduce a cinema dubbing quota system outlined by Corominas Piulats, Chapter 10). The rest of this chapter is devoted to exploring how this key tension provides a new and important outlet for research within minority language media studies by focusing on three specific themes: the rise of global English, the emergence of digital divide(s) and the impact of neo-liberal economic policy as well as the broader socio-economic processes linked to globalisation on minority language media.

The rise of global English

Cronin (1995) argues that the term minority language expresses a relation not an essence. As outlined in the Introduction (Chapter 1), we favoured the term minority language throughout this book, as it is the only term which makes clear what all the languages surveyed have in common – being dominated by a much larger language group. The contributors to this book have, by and large, used this term in the context of minority status within nation-states. However, with the increasing dominance of global economic institutions such as the World Trade Organisation (WTO) and the secession of political power to supranational structures such as the EU, it is clear that the global political context through which we evaluate language status has changed. The process of minoritisation, which Cormack defines as central to minority languages, is now being experienced by other more powerful language groups. National language groups in Europe have traditionally been able to rely on national terrestrial broadcasting networks and national newspapers to shore up their dominant position in a politico-linguistic context. Indeed, as Benedict Anderson (1991) has argued, the very dominance of these national languages originated with the emergence of the printing press. However, the capacity of national media institutions to support national languages is being challenged by trans-national media services delivered through satellite, cable and digital networks and broadcasting predominantly in English.

Both Cormack and Cunliffe (Chapters 4 and 8) cite the work of David Crystal (1997) who has argued that one of the key linguistic results of the dominance of trans-national media is the emergence of English as a global language. Nearly a quarter of the world's population – between 1.2 to 1.5 billion people – are already fluent or competent in English. In his Chapter 3, Guyot noted that neither Chinese or Hindi enjoy the status of English, though both languages have numerically greater numbers of speakers. However, Crystal (1997) makes clear that the dominance of English has little to do with the numbers of people who speak it and more to do with who those people are. Pennycook comments:

> A review of critical work on English in the world has shown how it is linked to social and economic power both within and between nations, to the global diffusion of particular forms of culture and knowledge and to the inequitable structures of international relations. (1994: 26)

Some language groups seem to be more profoundly affected by the encroachment of English than others. In assessing overall patterns of language change within the EU, Witt (2000) notes the increasingly strong position of English as well as indigenous minority languages but a decline in the position of many official national languages. He comments that 'interestingly enough protests against English becoming dominant in certain areas, are especially strong in countries with so-called major languages, whose speakers are not used to not being able to use their own language' (2000: 13).

The continuing encroachment of English has already provoked a reaction in some smaller national language communities. Dutch and Flemish nationalists demonstrated against the use of English at Schiphol airport in 2002. The same group also disrupted a meeting of the Belgium parliament a few weeks later: their logo being an image of the Belgian flag in the toilet. Along with well-documented activities of the *Académie Francaise*, the German language protectionists *Verein Deutsche Sprache* have protested about the increasing number of Anglicisms in the German language including 'cent' and 'abgespaced'. However, because of the strong position of Spanish in South America, English appears to be less of a threat to Spanish speakers. Ross notes:

In Spain, there is no comparable fuss. It is true that the (negative) influence of English is a common subject among language specialists and academics, and they have little difficulty in finding examples to quote. Outside academia, however, no-one is really concerned [...] the reason, of course, is that Spaniards do not regard their language as being threatened by the English language or anything else. Theirs is the tongue of an entire continent (excepting Brazil) a large part of the US and a major European country. Its importance is increasing, not receding. The impact of English is therefore seen as a matter for chat-show linguists, not an issue of public concern. (1997: 26)

For those of us engaged in minority language media studies, the increasing dominance of English means that the experience of marginalisation and exclusion that was imposed on minority language speakers by national language groups is now being experienced by national language groups themselves. To paraphrase Manuel Castells (1996: 161) 'the excluders have themselves become the excluded'. It is clear that national language groups can learn much from the experience of Europe's indigenous minority language communities who have been successful in maintaining their languages without the support of dominant cultural institutions. In many cases, the creation of minority language media has been the central tenet in response to cultural marginalisation. The very fact that this book is written in English yet concerns minority language media indicates that language communities have to come to some reconciliation with the dominance of English while attempting to protect their linguistic identity.

As the chapters of Jones and O'Connell (Chapters 11 and 12) indicate, a number of indigenous minority language groups in Europe have direct experience of dealing with the global dominance of English and their responses could do much to inform policy currently being designed to protect smaller national language communities. Traditionally, indigenous minority and national language groups have regarded each other with suspicion, however, the onslaught of global English may provide a new basis for research and co-operation between national and minority language scholars.

Minority language media and the digital divide(s)

Andrew Feenberg (1991) argues that new technologies represent a site of social struggle rather a neutral tool, or a coherent force for diversity or homogenisation. Within the social struggles being provoked by new media, some ethno-cultural communities appear to be more effectively equipped to utilise information and communication technologies (ICTs) to their advantage than others. As contributions by Williams and Cunliffe (Chapters 6 and 8) to this volume indicate, a number of indigenous minority language groups in Europe have begun to invest substantial sums in new digital technologies as an aid to language maintenance. Welsh and Catalan language groups have been at the forefront of the creation of digital television services, on-line newspapers, virtual libraries and minority language websites. However, there is some evidence that these policy-makers have failed to consider the broader questions relating to the 'digital divide' that are troubling technology analysts.

The term 'digital divide' may be taken at the broadest level to refer to the gap between those individuals and communities who own, access and effectively use ICTs and those who do not.[6] As the range of ICTs and their capabilities increase, it is recognised that there are now multiple digital divides relating not just to access to computers but also to computing skills, literacy and accessible content. Bridging the digital divide is considered necessary because lack of access to ICTs entrenches and reinforces existing socio-economic divisions. The consequences of this process are quite serious as the proliferations of ICTs in education and the increasing range of services available exclusively on the Internet, further amplifies the chasm between the information 'haves' and 'have nots'. Those on the wrong side of the divide(s) may have less opportunity to engage in formal education and training (Damarin, 2000). Exclusion from the arena of ICTs threatens the whole notion of citizenship in this context and Damarin argues that the digital divide 'is the most pressing civil rights issue of the millennium' (2000: 20).

There are a number of reasons why indigenous minority language speakers in Europe should be particularly concerned about the consequences of the digital divide for their own linguistic communities. Minority language speakers in Europe are often forced to operate in their second language, a national European language, in a variety of daily contexts such as work, education and public administration. Currently, the growing importance of the Internet requires the acquisition of literacy in a third language, English. Therefore, the dominance of English on the Internet is creating a dual burden of language marginalisation for minority language speakers. Although the most recent statistics indicates that linguistic diversity is increasing on the web,[7] English still accounts for approximately 85% of web content. Joe Lockard comments:

> English remains as irreplaceably central and monopolistic in electronic development today as it did fifty years ago when the first computer

builders start their project in West Philadelphia. Anyone who has watched the weirdly funny site of a high speed printer belting out a Semitic text the wrong way, from left to right, know whose language code is running the show. (1996: 13)

It is not just the linguistic content of much of the material on the Internet but the very structure of the medium that contributes to the marginalisation of minority language speakers. Marshall McLuhan (1962) argued that the 'medium is the message' noting that the form of new media can have as much impact as content. Most websites and on-line discussion groups still rely on printed rather than aural or visual formats. Some minority language cultures in Europe are still predominantly oral/aural cultures and bilingual speakers of minority languages often do not have highly developed literacy skills in their minority language. Although minority language speakers can acquire literacy skills, a number of cultural theorists has argued that the requirement for literacy devalues oral culture and constitute a force for cultural homogenisation.

A large proportion of minority language speakers in Europe are still located in rural peripheral communities where computer access and connectivity is low and computers skills are difficult to acquire. The digital divide not only builds on these existing socio-economic divisions but also feeds into an intergenerational divide. National Telecommunications and Information Administration (NTIA) surveys show that the digital divide between young and old people is much more pronounced in Europe than the US with 44% of people in the 55–64 age group on-line in the US compared to 12% in Europe.[8] This particular divide may have profound consequences for minority language communities who often have a higher than average proportion of people in these older age categories.[9]

It is clear that for minority language speakers, the low cost of creating discursive spaces on the Internet makes it a medium with enormous potential for language maintenance. Hawaiian speakers for instance, have used the Internet to provide cost-effective on-line education. However, this language group live in a society where access to computers is relatively widespread in schools and public institutions such as libraries (Villa, 2002). This situation may not be replicated in many other minority language situations, as Mark Warschauer comments:

The Internet necessitates access to and knowledge of, expensive computer equipment. It also demands a high degree of language and literacy skills in order to use well. Thus the Internet is accessible to a relatively small percentage of the population of the world compared to other media such as television, radio or newspapers and that population tends to be disproportionally affluent and educated. Even in industrialised countries, only a minority of the population uses the Internet on a regular basis. (1998: 6)

ICT policy-makers and minority language media analysts in Europe may have to conduct a good deal of research into whether, given the resources and infrastructure currently available to minority language communities, the Internet is ideal tool for language maintenance.

An area of the digital divide that has received less attention within media research is the question of whether digitisation will create a new hierarchy of television services. The arrival of digital television has been heralded as the solution for many of the problems plaguing minority language media in Europe, particularly amongst smaller language communities such as Scots Gaelic speakers. Terrestrial broadcasting frequencies have historically been controlled by national governments who allowed only a limited number of broadcasters access to television airwaves. However, with the arrival of digital television, many homes will be able to receive up to 1000 channels providing much greater space for minority language broadcasting services. Digitisation may provide a crucial opportunity for smaller minority language groups who have not been able to create a space of national broadcasting frequencies. However, it is also possible that a new digital divide may be emerging between long-established television services with considerable resources to devote to programme production and marketing, and new low-budget services that could potentially occupy a very marginal position within digital networks.

In their assessment of S4C in Wales, Grin and Vaillancourt (1999) note that while it is difficult for a minority language television service to compete with three or four national terrestrial services in a nation-state, the use of clever and original content may create enough interest to convince the sceptical channel surfer to remain as a viewer. However, with over 1000 channels to choose from, it is unlikely that many channel surfers will ever alight on a minority language service or even be aware of its existence. The greater availability of space on a network does not reduce the high cost of producing quality television programmes. In an increasingly competitive advertising market, minority language television services may be even less likely to attract the type of advertising revenue that would allow them to produce quality programmes in the new digital context.

Questions relating to emerging digital divide(s) in Europe highlight a number of potentially crucial areas of research. It is clear that some of this

---

scholarship must be completed before minority language communities can make decisions about the future allocation of resources to develop content for the new media technologies available. However, despite difficulties in terms of connectivity, skills and resources, it appears that minority language communities are anxious to assert their presence and their linguistic distinctiveness in the new discursive spaces created by digital television and the Internet.

Minority language media and globalisation

Globalisation is commonly used as shorthand to describe the spread of connectedness of production, communication and technologies around the world (Giddens, 1994; Waters, 2001). Rather confusingly, globalisation has also been used to refer to the effort of the International Monetary Fund (IMF), World Bank and others to create a global free market for goods and services (Stiglitz, 2002). This political project, while being significant and potentially damaging for economically marginalised groups, can be viewed a mechanism for exploiting the larger process.

In terms of the neo-liberal economic project of globalisation, it is clear from global trade agreements such as the General Agreement on Tariffs and Trade (GATT) and deals brokered by the World Bank and the IMF, that the key players within the global economy are becoming increasingly antagonistic towards protectionism particularly when these policies obstruct the expansion of global trade. The controversy surrounding the exclusion of audio-visual products from the GATT agreement during the 1993/1994 period indicates that US-dominated global media organisations have little understanding of the sensitivities that provoke European calls for cultural and media safeguards. In reviewing the GATT debate, Morley and Robbins comment:

> Whilst the United States was calling, in the name of free trade and the free circulation of ideas, for the scrapping of quota restrictions, European interests were resolved to preserve them in order, as they saw it, to defend the cultural specificity and integrity of European civilisation. (1995: 10)

Management figures in global media organisations tend to characterise European public service broadcasters as antiquated institutions obstructing capitalist progress. Stephen Ross, the late head of Time Warner clearly articulated this perspective stating that global media corporations stood for 'complete freedom of information', and 'the free flow of ideas, products and technologies in the spirit of fair competition'.

National frontiers he regarded as a relic of the past arguing that 'the new reality of international media is driven more by market opportunity than by national identity'. Ross argued that European media systems were 'on the path to a truly free and open competition that will be dictated by consumers' tastes and desires'.[10]

While this type of observation is rooted in hostility to national television services, a hostility that many minority language speakers share, the general distaste for public service broadcasting goals linked to identity, culture and education represents a potential point of conflict between minority language broadcasters, and global media organisations. Most minority language media advocates have been highly critical of national broadcasting services for excluding their language and culture from mainstream media. However, in terms broadcasting ideology, minority media providers share the conceptual emphasis on education and cultural protection espoused by public services broadcasters.

Very few minority language media services are commercially viable or fully integrated into the global media economy. The economic structures of these services are rooted in an ethos of protectionism and rely on state or European subsidies in some form. However, technological and economic changes are facilitating the increasing dominance of global media corporations who can not only produce cultural products such as TV programmes, films and popular music but also the hardware on which these cultural products are enjoyed such as DVD players, MP3 units etc. The multiplicity of roles played by global media organisations in the media markets of the future may make the current protectionist policies difficult to sustain. Thus, there is some evidence that minority language broadcasters have much to fear from the global capitalist economic project as currently espoused by trans-national economic institutions such as the IMF, which is essentially hostile to all forms of protectionism.

Viewed in terms of broader debates about connectivity and politico-spatial changes, however, it appears that minority language media organisations have less to fear. Globalisation has provoked a re-configuration of global geographies creating a process of glocalisation where power is located at the global and local level but eroded at national level. From this perspective, it is possible to argue that minority media services and their associated language groups are accomplishing from below the same erosion of national structures that globalisation is accomplishing from above. Smith (1995) has argued that the recognition of growing diversity within nation-states is actually contributing to their increasing weakness and decline. He comments, 'the co-resident peripheral ethnies are increasingly felt to undermine the fabric of the nation by their demands for separate but equal treatment, their cultural differences and their aspirations for diversity and autonomy' (1995: 95).

Despite the corrosive impact of minority language media on national identities and national broadcasting culture, analysts have tended to characterise these services and the revival of interest in minority languages as defensive reactions to globalisation. Manuel Castells (1997: 65) characterises the increasing dominance of minority language identities as evidence of the growing influence of 'identities of resistance'. He couples indigenous minority language movements with religious fundamentalist organisations, arguing that they are defensive reactions to modernisation and globalisation. He argues:

> Religious fundamentalism, cultural nationalism, territorial communes are, by and large, defensive reactions...Reaction against globalisation, which dissolves the autonomy of institutions, organisations and communications systems where people live. Reaction against networking and flexibility which blur the boundaries of membership and involvement, individualise social relationships of production and induce the structural instability of work, space and time...When the world becomes too large to be controlled, social actors aim at shrinking it back to their size and reach. When networks dissolve time and space, people anchor themselves in places and recall their historic memory. (1997: 66)

In reviewing the Catalan case, he identifies global media in particular as a key factor in prompting the emergence of these defensive reactions. He states

> [I]f nationalism, most often, a reaction against a threatened autonomous identity, then, in a world submitted to cultural homogenisation by the ideology of modernisation and the power of global media, language, as a direct expression of culture, becomes the trench of cultural resistance, the last bastion of self-control, the refuge of identifiable meaning. (1997: 52)

The characterisation of minority language media as manifestations of identities of resistance is very attractive. However, despite the potency of this image, it is difficult to reconcile this perspective with the enthusiastic manner in which indigenous minority language groups have embraced broadcast media. Historically, minority language activists have regarded nation-states and national broadcasting organisations as the key oppressor. In some cases, they have welcomed the challenge that supra-national organisations provided to nation-states and found trans-national institutions such as the EU to be much more receptive to their aims and ideologies. Rather than being defensive reactions to globalisation, the establishment of minority language media could be characterised as opportunism in a media context. These services have taken advantage of niches created as a result of the dismantling of national media infrastructures.

The ongoing process of globalisation has already had a varied impact on minority language media. The immediate opportunities created by globalisation have allowed minority language communities to create their own public spheres where cultural identities can be cherished and celebrated. For many minority language speakers, these services have resulted in a modernisation that has created new associations between their cultures and images of youth, glamour and modernity. However, the creators of minority language media may come to regret the decline of national broadcasting structures and their associated broadcast ideologies. Minority language broadcasters in Europe share with their public service counterparts a belief in the primacy of identity, language and culture over market ideologies and economic imperatives. As the power of the nation-state declines and the influence of trans-national economic institutions grows, minority language communities may find themselves in the vanguard of opposition to the creation of a global free market unfettered by any form of cultural safeguard to protect linguistic distinctiveness.

Given the impact of the changes outlined above, it is clear that minority language media studies face a number of key challenges in the future. The challenge for policy-makers concerns the perennial question of whether minority language media can save a language or as outlined by Cormack, whether we understand how minority language media engage with the community in order to support its linguistic identity. Minority language media advocates will have to devote increasing attention to interrogating the subtleties of engagement between specific media and class, gender and age strata within minority language communities in order to sustain and increase claims for funding. For language and media scholars currently engaged in minority language media studies, the key challenge remains the assertion of the legitimacy of minority language media studies as a field of research and the creation of new academic and institutional supports to promote further analysis and investigation.

Notes

1. The EU began to devote attention to indigenous linguistic minorities in the 1980s with the adoption of the European Letter on Regional Languages and Cultures from the Arfe Report. The Report also initiated subsequent interventions including most importantly the establishment of the European Bureau

for Lesser-Used Languages. For further discussion see Chapters 4 and 5 by Cormack and Hourigan.
2. Council of European Union Press Release, 2618th Council Meeting, Justice and Home Affairs, Brussels, November 2004.
3. Council of European Union Press Release, 2618th Council Meeting, Justice and Home Affairs, Brussels, November 2004.
4. Extra and Yagmur comment:
   As yet, specific documents on the language rights of immigrant groups in Europe hardly exist. The major document is the *Directive of the Council of the European Communities* (now the EU) on the schooling of children of migrant workers, published in Brussels, July 1977. Although this Directive has promoted the legitimisation of immigrant language instruction and occasionally also its legislation in some countries, the Directive was very limited in its ambitions regarding minority language teaching and has meanwhile become completely outdated. (2002: 44)
5. Within the general field of minority language studies, one of the most significant texts that deals with impact of indigenous minority language policy on immigrants is K. Woolard (1989).
6. BECTa (2001: 3).
7. Global Internet Statistics by Language: http://www.glreach.com/globstats.index.php3
8. NTIA (2000).
9. The absence of the contributions of older members of minority language communities to message boards and on-line discussion groups highlights a problem that may also be affecting the more passive media of television and radio. Content within these media often reflects the preoccupations and concerns of youth rather than those of older groups. Thus, the very interactivity of the Internet as a medium may allow minority language media analysts to develop a much clearer profile of users and identify lacunae within the current orientation of content.
10. The content of this speech is paraphrased from Morley and Robbins, K. (1995).

References

Anderson, B. (1991) *Imagined Communities* (2nd edn). London: Verso.
BECTa (2001) The digital divide: A discussion paper. Prepared for the Department for Education and Skills (DfES) by the British Educational Communications and Technology Agency (BECTa). On www at: www.BECTa.org
Castells, M. (1996) *The Rise of the Network Society* (Vol. 1 of *The Information Age*). Oxford: Blackwell.
Castells, M. (1997) *The Power of Identity*. (Vol. 2 of *The Information Age*). Oxford: Blackwell.
Cronin, M. (1995) Altered states: Translation and minority languages. *Tradúction, Terminology, Rédaction* 8 (1), 85–103.
Crystal, D. (1997) *English as a Global Language*. Cambridge: Cambridge University Press.
Damarin, S. (2000) The digital divide versus digital differences: Principles for equitable use of technology in education. *Educational Technology* 40 (4), 17–21.

DeBruin, J. (2000) We just couldn't behave like that: Dutch soap opera, adolescence and ethnicity. Paper presented to the *Crossroads in Cultural Studies* conference, Birmingham, June 2000.

Extra, G. and Yagmur, K. (2002) *Language Diversity in Multicultural Europe: Comparative Perspectives on Immigrant Minority Languages at Home and at School.* Paris: UNESCO.

Feenberg, A. (1991) *Critical Theory of Technology.* New York: Oxford University Press.

Frachon, C. and Vargaftig, M. (1995) *European Television: Immigrants and Ethnic Minorities.* London: John Libbey.

Giddens, A. (1994) Living in a post-traditional society In U. Beck, A Giddens and S. Lash (eds) *Reflexive Modernisation: Politics, Tradition and Aesthetics in the Modern Social Order.* Cambridge: Polity Press.

Grin, F. and Vaillancourt, F. (1999) *The Cost-effectiveness of Evaluation of Minority Language Policies: Case Studies in Wales, Ireland and the Basque Country.* European Centre for Minority Issues Monograph No. 2. Flensburg: European Centre for Minority Issues.

LMP (Linguistic Minorities Project) (1985) *The Other Languages of England.* London: Routledge and Kegan Paul.

Lockard, J. (1996) Resisting cyber-English. *Bad Subjects* 24. On www at: http://eserver.org/bs/24/lockard.html

McLuhan, M. (1962) *The Gutenberg Galaxy: The Making of Typographic Man.* Toronto: University of Toronto Press.

Morley, D. and Robbins, K. (1995) *Spaces of Identity: Global Media, Electronic Landscapes and Cultural Boundaries.* London: Routledge.

NTIA (2001) *Falling through the Net: Towards Digital Inclusion.* Washington, DC. US Department of Commerce.

Ogan, C. (2001) *Communication and Identity in the Diaspora: Turkish Migrants in Amsterdam and their Use of Media.* Lanham, MD: Lexington Books.

Pennycook, A. (1994) *The Cultural Politics of English as an International Language.* London: Longman.

Riggins, S.H. (1992) *Ethnic Minority Media.* London: Sage.

Ross, R. (1997) Why black English matters. *Education Weekly,* 29 January, 31–48.

Sahraouri, M. (1998) Putting more colour into the Dutch media. *Media Development* 45 (3), 22.

Slowinski, J. (1998) Socrates invades Central Europe. *Educational Policy Analysis Archives* 6 (9), 1–24.

Smith, A. (1995) *Nations and Nationalism in a Global Era.* Cambridge: Polity Press.

Stiglitz, J. (2002) *Globalization and its Discontents.* New York: Penguin.

Tomlinson, J. (1999) *Globalisation and Culture.* Cambridge: Polity Press.

Villa, D. (2002) Integrating technology into minority language teaching and preservation efforts: An inside job. *Language, Learning and Technology* 6, 92–101.

Warschauer, M. (1998) Technology and indigenous language revitalisation: Analysing the experience of Hawai'i. *Canadian Modern Language Review* 55 (1), 140–161.

Waters, M. (2001) *Globalization.* London: Routledge

Witt, Jorg (2000) English as a global language: The case of the European Union. *Erfurt Electronic Studies in English* 11, Article 20.

Woolard, K. (1989) *Double Talk: Bilingualism and the Politics of Ethnicity in Catalonia.* Stanford, CA: Stanford University Press.

Contributors

Edorta Arana is a lecturer in journalism at the University of the Basque Country.

Patxi Azpillaga is a lecturer in economics at the University of the Basque Country.

Donald R. Browne is Professor at the Dept of Communication Studies, University of Minnesota.

Mike Cormack is Senior Lecturer and Course Director of BA in Gaelic and Media Studies, Sabhal Mòr Ostaig, UHI Millennium Institute, Scotland.

Maria Corominas Piulats is a lecturer at the Dept of Journalism and Communication Sciences, Universitat Autonoma de Barcelona.

Daniel Cunliffe is Senior Lecturer in Multimedia Computing at the School of Computing, University of Glamorgan.

Jacques Guyot is Professor of Information and Communication Sciences at the University of Paris 8 – Vicennes.

Elin Haf Gruffydd Jones is a lecturer at the Dept of Theatre, Film and Television Studies at the University of Wales, Aberystwyth.

Niamh Hourigan is a lecturer at the Dept of Sociology, University College Cork, Ireland.

Paddy Ladd is Director of Postgraduate Research at the Centre for Deaf Studies, University of Bristol.

Tom Moring is Professor of Journalism at the Swedish School of Social Science, University of Helsinki.

Beatriz Narbaiza is a media lecturer at the University of the Basque Country.

Eithne O'Connell is Senior Lecturer in Translation Studies at Dublin City University Ireland.

Glyn Williams is a research professor at University Ramon Llul, Barcelona.

Index

GOIENA 163
Gooskens, I. 118
Gothenburg 116
Grame, T. 110
Granada Television 112
Greece 123
Greenlandic 5
Grillo, R. 2
Grimes, B.F. 40
Grin, F. 1, 2, 3, 12, 18, 21, 24, 25, 29, 30, 52, 53, 193, 259
Guinea 122
Gumicio-Dagron, A. 127
Guyot, J. 13, 37, 39, 40, 47, 117

Haavikko, P. 24
Habermas, J. 11, 45, 49
Haiti 132
Hall, P. 144
Harrie, E. 23
Harries, R. 140
Haugen, E. 63, 64
Hayek, F. 89
Hawaiian 258
Heatta, O.M. 109
Hein, K. 120
Heller, M. 2
Hind, J. 127
Hindi 9, 42, 121, 249, 255
Hinton, L. 141
Hmong 128
Hnahnu 119
Hobsbawm, E. 35
Hoffman, C. 216
Holten, G. 110
Horkheimer, M. 24
Hourigan, N. 1, 8, 11, 12, 13, 15, 54, 69, 189
How Green Was My Valley 197
Human Language Technology 105
Humphreys, E. 192
Hungary 20, 23
Husband, C. 22, 26
HTV 74, 237

Iceland 132
ICANN 142
ICT 91, 93, 94, 95, 256-260
IMF 84, 260, 261
immigrant languages 22, 36, 41, 43, 116, 248, 249-254
Incan 119
India 43, 121
indigenous languages 1, 2, 7, 15, 108, 120, 248, 251, 253, 255, 256

Indonesia 121
Information and Communication Technology *see* ICT
Innes, H. 19, 20, 22
International Monetary Fund *see* IMF
Internet 12, 14, 21, 22, 23, 37, 47, 49, 57, 58, 59, 62, 100, 102, 126, 128, 132-147, 164, 182, 245, 252, 257, 258
Inuit 46, 114, 123, 126, 127, 128, 253
Iran 109
Iraq 109
Ireland 13, 21, 27, 30, 36, 54, 69, 70, 124, 212-228,
Irish 3, 27, 30, 36, 54, 71, 74, 75, 76, 113, 140, 196, 212-228
Issacs, J. 191
Isin, E.F. 25
Italian 20, 59, 108, 110, 117, 138, 170
Italy 37, 38, 121, 123, 233, 250
ITV 112, 237, 239

Jackson, J.D. 20
Jakobson, R. 212
Jakubowicz, A. 115
Japan 121, 123, 128
Japanese 138
Jenkinson, B. 220
Johnston, H. 69

Kabyle 126
Kayes 120
Kazakh 127
Kelly-Holmes, H. 139, 141
Khoisan 120
Kibbee, D. 117
Korea 132
Koutsogiannis, D. 137
Krasny Most 127
Kurdish 109, 118
Kurds 109, 116
Knowledge Intensive Business Services 90
Korean 138
Kweekeh, F. 120
Kymlicka, W. 18, 26, 43, 44

Labour Party (UK) 74, 83
Ladd, P. 15
Ladin 38
Langer, S. 139
language maintenance 13, 52, 53, 57, 58, 60, 62, 63, 64, 66, 213, 219, 222, 223, 224, 257, 258
language planning 9, 10, 11, 60, 65, 106, 146, 213, 216, 223, 224